JAMES JOYCE

JAMES JOYCE

PATRICK PARRINDER

Reader in English, University of Reading

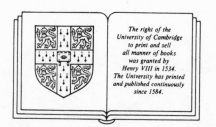

The right of the
University of Cambridge
to print and sell
all manner of books
was granted by
Henry VIII in 1534.
The University has printed
and published continuously
since 1584.

CAMBRIDGE UNIVERSITY PRESS

Cambridge

New York   Port Chester   Melbourne   Sydney

Published by the Press Syndicate of the University of Cambridge
The Pitt Building, Trumpington Street, Cambridge CB2 1RP
40 West 20th Street, New York, NY 10011, USA
10 Stamford Road, Oakleigh, Melbourne 3166, Australia

First published 1984
Reprinted 1987, 1990

Printed in Great Britain at
the University Press, Cambridge

Library of Congress catalogue card number: 84 – 9481

British Library Cataloguing in Publication Data

Parrinder, Patrick
James Joyce.
1. Joyce, James, *1882-1941*
I. Title
823′.912   PR6019.09Z/

ISBN 0 521 24014 X hard covers
ISBN 0 521 283981 paperback

GG

Contents

PART III

PART IV

Preface and acknowledgements

This book contains several features which have not been usual in introductory critical studies of Joyce. For example, I believe that understanding of his achievement should be firmly based on his two major works, *Ulysses* and *Finnegans Wake*, even though they present features which are unexpected, and even forbidding, to admirers of his early writings. For this reason my opening chapter, 'Joyce and the Grotesque', refers much more to *Ulysses* and *Finnegans Wake* than to their predecessors.

Joyce's rich and complex books set many traps for the unwary. His work is a standing rebuke to the parochialism of much modern writing, and it is possible for students of the English and American novel, for example, to come to him with quite inappropriate assumptions. In some of the following chapters my reading of the Joyceian text is prefaced with a more historical and/or theoretical discussion of ways of approaching it. Moreover, I have avoided referring to *Ulysses* and *Finnegans Wake* as 'novels', believing this to be largely unhelpful — though admittedly it is hard to settle on any satisfactory alternative. Whether or not Joyce is a novelist he is, I believe, one of the greatest masters of modern prose.

It would be impossible to list the debts to teachers, students, friends, and colleagues which have been incurred during the gestation and writing of this book. Among those to whom I am most grateful are Richard Brown, David Gervais, and Bonnie Kime Scott for their penetrating comments on earlier drafts; to the University of Reading Research Board for financial assistance; to Berni and Shari Benstock, James Hurt, and Giorgio Melchiori for the many hospitable occasions on which they shared with me their knowledge of *Finnegans Wake*; to my wife, above all for stimulating my interest in Joyce's Scandiknavery; and to Christopher Rolfe and Colin MacCabe. But there have been many, many others.

The primal debt, however, is to my father, who first encouraged me to read *A Portrait of the Artist* at the age of fifteen (when Stephen's experiences at boarding school could be contrasted with my own). The handful of Faber & Faber pamphlets that my father bought as a young man lies on my desk as I write. This book is dedicated to his memory.

Reading, England
January 1984

References to Joyce's works

References in the text and notes are to page numbers in the following editions, except that in the case of *CM*, reference is to the poems as numbered, and in the case of *FW*, to page and line.

Abbreviations

CM	*Chamber Music*, London (Jonathan Cape) 1971.
CW	*The Critical Writings of James Joyce*, ed. Ellsworth Mason and Richard Ellmann, New York (Viking Press) 1964.
D	*Dubliners: The Corrected Text with an Explanatory Note by Robert Scholes*, London (Jonathan Cape) 1967.
E	*Exiles: A Play in Three Acts*, introduced by Padraic Colum, London (Jonathan Cape) 1952.
FW	*Finnegans Wake*, 4th edn., London (Faber & Faber) 1975.
GJ	*Giacomo Joyce*, ed. Richard Ellmann, London (Faber & Faber) 1968.
Letters	Vol. I, ed. Stuart Gilbert, London (Faber & Faber) 1957. Vols. II and III, ed. Richard Ellmann, London (Faber & Faber) 1966.
P	*A Portrait of the Artist as a Young Man*, New York (Viking Press) 1964. This is the definitive text, corrected from the Dublin holograph by Chester G. Anderson and edited by Richard Ellmann. However, at no point does the pagination differ by more than one page from that of other recent editions, such as those published in England by Penguin Books.
PP	*Pomes Penyeach and other verses*, London (Faber & Faber) 1966.
SH	*Stephen Hero*, London (Jonathan Cape) 1969.
SL	*Selected Letters*, ed. Richard Ellmann, London (Faber & Faber) 1975.
U	*Ulysses*, Harmondsworth (Penguin Books) 1971.

Does the man exist who is able . . . to encompass *Finnegans Wake* or even *Ulysses?* I do not mean on the literal level, but all the allusions, all the associations and cultural–mythic symbolisms, all the combined paradigms and archetypes on which these works stand and grow in glory? Certainly no one could manage it alone. No one, for that matter, could wade through the entire body of criticism that the prose of James Joyce has accumulated to date!

Stanislaw Lem, *A Perfect Vacuum*,
translated by Michael Kandel

1 Introduction: Joyce and the grotesque

'After God Shakespeare has created most', says John Eglinton in *Ulysses*, echoing Dumas *fils* (or is it Dumas *père*?). Among the select band of writers of English who can legitimately be named 'after Shakespeare' are two whose peculiar province was the modern city. They are comic and visionary writers, powerfully aware both of the plasticity of words and of the mass and texture of things. They are so individual that their work defies direct comparison, though it makes a suggestive initial contrast. They are Joyce and Dickens.

Dickens needed the actual physical input of London or, as he put it, of 'streets' to fuel his writing.[1] Joyce, living in exile, told a friend that 'I want . . . to give a picture of Dublin so complete that if the city one day suddenly disappeared from the earth it could be reconstructed out of my book'.[2] We can get some idea of the intensity of Dickens's imagination from his remark that 'I don't invent it − really do not − *but see it*, and write it down'.[3] G. H. Lewes remembered him stating that 'every word said by his characters was distinctly *heard* by him'.[4] There is evidence that Joyce, too, may have heard the voices that resound in his books. Imaginary voices are prominent in his two most directly autobiographical works, the *Portrait of the Artist* and *Exiles*. In *Exiles* Richard Rowan, a writer, works all night and then goes out onto the strand, before dawn, to be plagued by the demonic voices of 'those who say they love me' (*E* 157). The voices recur in a letter Joyce wrote twenty years later to his old college friend Constantine Curran. Joyce was declining Curran's suggestion that it was time he revisited Ireland:

I am trying to finish my wip [Work in Progress] . . . and I am not taking any chances with my fellow-countrymen if I can possibly help it until that is done, at least. . . . But every day in every way I am walking along the streets of Dublin and along the strand. And 'hearing voices'. (*Letters*, I, 395)

Voices reverberate in Stephen Dedalus's imagination. Character in parts of *Ulysses* is reduced to the rambling voices of the interior monologue. In *Finnegans Wake*, where Joyce said that 'time and the

1

river and the mountain'[5] are the real heroes, the voices of Anna Livia, Shaun, Issy, and many others make an immediate impression on us. No doubt Joyce as a young man emulated Dickens and roamed the streets of Dublin for hours at a stretch, since this is what the protagonist of *Stephen Hero* does (*SH* 42). In adult life he was content to be absent from the city, but he depended utterly on remembering and hearing it. The Joyceian artist is a 'penman' who can bring back the dead to life (a recurrent motif) and invest them with the gift of tongues: 'He lifts the lifewand and the dumb speak' (*FW* 195:5).

Richard Rowan heard the voices of 'those who say they love me'. All Joyce's fiction has its roots in autobiography (though it all diverges, in greater or lesser degree, from 'straight' autobiography if such a thing exists). He knew suffering and bitterness in his early life, and occasionally spoke about it with raw and passionate feeling. Here is a passage from a letter to Nora Barnacle, written when they had just met, in which he set out to describe his character:

My home was simply a middle-class affair ruined by spendthrift habits which I have inherited. My mother was slowly killed, I think, by my father's ill-treatment, by years of trouble, and by my cynical frankness of conduct. When I looked on her face as she lay in the coffin – a face grey and wasted with cancer – I understood that I was looking on the face of a victim and I cursed the system which had made her a victim.   (*Letters*, II, 48)

'Cursing the system' was not uncommon (in life and in English fiction) around 1900. George Gissing, for example, had responded to the death of his first wife with a similarly resolute imprecation.[6] The 1880s and 90s had seen the heyday of literary naturalism when writers as various as Gissing, Zola, Maupassant, and George Moore showed their characters as being both moulded and trapped by circumstances. Yet there is a difficulty in Joyce's outburst, since he himself seems to be part of the 'system'. He knows he is partly to blame for his mother's unhappiness. And he was incapable of the rhetorician's trick of turning a caustic eye on society while keeping it strenuously averted from himself. In his novels he is not a passionate declaimer, as Dickens had been. Dickens began as a parliamentary reporter and, just as he needed the input from the streets, so he seems to have needed the rhetorical excitement associated with the editor's chair, the bar, the pulpit, and the platform. Joyce too had some newspaper experience and incorporated many sorts of hack writing and speech-making into his fiction. Yet Joyce was not a natural journalist; what he wrote for the press is usually inhibited and musclebound. Whenever newspaper oratory appears in his fiction it is as a borrowed style, ironically distanced – a bombast which he loves to parody but would never commit *in propria persona*. For Joyce's irony (much more genial than that of Swift, with which it has often been compared) is that of a connoisseur of the absurdities of others who, for himself, instinctively avoids self-exposure. Was he a socialist? An atheist? An anti-imperialist? The proper answer to these questions is almost certainly 'yes', but he had not the least inclination to blurt out such answers in public. In the letter to Nora quoted above he went on to say that 'One brother alone is capable of understanding me'. His art is constructed out of self-division and complexity.

This is not to say that his response to oppression and injustice was a supine one. He took some pride, quite rightly, in being less gullible in political matters than such artistic contemporaries as Pound and Wyndham Lewis. Leopold Bloom is to some extent a political spokesman for Joyce, and Bloom's prudence and moral sense are reminiscent of the humble Dickensian 'man in the street' such as Mr Plornish in *Little Dorrit*: 'As to who was to blame for it, Mr Plornish didn't know who was to blame for it. He could tell you who suffered, but he couldn't tell you whose fault it was'.[7] Joyce might laugh a little at Bloom's ingenuousness, but he lacked the sort of journalistic instinct which led Dickens to propose for *Little Dorrit* the sarcastic title of *Nobody's Fault*. His creed of 'silence exile and cunning' suggests, not an art of social impeachment, but one of subtly subversive effects.

Dickens was both a highly opinionated writer and one with an exceptional commercial flair. The occasions on which Joyce showed a genuinely commercial attitude to his fiction are remarkable for their rarity. One of the few blatant false starts in his career was his intention of following up *Dubliners* with a further collection of short stories to be called *Provincials* (*SL* 63). (The eight-year 'censorship' of *Dubliners* put paid to that.) By the time he was finishing *Ulysses*, the writer who made fun of the newspaper market for 'prize stories', such as 'Matcham's Masterstroke' by Philip Beaufoy, was protected by patronage from the full pressures of the literary market-place. Thanks to Miss Weaver's generosity he could provide for his family better than his father had done, while at the same time being saved from the financial necessity of writing conventional or even publishable fiction. After 1918 Joyce was not only a leader of the avant-garde but was peculiarly well-placed to follow T. S. Eliot's injunction that artists 'in our civilization, as it exists at present, must be *difficult*'.[8]

Could Dickens have avowed that he wished to give a picture of London so complete that if the city one day disappeared it could be reconstructed from his books? Presumably not. Not only were his settings and characters more exaggerated than Joyce's but he left behind too many versions of his London. His city is a prodigal, pulsating, shapeshifting place which he can go on creating afresh so long as there is the need to get a new book out of it. Joyce's two later books, by contrast, have a static and monumental quality which makes it inappropriate to describe them as 'novels'. The peculiarity of these works (as Ruskin said of St Mark's in Venice) is that of an architectural principle of confessed *incrustation*. Each interstice of their structure is meticulously crammed with detail and colour. The order they reveal is one of decorative intensity rather than of mere narrative sequence. An extraordinary labour of compilation and collation went into their making. *Ulysses* especially is an encyclopaedic representation of a day in Dublin – even if its relationship to the actual city is less straightforward than is implied by Joyce's boast.

But there is one point on which Dickens and Joyce are in profound agreement. Their recreation of the cities they loved would – in contrast to those of most other writers – be unashamedly populist and plebeian. Their books take us into the streets and pubs of their cities because they share a fascination with the lives, experiences and modes of expression of ordinary people. Both writers had an unlimited appetite for popular culture, whether in the forms of music and song, handbill and ballad, pantomime and melodrama, repartee and humour, or of sentiment and – in Joyce's case – pornography. Both are popular historians in the sense of giving written form to much that would otherwise perish, being in its nature oral, ephemeral or throwaway. Yet Joyce's activity as a cultural chronicler is much more deliberate than Dickens's. *Ulysses* is not only a novel of the recent past but one with a precise date (16 June 1904). Where for Dickens popular culture had been part of the irresistible material of storytelling, for Joyce it was something to be collected and exhibited; his work thus functions as a library or archive which confers permanence on the material deposited in it.

We may explain this more intellectual development in Joyce's art both in terms of his temperament and of the society and period in which he grew up. Stephen Dedalus, the 'artist as a young man', is necessarily an intellectual elitist and prig. Joyce, too, took pride in his Jesuit training and modelled himself on the rigour (if not the theology) of

St Thomas Aquinas. As a poet, he followed Pater and the Decadent school who saw the artist as a privileged being set above social and moral responsibilities. In drama he spurned what he saw as the political opportunism of the newly-formed Irish national theatre. Like Ibsen, he believed it might be necessary to appear as an 'enemy of the people'; so much is explicit in the title of his theatre pamphlet, 'The Day of the Rabblement' (1901). Yet this aloof intellectualism was a pose reflecting only part of Joyce's complex personality. *A Portrait of the Artist* shows Stephen rejecting his natural father in favour of Daedalus, the legendary embodiment of the lonely and innovating artist. But for Joyce a reconciliation with his father's world, and a determination to recreate the Irish urban culture his father personified, was the precondition of *Ulysses*.

Where Joyce did not deviate from Stephen's views was in his repudiation of the cultural ideology which had seized middle-class Catholic Ireland at the end of the nineteenth century. Douglas Hyde's Gaelic League, dedicated to the 'de-Anglicization' of Ireland, was formed in 1893. The folklore which interested Joyce, however, was not that of the peasantry and the Celtic twilight but of his own circle. He had no time for the language revival, which was intent on creating an artificial culture in order to nurture the myths of Irish nationalism. Stephen Dedalus vows to fly by the 'nets' of nationality, language and religion which would hold him prisoner in provincial Ireland. Though British rule was part of the 'system' he cursed, he had even less sympathy for what he called the 'old pap of racial hatred' (*SL* 111). He inclined towards international socialism rather than the chauvinistic project of 'de-Anglicization', and found no magnetism whatever either in the League or in one of its principal activists, the future rebel Patrick Pearse, whose Irish language class he briefly attended.[9] He certainly did not admit – what even Yeats, in his play *Cathleen ni Houlihan* (1902), was to imply – that he should be prepared to sacrifice himself in the cause of national independence. Yet Joyce was neither unpatriotic nor indifferent to the Irish cultural heritage. To a friend such as Arthur Power he did indeed appear a 'literary Fenian' in revolt against the English conventions.[10] The sort of patriotism he felt can be more easily understood when we remember his lifelong reverence for the drama of Ibsen. Far from being the prisoner of a nationalist party-line, Ibsen was a cosmopolitan artist who nevertheless drew profoundly on Norwegian legends, traditions, and ways of life. Joyce returned to traditional Irish folklore in *Finnegans Wake* – written once Ireland had gained its independence – but in *Ulysses* he combines Greek mythology and the intellectual detritus of two thousand years with a wholly modernized, pragmatic and unidealized notion of culture. Through the device of a Jewish, deracinated hero he shows how inherited values, aesthetic tastes and half-remembered 'lessons of history' are forced to find their own level amid the blare of slogans, street-signs and advertising jingles produced by modern capitalism. His hero, an advertising agent, is a 'cultured allroundman' generously hospitable both to the high-points of literature, the sciences, and grand opera, and to such ephemera as Kino's eleven-shilling trousers and Plumtree's potted meat:

> *What is home without*
> *Plumtree's Potted Meat?*
> *Incomplete.*
> *With it an abode of bliss.*   (*U* 76)

Bloom, sentimental and bourgeois, enjoys the jingle and would dearly like to preside over an 'abode of bliss'. For him, Home Rule takes second place to home comforts – even though he knows that the latter depend on something more substantial than Plumtree's potted meat.

Bloom unfolds his newspaper and reads the Plumtree's advertisement in the middle of talking to an acquaintance. Equally natural, and equally defiant of conventional etiquette, is the literary gesture Joyce makes by including such doggerel in a work of art. In his time Joyce was much criticized for his anarchic, debunking attitude toward literary pieties. More recently he has been much admired for it. Without dismissing such reactions (which Joyce clearly intended to provoke) we should also remember his comment that *Ulysses* was fundamentally a humorous work, and that this would become obvious when the critical confusion about it had died down.[11] For Joyce's is what may be called anarchic humour – a humour which subverts existing structures and hierarchies *without taking up a political stance*. The time-honoured place of anarchic humour in Western societies is represented by the institution of the carnival. Of Joyce's two major works, the first takes place on the day when its hero is cuckolded – traditionally an occasion for bawdiness and ridicule – while the second is a 'funferal' based on the Irish wake or funeral merrymaking.

Laughter goes with licence, and licence in all its forms – from the most disorganized to the most highly organized – takes a curiously parallel course to acts of political revolt and rebellion. The drunken orgy parallels the political riot (words like *mob* and *hooligan* are conventionally used of both), and, among the more stage-managed forms of festivity, the modern carnival queen is a descendant of the medieval Lord of Misrule. The coronation ceremony for beauty queens parodies the sanctification of the monarch's authority. The whole point of such parodic occasions is to provide a forum in which behaviour that is normally frowned upon -- such as ogling another person's physical attributes, or flaunting one's own -- becomes sanctioned and overt. The world, as ordinarily experienced, is turned bottom upwards. Such a bottoms-up view deeply appealed to Joyce, for all sorts of reasons. He was no respecter of sexual conventions, and some of his letters to Nora, written during their brief separation in 1909, go far beyond the usual bounds of discretion even in our present permissive half-century. A letter to his brother Stanislaus in 1904 contains the following abrupt, though eloquent, conclusion:

I really can't write. Nora is trying on a pair of drawers at the wardrobe
Excuse me   *JIM*   (*SL* 44)

Joyce's experiments with form are, in part, a successful attempt to get material as profane as this into fiction.

There is a more sombre reason for the comic form of Joyce's major works: not only the recording of unsanctified pleasures but the lightening of unavoidable pain. Joyce, as any biographical summary will show, did not have an easy life despite a fair ration of success and good fortune. He portrayed Stephen Dedalus with full sincerity as a haunted young man, guilty, insecure, and obsessed with the recent death of his mother. New troubles -- the loss of his eyesight, his estrangement from his brother, his daughter's schizophrenia -- came to him as he grew older. But in his writing, as to a certain extent in his life, laughter and excess could hold misery at bay. It is no accident that Leopold Bloom, that masterpiece of comic fictional characterization, is the son of a suicide. The Irish wake, with its upside-down antidote to the gravity of mourning and bereavement, is the perfect symbol of Joycean comedy.

Joyce's humour cannot be reconciled with the notion that his is a 'classical' art, despite the well-known passage in *Stephen Hero* which speaks of the 'classical temper' (*SH* 83). Joyce did have leanings towards what (using the analogy of a style of architecture) we might call 'romantic neoclassicism'; this is evident from such things as his adoption of the name Daedalus or Dedalus, his study of Aristotelian and Thomist aesthetics, and his decision to write a new version of the

Odyssey. But classical proportion and classical decorum are alien to most (though not quite all) of his writing. ('For classicism is dead', he declared to his friend Power; 'It was the art of gentlemen, and gentlemen are out of date'.[12]) Many critics have remarked on his affinities with medieval art, especially that of the Irish *Book of Kells* with its astonishingly intricate marginal designs and illuminated letters. The *Book of Kells* is a manuscript of the Gospels, and W. B. Stanford has compared its transformation of the sacred text with Joyce's transformation of Homer.[13] Both the *Book of Kells* and *Ulysses* are 'copies' in which the original text is overlaid with an unprecedented degree of decorative extravagance.

The reason why the *Book of Kells* appealed so strongly to Joyce is, almost certainly, that it is one of the greatest traditional examples of the art of the grotesque. The word *grotesque* derives from a type of Roman ornamental design first discovered in the fifteenth century, during the excavation of Titus's baths. Named after the 'grottoes' in which they were found, the new forms consisted of human and animal shapes intermingled with foliage, flowers, and fruits in fantastic designs which bore no relationship to the logical categories of classical art. For a contemporary account of these forms we can turn to the Latin writer Vitruvius. Vitruvius was an official charged with the rebuilding of Rome under Augustus, to whom his treatise *On Architecture* is addressed. Not surprisingly, it bears down hard on the 'improper taste' for the grotesque. 'Such things neither are, nor can be, nor have been', says the author in his description of the mixed human, animal, and vegetable forms:

For how can a reed actually sustain a roof, or a candelabrum the ornaments of a gable? or a soft and slender stalk, a seated statue? or how can flowers and half-statues rise alternately from roots and stalks? Yet when people view these falsehoods, they approve rather than condemn, failing to consider whether any of them can really occur or not.[14]

We have here a confrontation between the logic of imperial classicism and what is condemned as a meretricious popular taste. Classicism demands the analytical and ordered representation of 'things as they are'. The grotesque involves a blurring of distinctions, a continual change from one type to another, a riot of incompleted forms. In modern aesthetics the term has become a generic one extending to the art of any period or nation. Hegel, for example, defined the grotesque with reference to Hindu sculpture. For him it had three characteristics, 'the unjustified fusion of different realms of being', 'excess and distortion', and the 'unnatural multiplication of one and the same function', as in the presence of numerous arms and heads.[15] The decorative complexities of the *Book of Kells* would fit this definition very well. Like the Hindu temple sculptures, this ancient Irish art contains strong overtones of fertility symbolism.[16]

The most remarkable modern discussion of the grotesque in literature is that offered by the Soviet critic and theorist Mikhail Bakhtin. In his book on Rabelais, Bakhtin shows how the confrontation of the classical and the grotesque may be exemplified by a difference in bodily imagery. Classical art

presents an entirely finished, completed, strictly limited body, which is shown from the outside as something individual. That which protrudes, bulges, sprouts, or branches off . . . is eliminated, hidden, or moderated. All orifices of the body are closed. The basis of the image is the individual, strictly limited mass, the impenetrable facade.

The grotesque body, by contrast,

is cosmic and universal. It stresses elements common to the entire cosmos: earth, water, fire, air; it is directly related to the sun, to the stars. . . . This body can merge with various natural phenomena, with mountains, rivers, seas, islands, and continents. It can fill the entire universe.[17]

If Rabelais is a grotesque artist − as both Bakhtin and Wolfgang Kayser have powerfully argued − then so, in large measure, is Joyce. The critical comparison of Joyce and Rabelais, and the description of aspects of Joyce's art as Rabelaisian, has been a commonplace since the 1920s. The first thing we learn about Mr Leopold Bloom is that he 'ate with relish the inner organs of beasts and fowls'. In the course of *Ulysses* we see or hear him eating, drinking, defecating, micturating, belching, farting, and masturbating. Stephen may show a romantic inclination for the classic, but Bloom and Molly (who, in addition to the above-named activities, copulates and menstruates) plainly belong to the grotesque. Their orifices are all too blatantly open, and so − for that matter − are Stephen's. At the end of the 'Proteus' episode the young artist feels his cavity-ridden teeth and then picks his nose, the first fictional hero ever to do so.

At least two incidents in *Ulysses* turn on the distinction between the classical and the grotesque body. The first is Bloom's curiosity about the Greek statues in the National Museum. In the 'Lestrygonians' episode we see him thinking of ambrosia and nectar, the 'food of the gods', and whether this food does not entail a digestive process. How did the Greek deities relieve themselves of bodily wastes, he wonders?

Do the statues throw any light on this murky problem? 'They have no. Never looked. I'll look today. Keeper won't see. Bend down let something fall see if she' (*U* 176). The keeper may not see, but apparently Buck Mulligan does; and the results of Bloom's hastily concluded investigation are inconclusive (*U* 650). Nevertheless, the classical doctrine holds (in the words of the Nymph in 'Circe') that 'We immortals . . . have not such a place and no hair there either. We are stone cold and pure. We eat electric light' (*U* 499). Anyone less vulgar and more classically minded than Bloom should have known instinctively that the Greek statues would possess no anal orifice.

The aesthetic theory of Stephen Dedalus in the *Portrait* distinguishes between impure or 'kinetic' art and the classical mode of 'aesthetic stasis'. Nietzsche in *The Genealogy of Morals* had made fun of the Kantian view that the spell of beauty enables us to view even nude female statues 'disinterestedly'.[18] Leopold Bloom pays lip-service to this aesthetic when he shows Stephen Molly's photo, conceding that it 'simply wasn't art' (*U* 573). Be that as it may, the slightly soiled snapshot carried around by this amateur of the female form provides another instance of the grotesque as opposed to the classical. Molly's parted lips, her winsome look aimed directly at the camera, and most of all her opulent bosom 'with more than vision of breasts' are a direct affront to the classical separation of art from life, or of aesthetic appreciation from lust. Earlier Bloom has expressed his admiration for the splendidly proportioned hips and bosoms of Greek statuary. His dubious motives for showing Stephen Molly's picture are a further example of his instinctive reduction of the classical to the erotic.

Ulysses, as I shall argue later, is full of grotesque humour, much of it based on distorted or incongruous views of the body. But *Ulysses* is a comparatively realist work and classical art still retains an important place in it. *Finnegans Wake*, by contrast, is entirely given over to the grotesque, and contains many renderings of the body merged into landscape. The heroine is a river – or rather, all rivers – and the hero an extinct volcano or legendary giant buried (in one of the many versions) with his head at Howth and his toes sticking up in Phoenix Park. Hero and heroine both have a multiple, not an individual, identity. This opening-up of the body and of identity belongs naturally with an opening-up of the word – a systematic deformation and reformation of language. Kayser sets Joyce in a tradition of 'verbal grotesques' going back to Rabelais and Sterne.[19] Rabelais, according to Leo Spitzer, 'creates word-families, representative of gruesome fantasy-beings, copulating and engendering before our eyes, which have reality only in the world of language'.[20] Something similar happens when Joyce – to take an almost random example – puns on *incest* and *insect* and calls the hero of his 'Eyrawyggla saga' 'humile, commune and ensectuous' (*FW* 48:16–17, 29:30).

Joyce turned increasingly to the mode of grotesque humour as he grew older. The decisive break with his early style would seem to come somewhere between the end of the *Portrait* and the later chapters of *Ulysses*. But we can trace grotesque elements in his imagination from the beginning. The hell-fire sermon in the *Portrait*, the *double entendre* in the title of *Chamber Music*, and the lampoon 'The Holy Office' (1904) in which he assumes the role of 'Katharsis–Purgative' are three cases in point. In each of them Joyce's vision is one of incongruity, of Eliot's 'recognition, implicit in the expression of every experience, of other kinds of experience which are possible'.[21] Yet the incongruity is also a debunking – an act of deliberate vulgarity. There are similarities between aspects of *Ulysses* and the worm's-eye or custard-pie view of life which George Orwell described in his essay on comic seaside postcards, 'The Art of Donald McGill'. Grotesque humour, like the carnival, debunks the established social order and its necessary hypocrisies:

Codes of law and morals, or religious systems, never have much room in them for a humorous view of life. . . . A dirty joke is not, of course, a serious attack on morality, but it is a sort of mental rebellion, a momentary wish that things were otherwise. So also with all other jokes, which always centre round cowardice, laziness, dishonesty or some other quality which society cannot afford to encourage.[22]

Joyce is not at one with the tellers of dirty jokes in his fiction, any more than Orwell was at one with Frank Richards or Donald McGill. He portrays his scroungers and barflies against a background of classical epic, and mixes profanity with the extremes of learning and literary sophistication. In his erudition, his love of pedantry, and the battery of scholarship he brings to bear on the coarsest matters, he is reminiscent of such earlier Irish comic writers as Swift and Sterne.[23] Neither Swift nor Sterne, however, shared Joyce's encyclopaedic aims. To find a precedent for these we must again turn to Rabelais, whose *Gargantua and Pantagruel* is described by Bakhtin as an 'encyclopaedia of folk culture'.[24] Exactly the same phrase may be applied to *Ulysses* and *Finnegans Wake*, provided we remember that folk culture in Joyce is an urban and industrial phenomenon, permeated at all levels by the press, advertising, popular fiction, opera and music-hall. In *Ulysses* this culture is summed up in the marriage of a newspaper advertisement canvasser and a professional soprano. In *Finnegans Wake* we encounter still more recent forms of discourse and popular expression: the telephone, radio and television.

For a further example of Joyce's grotesque art we may look at his treatment of Shakespeare. Shakespeare has little importance in the early works; he does not make a full appearance on the Joyceian stage until *Ulysses*. Stephen identifies with Hamlet – he is wearing a 'Hamlet hat', whatever that may be – and in the Library chapter, with dazzling erudition, he develops his theory of Shakespeare's art. The theory has already been ridiculed by Buck Mulligan, who tells Haines that 'He proves by algebra that Hamlet's grandson is Shakespeare's grandfather and that he himself is the ghost of his own father' (*U* 24). (It may be noticed that this sentence in itself embodies the three characteristics of the grotesque – unnatural fusion, distortion, and multiplication – specified by Hegel.) Mulligan's travesty is hardly more absurd, as it turns out, than the theory itself. Stephen deconstructs Shakespeare's plays to show that their author's experience of cuckoldry is the motive power of his art from first to last. His argument is parodied later, in the séance-like atmosphere of Nighttown, where one of the many spirits called up from the dead is the face of William Shakespeare 'crowned by the reflection of the reindeer antlered hatrack in the hall' (*U* 508) – in other words, wearing horns. Shakespeare speaks (''Tis the loud laugh bespeaks the vacant mind'), but then his face dissolves into that of Bloom's friend Martin Cunningham. In *Finnegans Wake* Shakespeare is subjected to further grotesque indignities, though now they are verbal rather than intellectual and melodramatic. *Macbeth* is epitomized in the following passage:

For a burning would is come to dance inane. Glamours hath moidered's lieb and herefore Coldours must leap no more. Lack breath must leap no more. (*FW* 250: 16–18)

If Macbeth can become 'Lack breath' we need not be surprised that Shakespeare himself appears variously as shaggspick, Shakhisbeard, Scheekspair, Shikespower, Shopkeeper, and Shapesphere.[25]

Shakespeare was included in *Ulysses* and *Finnegans Wake* not only because of his comic potential but because Joyce wished these books to be all-embracing. God, in the form of the world's major sacred books and scriptures, is in them too. Joyce was a lifelong admirer of the Italian Renaissance philosopher Giordano Bruno, whose teaching can be summed up in the proverb 'Extremes meet'. One of the best-known grotesque examples of a meeting of extremes in the English language is the fact that *god*, spelt backwards, becomes *dog*. If the principle of a meeting of extremes is accepted it is possible to see a direct continuity between the early romantic phase in which Stephen Dedalus vowed to forge the 'uncreated conscience' of his race, and the monumental profanities of the later Joyce. The late books are both the fulfilment and the inversion of Joyce's early ambitions. His main anxiety, as a young man, is that he may prove equal to his artistic calling − that the fecundity of his imagination shall match the demands made on it by his youthful dreams. The central subject of *Ulysses* and *Finnegans Wake*, however, is the celebration not of artistic but of ordinary human fecundity. These books are as profuse as the *Book of Kells* and as priapic as the sculptures and emblems found in the Italian grottoes.[26] Their sexual symbolism and supposed obscenity is part of a primordial concern with succession, generation and fecundity.

In his *Autobiographies* W. B. Yeats said that in the 1890s, under the French symbolist influence, he believed that 'our whole age is seeking to bring forth a sacred book'.[27] Of all his contemporaries only Joyce seems to have fully grasped that such a book could be made, not out of aesthetic ideals such as the young Stephen's, but of debunking, parody, coarseness, and comedy. Its justification would lie not in delicacy and good taste (though a place somewhere in the great edifice would be reserved for these things) but in sheer abundance and creative power, not diffused in the Dickensian manner from book to book, but incrusted as thickly as the author could make it. The whole of modern experience and verbal expression would be epitomized within a single enigmatic pair of covers. The aura which *Ulysses* and (in its more esoteric way) *Finnegans Wake* have acquired in the half-century since Joyce's death suggests a virtual realization of Yeats's dream. The place of Joyce's books in the cultural Holy of Holies is attested to by literary influence, by the accumulation of criticism and scholarship, and by the fascination they hold for their readers. Yet these books are pagan to the core and turn conventional notions of sacredness upside down. Their author excelled as a literary comedian, and was a high priest of burlesque and profanity. He was, also, an Inimitable.

PART I

2 The student

University College

James Joyce embarked on his career as an artist soon after entering University College, Dublin, in 1899. He did so by writing essays and verses, by championing modern drama in the college debating society, and by teaching his contemporaries to regard him as a poet and genius. It was not long before the news of a brilliant student at the Catholic university – a small group of Georgian town houses on the south side of St Stephen's Green, close to the intellectual and fashionable heart of the city – began to spread in Dublin literary circles. In 1902, for example, Joyce had his first meeting with W. B. Yeats, who was already in his late thirties and Ireland's leading poet. The meeting was somewhat ruefully described by Yeats in an unpublished preface,[1] and became legendary over the years. Later, in *Stephen Hero* and *A Portrait of the Artist as a Young Man*, Joyce gave an unsurpassed fictional account of what it is like to be a student; but though his fiction added substantially to the legend of its author as a very formidable young man, it was not the original source of that legend. Joyce's direct impact on those who knew him is exemplified by this extract from a diary kept in 1903–4 by his younger brother:

Jim is, perhaps, a genius though his mind is minutely analytic. He has, above all, a proud, wilful, vicious selfishness, out of which by times now he writes a poem or an epiphany, now commits the meannesses of whim and appetite . . . He has extraordinary moral courage – courage so great that I have hopes that he will one day become the Rousseau of Ireland.[2]

It is not hard to recognize in this proud, egotistical and courageous figure the 'Stephen Dedalus' who at the end of the *Portrait* dedicates himself to the path of 'silence exile and cunning'. Stephen's growth to artisthood and departure from Ireland in the *Portrait* are felt – like the coming of a prophet – to answer the needs of the time; he goes to forge the 'uncreated conscience' of his race. Stanislaus Joyce, too, sees his brother as a future liberator and sage, if not a prophet. Ireland,

17

he implies, is awaiting its Rousseau. Certainly both Ireland and
Stanislaus found it hard to accustom themselves to the emergence, not
of a Rousseau, but of the author of *Ulysses*.

Born in 1882, Joyce had passed through Clongowes Wood College
and Belvedere College, perhaps the best schools in middle-class
Catholic Ireland. University College was his third educational
institution run by the Jesuit order and basing its instruction on the
supreme authority of the church fathers. University College, however,
had been founded with very different aims from a Clongowes or a
Belvedere. Its decline into a 'day-school full of terrorised boys' (*SH*
238) – as Stephen sardonically and contemptuously describes it – is
intimately connected with the establishment of the Joyce legend. At
University College the self-proclaimed artist stood out all the more
sharply in a timid and censorious institution which fell far short of its
own ideals.

University College was, in intention if not in achievement, one of the
class of great Victorian foundations which transformed education and,
in doing so, helped to create the modern world. It was modelled on
another new university, the Catholic University of Louvain in Belgium,
which opened in the 1830s. Two aspects of its foundation were to
influence all of its alumni, including Joyce and his contemporaries who
entered the college forty-five years after it took in its first students in
1854. First, it was a Catholic institution, governed by the Irish bishops
who saw it as an essential counterweight to Trinity College and to the
new Protestant 'godless colleges' at Belfast, Cork and Galway. Then
there was the abiding memory of its first rector, John Henry Newman,
one of the most powerful and original of Victorian minds. Newman's
high and liberal aspirations for University College had received
unforgettable expression in the lectures usually known as *The Idea of
a University* (1852). Yet he had resigned and left Dublin after a brief
tenure, exhausted by his failure to win a measure of academic
autonomy and to wrest control from the bishops. Newman's dream of
an imperial Catholic university attracting students from throughout
the English-speaking world was never realized.[3] In 1879 it became part
of the Royal University, a purely examining body, and in 1883 the
management of the college was entrusted to the Jesuits, with Father
William Delany as President.

Many other writers born after 1850 attended new universities – in
England, for example, one thinks of Gissing at Manchester, Wells at
South Kensington, and D. H. Lawrence at Nottingham – but only

perhaps in Wells's case was the intellectual and imaginative impact as decisive as it was on Joyce. Both Newman's university and T. H. Huxley's Normal School of Science in South Kensington (now Imperial College) were, and in some ways still are, strongly ideological institutions. The religious framework of studies at University College was part of Newman's original plan, as is evident from the following decision of the steering committee set up soon after his initial appointment as rector:

As all academic instruction must be in harmony with the Principles of the Catholic Religion, the Professors will be bound, not only not to teach anything contrary to religion, but to take advantage of the occasion the subjects they treat of may offer, to point out that Religion is the basis of Science, and to inculcate the love of Religion and its duties.[4]

Under the direction of a great intellect such as Newman, the 'Principles of the Catholic Religion' might have enriched a modern liberal and scientific education; but this was by no means the case under Father Delany. Kevin Sullivan has described the Jesuits as 'little more than educational caretakers . . . for a student as talented as Joyce, the curriculum at University College was intellectually contemptible'.[5] In the key subject of Philosophy, where the text used was Rickaby's *General Metaphysics*,[6] students were carefully shielded from having to confront any of the intellectual difficulties surrounding the Catholic faith in the modern world. Virtually every development in European philosophy since the Renaissance was condemned *a priori*, being the product of heretics, atheists, Protestants or Jews.

In *Stephen Hero* Joyce imagined a confrontation between his protagonist and the President of University College. In reality Joyce's interview with Father Delany over his paper 'Drama and Life' took place before his eighteenth birthday and was, no doubt, much embellished in retrospect. Stephen's conversation with the President is in some respects reminiscent of Newman's battles with the Catholic bishops fifty years earlier. Stephen demands freedom from censorship, just as Newman had tried, and failed, to win a free hand in the appointment of his professors. The President's manner is urbane, condescending and wholly unshakeable. Stephen lives up to his reputation as a brilliant young paradoxist with considerable finesse, never more so than when he defends his 'Art for Art's sake' heresies with the contention that 'I have only pushed to its logical conclusion the definition Aquinas has given of the beautiful' (*SH* 100). It is highly unlikely that Joyce ever said such words to Father Delany, though no doubt he would have wished to have done so. His intellectual development immediately after leaving university shows that he had retained his respect for the Jesuits, whatever the defects of University College. In a verse satire, 'The Holy Office' (1904), we find him disparaging

> Those souls that hate the strength that mine has
> Steeled in the school of old Aquinas.   (*PP* 38)

Despite a certain sardonic edge, these are surprising lines. Joyce and a handful of his fellow-undergraduates had been present on 27 November 1901 when Father Delany inaugurated the Academy of St Thomas Aquinas, a new college society.[7] Joyce's private study of Aristotle and Aquinas, however, is not recorded until the so-called Paris and Pola notebooks that he kept in 1903 and 1904. Despite the evidence of *Stephen Hero* and the *Portrait*, his undergraduate writings show only the first stirrings of the aesthetic theories that Stephen Dedalus expounds. In his novels Joyce seems to have heightened the contrast between Stephen's precocity and his benighted fellow-students and teachers by advancing his own intellectual development two or three years.

At the turn of the century University College, as the only Catholic university in a predominantly Catholic country, was becoming a breeding-ground for cultural nationalism. Far from being the cosmopolitan centre that Newman had conceived, it was – Joyce felt – an insular and inward-looking establishment. The Gaelic League flourished there and, some years after Joyce left, University College students would play a leading part in the formation of a nationalist militia, the Irish Volunteers. (Davin, in the *Portrait*, is already practising military drill.) In later life Joyce's student contemporaries were to become a cross-section of the professional and ruling elite of the Irish Republic. Still more significantly, no less than three of his closest associates eventually met with sensational and violent deaths. The pacifist Francis Skeffington (McCann in the *Portrait*) was murdered by a British officer when trying to stop soldiers from looting during the Easter Rising. (His 'treason' became so notorious that members of the English branch of the Skeffingtons, including some of my own relatives, changed their names.) Thomas Kettle, a pugnacious advocate of the 'parliamentary road' to Home Rule, enlisted in the British Army and was killed leading his company of Dublin Fusiliers in the Battle of the Somme. George Clancy (Davin in the *Portrait*) became mayor of Limerick and was murdered in front of his wife by Protestant irregulars (the Black and Tans). These subsequent deaths give, in retrospect, a very precise meaning to the 'nightmare of history' from which Stephen in *Ulysses* says he is trying to awake. Joyce's attitude as a student was that of an avant-garde artist who refused all commerce with the political vanguard of future militants, idealists, and potential martyrs. His pamphlet 'The Day of the Rabblement' was provoked by the Irish Literary Theatre's readiness to lower its artistic standards in the interests of nationalism. His eventual decision to live in exile may well reflect a premonition that to stay in an Ireland torn by bloodshed and political hatreds would destroy his creative equilibrium. The countries in which he made his home, Italy, Switzerland, and France, were places where he could maintain his usually undemonstrative Irish patriotism undisturbed.

Joyce made a powerful impression on his fellow-students. So much is clear both from his own fiction and from the memoirs of those who knew him at this time. For all his celebrated aloofness he wrote, debated, joked, conversed, and plunged into the mêlée as a precocious intellectual and champion of unpopular causes (especially Ibsen and continental drama). The authoritarian nature of the college, reflected in the censorship of papers given to the students' Literary and Historical Society and of the unofficial college magazine *St Stephen's*, encouraged him to develop the role of gadfly and literary outlaw that he would pursue to the end of his life. Joyce's notion of a career, too, was formed to some extent in reaction against the middle-class ideal represented by University College.

In traditional European societies freedom of choice of a career was open only to the occasional rebel who ran away, either to the big city or to sea. The sons of the aristocracy entered the professions appropriate to their station and place in the family – estate management, the army, the church, politics, or the law. The lower classes were restricted either to a trade already practised in the family or to whatever menial occupation happened to be available. The increasing social mobility of the nineteenth century entailed the existence of a large middle class which had secured freedom of choice of career for its sons (not daughters); a fact which explains both the growing demand for higher education and the palpable tension surrounding the announcement, on the part of many a Victorian fictional hero, of what he intended to 'do'. Joyce's family had been part of the property-owning middle classes for several generations,

although at the time of his adolescence their fortunes were in steep
decline. His father had once been a student and was an earlier
beneficiary of bourgeois freedom of choice. No doubt, as Stephen
mockingly implies when he lists his father's occupations, he had
indulged it to excess:

> a medical student, an oarsman, a tenor, an amateur actor, a shouting politician,
> a small landlord, a small investor, a drinker, a good fellow, a story-teller,
> somebody's secretary, something in a distillery, a tax-gatherer, a bankrupt and
> at present a praiser of his own past.   (*P* 241)

Simon Dedalus's Micawberish progress contrasts with the discovery
of a true vocation which rounds off the nineteenth-century
Bildungsroman, whether it be *David Copperfield*, the Fred Vincy story
in *Middlemarch*, or Samuel Butler's *The Way of All Flesh*. In these
novels, the hero's freedom of choice is in the end freedom to make the
right choice. In *A Portrait of the Artist*, Joyce pushes this paradox to
the limit at which Stephen is given no choice except that between
following his deepest instincts and the logic of his given identity –
symbolized by the name Dedalus – and betraying his artistic 'soul' by
becoming a priest. Yet, unlike his more conventional contemporaries,
Stephen has to follow the traditional expedient of 'running away', or
going into exile, if he is to achieve true self-development.

Joyce's fiction does not pursue Stephen into exile. While he remains
in Dublin he lives a Bohemian existence – a form of artistic revolt
amongst the young which parallels the sponging of Simon Dedalus and
his cronies. (So we have the absurd situation that both Simon and his
eldest son despise one another as wastrels.) To put Stephen and his
friends, such as Buck Mulligan, Cranly, and Lynch, beside Simon and
his friends is to realize how much the ethos of the wastrel and the idler
informs Joyce's books. In Buck Mulligan's case we could easily
construct a list of occupations to parody Simon Dedalus's miscellany:

> a medical student, a swimmer, a congenital actor, a literary politician, a
> usurping tenant, a sponger, a drinker, a wit, an obscene story-teller, a hanger-
> on at Oxford, a gatherer of confessions, a Judas, an intellectual bankrupt and
> a praiser of his own present and future.

Ironically people like Simon and the Buck are 'artists' – 'characters',
luminaries, entertainers – in ordinary Dublin parlance. It is typical of
Stephen that he cannot admit his kinship with these gentlemanly
parasites, however much he appears to resemble them. Artisthood, for
Stephen, is the opposite of an 'allround' vocation such as Mulligan, his

father, and (in a slightly different sense) Leopold Bloom have chosen. It is a discipline still more demanding, constricting, and uncompromising than the priesthood which he had rejected.

Stephen's artistic vocation is predestined. It is the result of a 'call' he has received, not from divine authority, but from the heart of life itself. It would be wrong, however, to let the legend of the predestined artist obscure the reality of the process by which Joyce himself came to take up the bourgeois profession of letters. For Stephen's self-conscious display of genius is part of the licensed irresponsibility of student Bohemianism. The real test of his dedication and capacity for toil will come later. (The same is of course true of Buck Mulligan, the archetypal medical student. Having qualified as a doctor, Oliver St John Gogarty – the model for Mulligan – went on to become a noted surgeon and an Irish senator as well as an author and wit.) Joyce's student period was prolonged by his sojourn in Paris, ostensibly following a medical course, until he was summoned home to his mother's deathbed early in 1903. There followed another eighteen months' Bohemian existence in Dublin, which included a very brief stay in Gogarty's Martello Tower. In the summer of 1904, Joyce abandoned this hand-to-mouth existence, took an overseas teaching job, and soon had started a family. His brother Stanislaus, who followed him to the Berlitz School in Trieste, made his life there and eventually became a Professor of English. Not the least of Joyce's debts to University College was that it left him with the qualifications and the motivation to enter a moderately congenial profession which would support him and his dependants (however meagrely) until he had found his feet as an artist. He too was a beneficiary of bourgeois freedom of choice.

The old master in Christiania

Stephen's main intellectual interests in the student episodes of the *Portrait of the Artist* are in aesthetic theory. Yet, as we have seen, the evidence suggests that it was not until after he left University College that Joyce became a serious student of Aristotle and Aquinas. His student years were his Ibsen years, in which he attracted public notice by his fervent championship of European drama. Joyce adopted Ibsen as his artistic father-figure with a touching devotion which led him to learn Danish and to write an ardent fan-letter to his hero. His pamphlet 'The Day of the Rabblement', after savaging the Irish theatre, ends with the fire-breathing announcement that 'Elsewhere there are men who are worthy to carry on the tradition of the old master who is dying in Christiania' (*CW* 72). The year was 1901; Joyce was nearly twenty; the twentieth century was a few months old; and Joyce had skilfully chosen the grounds of his first intervention in Irish literature.

It is not surprising that Joyce, at this time, should have turned to the drama. The major Irish literary figures of the day were Wilde, Yeats, and Shaw. Wilde's glittering comedies were set among the British aristocracy from which Joyce, as a Dublin Catholic, felt infinitely remote. The Irish Literary Theatre (the precursor of the Abbey Theatre) was launched in May 1899 with Yeats's play *The Countess Cathleen*, which Joyce admired. His fellow-students, however, launched a petition against it, and soon Joyce had come to despise the new theatre's readiness to appease nationalist sentiment. The choice of Douglas Hyde's *Casad-an-Súgán* and of Yeats and George Moore's *Diarmuid and Grania* for its next productions led to his pamphleteering outburst. There was, he said, no genuine native Irish tradition in drama: 'A nation which never advanced so far as a miracle play affords no literary model to the artist, and he must look abroad' (*CW* 70). The implication of this cutting verdict on Irish provinciality is borne out in the portrayal of Stephen in the *Portrait of the Artist*: loyalty to art is a higher duty than loyalty to one's country.

Bernard Shaw, though only beginning to make his mark as a dramatist, was the leading English Ibsenite. Joyce regarded him as a fellow-townsman, though he had left Ireland years before. There are a few resemblances between the Ibsen whom Joyce idolized and the Ibsen portrayed in Shaw's *The Quintessence of Ibsenism* (1891). Both Joyce and Shaw delighted in Ibsen's courageous exposures of corruption, hypocrisy, the suppression of truth, and the oppression of women in his native country. Ibsen in *Ghosts* had scandalized Europe by putting hereditary syphilis on the stage; Joyce, also in the name of realism and of debunking bourgeois prudery, was to put defecation and masturbation into *Ulysses*. Joyce looked up to Ibsen, as his brother looked up to Rousseau, as an exemplar of the 'extraordinary moral courage' needed to become a great writer in unenlightened Ireland. Yet, if anything, Joyce's early essays on Ibsen played down his achievements as a reformer.

In these essays Joyce was looking for aesthetic, rather than moral and political, justifications of the realist movement to which Ibsen belonged. In a review of a painting then being exhibited at the Royal

Hibernian Academy – Munkacsy's 'Ecce Homo' – Joyce put forward truthfulness, objectivity and the portrayal of emotional conflict as the criteria of a 'dramatic' work of art (*CW* 31–7). A few months later, in the paper on 'Drama and Life' that he read to the Literary and Historical Society, he offered this definition of the dramatic:

By drama I understand the interplay of passions to portray truth; drama is strife, evolution, movement in whatever way unfolded; it exists, before it takes form, independently; it is conditioned but not controlled by its scene.   (*CW* 41)

He distinguished between drama and what he called 'literature', or *belles lettres*. Drama was the more classical and permanent art of the two. It is not hard to detect echoes of Aristotle and Samuel Johnson in the following passage:

Human society is the embodiment of changeless laws which the whimsicalities and circumstances of men and women involve and overwrap. The realm of literature is the realm of these accidental manners and humours – a spacious realm; and the true literary artist concerns himself mainly with them. Drama has to do with the underlying laws first, in all their nakedness and divine severity, and only secondarily with the motley agents who bear them out.
(*CW* 40)

This argument, which hinges on the distinction between 'accidental manners and humours' and 'underlying laws', could be turned either for or against bourgeois drama such as Ibsen's. Joyce's purpose, however, was to condemn the picturesque costume-theatre of historical romance (stretching, in his eyes, back to Shakespeare) and to assert that Ibsen's drab modern scene offered the 'nakedness and divine severity' for which he called. 'Drama and Life' dismisses nostalgia for the 'good old times' (*CW* 45) and claims that the present is one of the great ages of art. Joyce's defence of modern bourgeois drama was put still more forcefully in a passage from the lengthy critique of Ibsen's *When We Dead Awaken* which he published in the London *Fortnightly Review* in 1900:

Ibsen has chosen the average lives in their uncompromising truth for the groundwork of all his later plays. How easy it would have been to have written *An Enemy of the People* on a speciously loftier level – to have replaced the *bourgeois* by the legitimate hero! Critics might then have extolled as grand what they have so often condemned as banal. But the surroundings are nothing to Ibsen. The play is the thing.   (*CW* 63)

'The play is the thing'. Joyce wrote an Ibsenite play, *A Brilliant Career*, while on holiday at Mullingar in 1900. Stanislaus Joyce describes the play, which has not survived, as 'a rehash of ingredients borrowed . . . from *When We Dead Awaken*, *A Doll's House* and *The League of Youth*'.[8] Joyce sent it to William Archer, Ibsen's English translator, whose criticism was tactful but devastating. Evidently Joyce took this to heart since when, in late 1902, Yeats asked him to write a play for the Irish Literary Theatre, he replied that he would do so in five years' time.[9] (Yeats was more successful in recruiting J. M. Synge, eleven years older than Joyce, whose first play *The Shadow of the Glen* was performed in 1903.) Joyce showed that he had absorbed the technical lessons of Ibsen's work when he came to write 'The Dead' and, much later, his play *Exiles*. Nevertheless, for all his enthusiasm, it is only in the broadest and most symbolic sense that he can be considered Ibsen's heir. As early as 1907 he is on record as arguing that Ibsen's realism did not go far enough.[10] In strict terms of literary succession he had far more in common with Flaubert, whose novels he studied carefully but about whom he wrote almost nothing. We may hypothesize that Joyce's passionate Ibsenism had two root causes, neither of which had much to do with the neoclassical theory of drama. The first was the Norwegian writer's fearlessly individual stance as the artistic representative of a small country on the edge of Europe in the process of gaining its political independence. The second was a profound response on Joyce's part to aspects of Ibsen's dramatic symbolism: the syphilis-theme in *Ghosts*, the door-imagery of *A Doll's House* and *The Master Builder*, and the representation in several plays of the artist's essential solitude. In 'The Holy Office' (privately printed in 1904) Joyce mounted a furious attack on the Dublin literati. At the back of his mind, no doubt, was Goethe's comparison of the Irish to 'a pack of hounds, always dragging down some noble stag'.[11] But the self-image that emerges is unmistakably Ibsenite in expression:

> Where they have crouched and crawled and prayed
> I stand the self-doomed, unafraid,
> Unfellowed, friendless and alone,
> Indifferent as the herring-bone,
> Firm as the mountain-ridges where
> I flash my antlers on the air.   (*PP* 38)

Through his worship of Ibsen Joyce discovered not only the bourgeois hero but the artist as hero.

Chamber Music

In the *Portrait* Stephen expounds the neoclassical theory of the strict division of literary forms into the lyrical, the epical, and the dramatic. Perhaps the appeal of this theory for the young Joyce reflects the clarity with which his own student writings fall into separate compartments. His early verse, for example, shows no sign of the 'flashing antlers' and defiant doggerel of 'The Holy Office'. When he wrote an appreciation of the mid-Victorian Dublin poet James Clarence Mangan (published in *St Stephen's*, 1902), he could not prevent the Irish national question from rearing its head: caught up in the 'narrow and hysterical nationality' (*CW* 82) of his times, Joyce argued, Mangan had failed to meet the challenge of awaking from history's nightmare. 'History encloses him so straitly that even his fiery moments do not set him free from it' (*CW* 81). But the questions of nationality, language, and religion that beset Stephen Dedalus are altogether absent from Joyce's first volume.

Chamber Music (1907) is a sequence of lyrics written during his student years which Joyce later selected and arranged for book publication. The poems in the main are slight and mellifluous pieces modelled on the songs of Shakespeare and the Elizabethans. In them Joyce adopts the guise of a courtly lover and lutanist

> All softly playing,
>   With head to the music bent,
> And fingers straying
>   Upon an instrument. (I)

These are unexpected works for Joyce to have produced. Their delicacy and finesse is undeniable, yet reading them one wonders what all the fuss (by the young Joyce himself and those closest to him) was about. The last thing one would call the poet of *Chamber Music* is a future Rousseau of Ireland. Echoes of Blake, Keats and other nineteenth-century lyric poets are frequent, and the usually simple and graceful diction seems the work of a talented but by no means exceptional young poet. He had no difficulty in placing several of his 'capful of light odes' (*U* 412) in Dublin magazines. Perhaps it is significant that, in later life, Joyce gave contradictory accounts of *Chamber Music*. Writing to Stanislaus in 1907 he spoke of the 'expression of myself which I now see I began in *Chamber Music*'.[12] Much later, however, he told Herbert Gorman that 'I wrote *Chamber Music* as a protest against myself'.[13] Like some of the later *Pomes Penyeach*, these lyrics reveal the easily-moved, sentimental side of his personality which would have been more fully indulged had he taken up — as he might have done — a career as a singer. In most of his writings such powerful feelings would be very sparingly unleashed. *Chamber Music* is the least ironic of Joycean texts.

Even so there is deliberate pastiche, if not outright parody, in these poems. The sequence follows the progress of a love-affair and, in the first few poems, the lover's air is one of extreme and perhaps deceptive innocence. He longs to nestle in his beloved's 'sweet bosom' (VI) and watches entranced as

> My love goes lightly, holding up
> Her dress with dainty hand.   (VII)

'Light' appears in a later poem ('Lightly come or lightly go', XXV) with a subterranean ninetyish suggestion of the 'lights-o'-love' or harlots of whom Joyce might have read in George Moore's *Confessions of a Young Man* (1888). The growth of love described in the early lyrics leads quickly to thoughts of seduction. In XII his blandishments have a fairly obvious aim: he addresses his mistress as 'sweet sentimentalist' and invites her to

> Believe me rather that am wise
> In disregard of the divine.

The succeeding poems show a successful seduction followed by gradual disillusionment, discord, and a reluctant agreement to part. A few lyrics celebrate the joys of sex as openly as any poet, writing for the respectable public of turn-of-the-century Dublin, is likely to have done. Others are poignant evocations of loneliness and the selfish and narcissistic needs which sexual love is called on to appease. The progress of love, conventionally plotted against the cycle of the seasons, leads from the pastiche of innocence to the unresolved tensions of experience:

> Sleep now, O sleep now,
>   O you unquiet heart!
> A voice crying 'Sleep now'
>   Is heard in my heart.
>
> The voice of the winter
>   Is heard at the door.
> O sleep for the winter
>   Is crying 'Sleep no more!'

>My kiss will give peace now
>   And quiet to your heart —
>Sleep on in peace now,
>   O you unquiet heart!   (XXXIV)

This poem, like the rest of *Chamber Music*, is remarkable for its simplicity and obliquity. Two conflicting voices are heard, which cannot be reconciled. The meaning of the voices, however, is barely hinted at: only in the last poem in the volume, 'I Hear an Army' — a poem added later, and written in a different style — is the poet's reticence overcome, so that we hear the despair of his 'unquiet heart' and share his nightmares. The other, more conventional lyrics allude to feelings rather than evoking them directly. In *Pomes Penyeach* (1927) Joyce published a poem, 'Tilly', written in Dublin in 1904 but excluded from the earlier volume. Here he abandons the pastoral and musical decorum of *Chamber Music* for something far more expressionistic:

>He travels after a winter sun,
>Urging the cattle along a cold red road,
>Calling to them, a voice they know,
>He drives his beasts above Cabra.
>
>The voice tells them home is warm.
>They moo and make brute music with their hoofs.
>He drives them with a flowering branch before him,
>Smoke pluming their foreheads.
>
>Boor, bond of the herd,
>Tonight stretch full by the fire!
>I bleed by the black stream
>For my torn bough!   (*PP* 13)

Again there are two voices: the voice of the torn tree and the soothing tones of the herdsman urging his cattle homewards. The last stanza in which the poet speaks through the tree makes a radical break from the preceding stanzas. The poem reveals a defiant and disruptive impulse, a painful refusal to compromise, which is almost entirely suppressed in *Chamber Music*. It is a bitterly partisan poem and one which invites symbolic interpretation: the cattle-driver who has casually ripped off the branch, for example, may be God himself. Joyce wrote 'Tilly', according to Richard Ellmann, while 'bleeding' over his mother's death.[14]

A modern Daedalus

May Joyce died in August 1903, four months after her eldest son had been fetched home from Paris by telegram. By his twenty-second birthday, on 2 February 1904, Joyce had adopted the title *Stephen Hero* for the autobiographical novel he was writing. Soon he began signing letters with the name 'Stephen Daedalus'. Some early versions of the *Dubliners* stories were published in 'AE's' magazine *The Irish Homestead* under the same pseudonym. Joyce's adoption of this outlandish name (the spelling was later amended to Dedalus) represents a decisive moment in his artistic development.

That the genesis of a work of art might lie in the discovery of a 'strange name' is the theme of the following lyric, which has a density of image and literary allusion quite uncharacteristic of the other poems in *Chamber Music*:

> Thou leanest to the shell of night,
>   Dear lady, a divining ear.
> In that soft choiring of delight
>   What sound hath made thy heart to fear?
> Seemed it of rivers rushing forth
>   From the grey deserts of the north?
>
> That mood of thine, O timorous,
>   Is his, if thou but scan it well,
> Who a mad tale bequeaths to us
>   At ghosting hour conjurable –
> And all for some strange name he read
>   In Purchas or in Holinshed.   (XXVI)

The 'sound' that has upset the lady is, apparently, what Blake would have called the Voice of the Bard. Among the bardic voices present are those of Shakespeare, the Tennyson of 'In Memoriam' – who seems to me the main source of the poem's manner – and of Coleridge, who read the name of Kubla Khan in *Purchas His Pilgrimage*. Where, then, did Joyce read the name of Daedalus? Its bearer is one of the better-known Greek heroes and the question cannot be answered with any certainty. The notion that Dublin was, or might become, a 'modern Athens' was a commonplace at the time of the Irish literary revival. Oliver Gogarty, for example, was as ardent a 'modern Athenian' in real life as is his likeness, Buck Mulligan, in *Ulysses*. The Greek diphthong in Daedalus had been anticipated by 'AE' (the pen-name of the poet and theosophist George Russell). There is, as it happens, a fascinating potential literary source for Joyce's pseudonym which, if not known to the writer himself, might have been known to one of his friends. This is *A Modern Daedalus* (1885), a science-fiction adventure tale in which a young Irishman builds himself wings and heads across the Irish Sea to London. During his absence a nationalist rebellion breaks out, led by his brother. The hero flies back in time to rally the rebels, bombing Dublin Castle from the air and sinking a dreadnought in Dublin Bay. Tom Greer, the author of *A Modern Daedalus*, contested North Derry as a Liberal Home Ruler in 1892. It would be a remarkable coincidence if Joyce had never heard of the book.

'Your absurd name, an ancient Greek' (*U* 10), Buck Mulligan says. The legendary Daedalus was not only a pioneer of aviation but of genetic engineering as well. He built the wooden contraption which enabled Pasiphaë to mate with a bull and thus to produce the Minotaur. Joyce pays scant attention to this aspect of the legend. The 'fabulous artificer' whom he takes as his namesake is, specifically, an airman. In 1903, while Joyce, his brother, and a few Dublin contemporaries were nursing the knowledge of his proud, lonely genius, two other brothers on the far side of the Atlantic were successfully completing the first aeroplane. Stephen's 'epiphany' on Dollymount Beach in the *Portrait* shows him a 'hawklike man flying sunward above the sea' (*P* 169). The Wright brothers' first flight took place at Kitty Hawk. Joyce's hawklike man is a symbol of creative genius as an eternal force, capable not only of astonishing the ancient Greeks but of revolutionizing contemporary society. ('You're always talking about "modern" ', Cranly tells Stephen, *SH* 190.) The name Daedalus signifies a defiant individualism whose inventions the world will be forced to reckon with. Yet there is a deep gulf between the grand name and the early productions of 'Stephen Daedalus'.

Apart from his verse and critical essays, Joyce's apprentice writings consist of some early drafts of *Dubliners* stories, the *Epiphanies*, the 1904 essay 'A Portrait of the Artist', and *Stephen Hero*. All these except the short stories were posthumously published, so their survival is to some extent fortuitous. None of them – not even *Stephen Hero* – can be considered as free-standing works of art. Instead, they belong to the prehistory of the *Portrait* and *Dubliners*. Joyce as a collector of 'epiphanies' attained a certain biographical notoriety, as in Gogarty's memoir *As I Was Going Down Sackville Street* (1937) where he is shown rushing off to the lavatory to jot down his friends' conversation.[15] Stephen's theory of epiphanies will be considered

below. Joyce's epiphanies themselves, which were written down
between 1900 and 1904, were later treated as work-notes for his
autobiographical fictions, though not every one was used. The essay
'A Portrait of the Artist' (reprinted, like the epiphanies, in Scholes and
Kain's collection *The Workshop of Daedalus*) was submitted in 1904
to W. K. Magee (John Eglinton), the editor of *Dana*, but rejected on
grounds of incomprehensibility. It contains, among other matter, the
earliest version of Stephen's vision of the 'bird-like girl' on the beach
in the 1916 *Portrait*. The long fragment of *Stephen Hero*, almost
entirely concerned with Stephen's life as a university student, raises in
its most acute form the problem of autobiographical truth in Joyce's
fiction. Not only is the dialogue and pattern of relationships heightened
for dramatic purposes, but none of the chronology of *Stephen Hero*
can be taken on trust as authentic. Nevertheless, the painstaking
realistic narrative gives a sense of the specificity of Joyce's university
life, and (still more) of his relations with his family at that time, which
can be had from no other source.

The documentary fullness of *Stephen Hero* is so marked that it is easy
to underestimate Joyce's rewriting of his experiences. Critics have
dismissed the fragment as Joyce's most naive text, and perhaps it is.
Yet it contains some incisive and memorable episodes which, for
whatever reasons, he later expunged from the *Portrait*. For example,
there is the scene with his mother which forms the climax of Chapter
22, and is surely the most horrifying moment in the book:

One evening he sat [silent] at his piano while the dusk enfolded him. The dismal
sunset lingered still upon the window-panes in a smoulder of rusty fires. Above
him and about him hung the shadow of decay, the decay of leaves and flowers,
the decay of hope. He desisted from his chords and waited, bending upon the
keyboard in silence: and his soul commingled itself with the assailing,
inarticulate dusk. A form which he knew for his mother's appeared far down
in the room, standing in the doorway. In the gloom her excited face was
crimson. A voice which he remembered as his mother's, a voice of a terrified
human being, called his name. The form at the piano answered:
— Yes?
— Do you know anything about the body? . . .
He heard his mother's voice addressing him excitedly like the voice of a
messenger in a play:
— What ought I do? There's some matter coming away from the hole in
Isabel's . . . stomach . . . Did you ever hear of that happening?
— I don't know, he answered trying to make sense of her words, trying to
say them again to himself.
— Ought I send for the doctor. . . . Did you ever hear of that? . . . What ought
I do?

— I don't know. . . . What hole?
— The hole . . . the hole we all have . . . here.   (*SH* 168)

Who can doubt that some such event actually took place in the Joyce family? Yet the rawness owes as much to an art designed to shock as it does to naked experience. There is an earlier version of it in the *Epiphanies* – and there it is Joyce's brother Georgie, not Stephen's sister Isabel, who is dying. In each version the main effect is of the repression and physical shame implicit in the mother's inability to name the parts of the body when speaking with her son. Joyce's revision of the scene adds to its emotional power by carefully underlining the grotesque character of the moment. Stephen, the disembodied aesthete, appears as a Platonic 'form at the piano' ('his soul commingled itself with the assailing, inarticulate dusk') and his mother appears also as a 'form'. Her voice is that of a 'terrified human being' but it is also 'like the voice of a messenger in a play'. The 'play' here is obviously a neoclassical drama or its bourgeois equivalent (such as Ibsen's drawing-room tragedies) in which violent or disgusting action is not allowed on-stage. We move from the self-consciously decadent scene-painting of the beginning of the paragraph to the final inescapable gesture pointing at, not naming, the grotesque body. The overall impression is one of pain and shock and (I think) of private exorcism rather than the attainment of artistic sanity or balance. Mrs Daedalus's and Stephen's embarrassment in this scene throws up Swiftian perspectives of the horror of the flesh; Joyce, however, would turn away from this mode of disgust to the broad comedy of Leopold Bloom's interest in Greek statues.

The sequence portraying Isabel's death is omitted from *A Portrait of the Artist*. It would not easily fit in with the symbolistic mode of that book, being too clearly an expression of outrage and horror. Anger, frustration and a wound-up, taut energy characterize *Stephen Hero*, and all these things relate to the hatred of Catholicism which intensifies as the book progresses. Stephen is not attracted by the ideal of national liberation represented by Madden because

The Roman, not the Sassenach, was for him the tyrant of the islanders: and so deeply had the tyranny eaten into all souls that the intelligence, first overborne so arrogantly, was now eager to prove that arrogance its friend. The watchcry was Faith and Fatherland, a sacred word in that world of cleverly inflammable enthusiasms.   (*SH* 57–8)

He offends his mother by his mockery of the Faith, and refuses to make his Easter duty. He uses the term 'paralysis' to describe the grip exercised by Catholicism over Dublin and its University College.

Joyce wrote to Curran in July 1904 that he was calling his series of stories *Dubliners* 'to betray the soul of that hemiplegia or paralysis which many consider a city'.[16] At the same time he was sending Curran *Stephen Hero* to read in instalments. 'Hemiplegia or paralysis' is a medical concept and, in Joyce's mind, it seems to have been intimately associated with syphilis. Mental paralysis, symptomatic of the dreaded tertiary stage of syphilis, is what Oswald Alving succumbs to in the final minutes of Ibsen's *Ghosts*. Did Joyce see himself as a possible victim either of contagious or of hereditary syphilis? In *Stephen Hero*, Lynch warns Stephen of the danger of contracting the disease: 'You may get a dose that will last you your life. I wonder you have not got it before this' (*SH* 196). An entry in Stanislaus's diary, dated 13 August 1904, gives biographical substance to the idea that Joyce became obsessed with the subject:

He talks much of the syphilitic contagion in Europe, is at present writing a series of studies of it in Dublin, tracing practically everything to it. The drift of his talk seems to be that the contagion is congenital and incurable and responsible for all manias, and being so, that it is useless to try to avoid it.[17]

The idea that the contagion of Dublin is syphilitic is suppressed in Joyce's imaginative works, though it may explain the peculiarly personal pressure with which, in *Stephen Hero*, he develops the idea of paralysis.

The 'meaning' of *Stephen Hero* − insofar as this fragment of a manuscript can be said to possess a unity − is to be found in those passages in which Stephen braces himself to escape from an overwhelming condition of social pathology. 'The deadly chill of the atmosphere of the college paralysed Stephen's heart. In a stupor of powerlessness he reviewed the plague of Catholicism' (*SH* 198). Here Joyce is true to the programme he had announced in his letter to Curran. In reaction against the sense of powerlessness, Stephen decides to stake everything on the melodrama of individual rebellion.

He, at least, though living at the farthest remove from the centre of European culture, marooned on an island in the ocean, though inheriting a will broken by doubt and a soul the steadfastness of whose hate became as weak as water in siren arms, would live his own life according to what he recognised as the voice of a new humanity, active, unafraid and unashamed.　　　(*SH* 199)

It is important to understand why, at such a point, Stephen can only break out into humanist rant. His mind is still dominated by the 'plague of Catholicism'. He accepts the cultural values of the religion he is cursing; if Ireland is at the periphery of European culture, then Rome must be very close to the centre. He accepts its spiritual categories, speaking of the will and the soul and the lure of 'siren arms'. His 'voice of a new humanity' is the inverse of the old Catholic conscience, its dictates written out in negative terms ('Thou shalt be active, *un*afraid and *un*ashamed'), but still commanding obedience. This is the Stephen who will later be sardonically analysed by Buck Mulligan, who observes that 'You have the cursed jesuit strain in you, only it's injected the wrong way' (*U* 14).

Throughout *Stephen Hero* there is a gathering exposition of Stephen's aesthetic beliefs, culminating in the famous 'theory of epiphanies' with its transferred religious terminology. In the fictional version of his paper to the Literary and Historical Society Joyce allows Stephen to make an outright declaration of allegiance to the 'classical temper' such as he himself had avoided in his published critical writings: 'The classical temper . . ., ever mindful of limitations, chooses rather to bend upon these present things and so to work upon them and fashion them that the quick intelligence may go beyond them to their meaning which is still unuttered. In this method the sane and joyful spirit issues forth and achieves imperishable perfection, nature assisting with her goodwill and thanks' (*SH* 83). Later he is made to defend his somewhat heretical use of the term 'classical' at his interview with the President of the college.

It was in *Stephen Hero* that Joyce for the first time developed an aesthetic theory in the strict sense of a philosophical theory of beauty. Both here and in the *Portrait* his theory is essentially a commentary on Aquinas's three requirements for beauty (*Ad pulcritudinem tria requiruntur*). The three requirements are *integritas, consonantia, claritas*. Of these, only the third appears problematical. *Integritas* represents the unity and coherence of the aesthetic object; *consonantia*, its proportion or symmetry. For Stephen the remaining quality, *claritas*, appears mysterious, and he regards it as the supreme quality of the three. He approaches it empirically, or perhaps we should say intuitively; the result in *Stephen Hero* (but not in the *Portrait*) is the famous theory of epiphanies. The passage must be quoted as a whole:

He was passing through Eccles' St one evening, one misty evening, with all these thoughts dancing the dance of unrest in his brain when a trivial incident set him composing some ardent verses which he entitled a 'Vilanelle of the Temptress'. A young lady was standing on the steps of one of those brown brick houses which seem the very incarnation of Irish paralysis. A young gentleman was leaning on the rusty railings of the area. Stephen as he passed on

his quest heard the following fragment of colloquy out of which he
received an impression keen enough to afflict his sensitiveness very severely.
The Young Lady – (drawling discreetly) . . . O, yes . . . I was . . . at the . . .
    cha. . .pel. . . .
The Young Gentleman – (inaudibly) . . . I . . . (again inaudibly) . . . I . . .
The Young Lady – (softly) . . . O . . . but you're . . . ve. . .ry . . . wick. . .ed. . . .

This triviality made him think of collecting many such moments together in
a book of epiphanies. By an epiphany he meant a sudden spiritual
manifestation, whether in the vulgarity of speech or of gesture or in a
memorable phase of the mind itself. He believed that it was for the man of
letters to record these epiphanies with extreme care, seeing that they themselves
are the most delicate and evanescent of moments. He told Cranly that the clock
of the Ballast Office was capable of an epiphany. Cranly questioned the
inscrutable dial of the Ballast Office with his no less inscrutable countenance.

— Yes, said Stephen. I will pass it time after time, allude to it, refer to it, catch
a glimpse of it. It is only an item in the catalogue of Dublin's street furniture.
Then all at once I see it and know at once what it is: epiphany.

— What?

— Imagine my glimpses at that clock as the gropings of a spiritual eye which
seeks to adjust its vision to an exact focus. The moment the focus is reached
the object is epiphanised. It is just in this epiphany that I find the third, the
supreme quality of beauty.   (*SH* 216–17)

Here the 'third, the supreme quality of beauty' is experienced as an
'epiphany', and the prime example of an epiphany that Stephen offers
is the colloquy between a young lady and a young gentleman in Eccles
Street. What does this mean? The colloquy is trivial both in that it is
trifling and in the archaic sense of the *trivium*, or threefold course of
studies. It consists of three dramatic lines or speeches, it possesses (so
we are told) the three requirements of beauty, and it leads Stephen, as
an artist, in three different directions. The first is that of making a
realistic record, of 'collecting many such moments together'. The
second is that of writing a 'Vilanelle of the Temptress'. The third is that
of explaining *claritas* and thus of perfecting his theory of beauty; for
this purpose, the young couple in Eccles Street become
interchangeable, in his mind, with a momentary view of the clock of
the Ballast Office. It seems a great deal to hang on a 'trivial incident'.

Why, it may be asked, does Stephen feel the need of a theory of
beauty, and why does he base it on such unpromising material? Oscar
Wilde had stated in the preface to *The Picture of Dorian Gray* (1891)
that 'The artist is the creator of beautiful things'. Hence to define
beauty is to define the activity of the artist. But Stephen holds a
specifically modern view of the artist – one that is decisively influenced
by the various avant-garde movements of the *fin-de-siècle*. From the

interest he takes in a casual conversation, and in the clock of the Ballast Office, it is clear Stephen would subscribe to a second tenet to be found in Wilde's famous preface: 'No artist is ever morbid. The artist can express everything'. Put these two aphorisms together and we have a paradox which Stephen, like many other artists around 1900, was attempting to resolve.

Hence the scholastic terminology which he draws from Aquinas is something of a facade. As we follow the threefold directions of Stephen's response we shall discover the essential modernity of his artistic interests. First of all, we have the writing-down of an actual fragment of conversation, even though that conversation is inarticulate, apparently pointless, and largely inaudible. The Joyce who wrote down this conversation was, like many of his contemporaries, fascinated by the possibilities and pitfalls of an 'absolute realism'. In 1907, pointing to a drunken labourer and his mother in a restaurant, he was to tell Stanislaus that 'For me, youth and motherhood are those two beside us'.[18] What, then, is represented by the young lady and gentleman? Like the houses among which they live, they typify the social pathology of Ireland and are the 'incarnation of Irish paralysis'. The young gentleman, apparently, was not at the chapel. The young lady pretends to think him wicked, but she finds that wickedness roguishly attractive. Paying lip-service to religion, afraid to express their real feelings (the young gentleman indeed can articulate virtually nothing), these are stereotyped victims of a repression which Stephen can only view sardonically. At the same time, Stephen (and Joyce) would reject any suggestion that such people are unfit for artistic portrayal. Joyce told his brother in 1904 that 'It is my idea of the significance of trivial things that I want to give the two or three unfortunate wretches who may eventually read me'.[19]

If the conversation in itself was so trifling, why did Stephen receive 'an impression keen enough to afflict his sensitiveness very severely'? We cannot say. The precise content of the epiphany is – characteristically – unspoken and the artist's reticence creates an air of deliberate mystery. (Was Joyce himself perhaps the 'young gentleman'? His friend Mary Sheehy had once told him – so it is said – that he was 'very wicked'.[20] If that is so, it would support the impression we have of contradictory feelings at work in the passage.) Stephen aims to detach himself from the incident, claiming that as a 'man of letters' he is simply a delicate and precise recording instrument registering such 'moments' – a sort of literary seismograph. Yet his pose of scientific impartiality is belied by his other responses. The incident affects the highly-strung poet so severely as to set him composing 'some ardent verses which he entitled a "Vilanelle of the Temptress" '. (These verses are printed in the *Portrait*, where Stephen is shown writing them in far more narcissistic circumstances.) It follows that the epiphany is a moment of creative inspiration and that the young lady in Eccles Street bears some relation to an imaginary temptress. Stephen, we may surmise, is both attracted and repelled by his glimpse of the mildly flirtatious young couple. For all their vulgarity they represent the present enjoyment of something that he himself only knows as desire and absence: the relationship, that is, between himself as a poet and an imaginary *femme fatale* or Muse.

But Stephen is not content with finding creative material of two different sorts in the 'trivial incident'; he also intellectualizes it. The momentary conversation, he asserts, constituted an 'epiphany' or sudden spiritual manifestation; and it was, in addition, a moment of beauty. Hence it must display the three qualities of *integritas, consonantia*, and *claritas*. Stephen now solves the mystery of *claritas* to his own satisfaction:

Claritas is *quidditas*. After the analysis which discovers the second quality the mind makes the only logically possible synthesis and discovers the third quality. This is the moment which I call epiphany. First we recognise that the object is *one* integral thing [*integritas*], then we recognise that it is an organised composite structure, a *thing* in fact [*consonantia*]: finally, when the relation of the parts is exquisite, when the parts are adjusted to the special point, we recognise that it is *that* thing which it is [*claritas/quidditas*]. Its soul, its whatness, leaps to us from the vestment of its appearance. The soul of the commonest object, the structure of which is so adjusted, seems to us radiant. The object achieves its epiphany.   (*SH* 218)

Earlier in the book Stephen had declared that 'The modern spirit is vivisective. Vivisection itself is the most modern process one can conceive' (*SH* 190). The modern theory of beauty, by the same token, is analytical or diagnostic. To perceive the radiance or beauty of an object is to recognize its quiddity or whatness: the essential nature behind the appearance. Such is the moment of 'epiphany'. As a contribution to aesthetics this is, of course, hard to take seriously. In equating beauty with understanding (whether scientific or mystical understanding), Stephen is performing a conjuring trick and, effectively, squaring the circle. His argument does not invite detailed refutation; instead, we must try to assess just what sort of intellectual satisfaction Stephen derives from this theory of beauty.

The epiphany is a transferred religious conception – hence it surrounds the artist's pursuit with an atmosphere of sanctity. It speaks of a moment of intuitive perception, inexplicable in rational terms and to be represented in the fewest possible words; the main shared characteristic of Joyce's surviving 'epiphanies' is their pregnant terseness. Beauty, therefore, is an enigma. Like an Imagist poem, it is both made manifest in words, and it manifests distrust in words. Yet we are not concerned with a mere 'impression' but with a moment of diagnosis or clairvoyant insight. Like other romantics before him, Stephen is asserting that the artist is a seer and that beauty is truth.

During his Ibsen years Joyce had sought to justify the modern theatre by appealing to a neoclassical theory of drama. Drama was truthful, objective, and based on the interplay of passions. The passage we have been discussing in *Stephen Hero* may have been written about four years after 'Drama and Life'. Yet as Joyce, through Stephen, elaborated his theory of beauty he used the short cut of '*Claritas* is *quidditas*' to reintroduce his earlier concern with art as truthful and objective representation. The impulse behind his search for a theory of beauty, I have suggested, lay in his response to the romantic aestheticism of the later nineteenth century, as represented by the 'decadent' preface to *Dorian Gray*. In his 1902 essay on Mangan, Joyce had already argued that neither romanticism nor classicism could be accepted in its entirety. The dispute between the two schools, he had written, 'presses slowly towards a deeper insight which will make the schools at one' (*CW* 74). In formulating the theory of epiphanies Stephen was aiming for this 'deeper insight'. He was combining the 'classical temper' – advocated in an earlier passage of *Stephen Hero* – with the romantic temper.

A crucial feature of the theory is that – so it claims – beauty may be found literally anywhere. Joyce was not alone, at this time, in suggesting that the 'delicate and evanescent moments' of beauty had no necessary connection with rare and delicate objects. The search for beauty should mean, not a turning away from ordinary life, but a heightened appreciation of the typical and the commonplace. Here Stephen's attitude resembles that of the realist and naturalist school, whose Anglo-Irish representative was the George Moore of *Esther Waters* (1894). At the turn of the century similar views to Stephen's were being expressed by the young English novelist Arnold Bennett, who praised Moore's realism in the essays collected as *Fame and Fiction* (1901). It was in *Dubliners*, his first completed work of fiction, that Joyce would come closest to the world of Moore and Bennett. In *Dubliners*, too, he showed that he had outgrown both his period as a student and his versatile literary apprenticeship. The 'modern Daedalus' was about to put on his wings.

3   *Dubliners*

Joyce and the short story

In *Stephen Hero* the intensity of Stephen's artistic ambition leads him to try out a whole series of aesthetic positions. He is the vivisectionist, dedicated to uncover the 'significance of trivial things' and their embodiment of the pathological condition of social paralysis. He is the unfrocked theologian, reinterpreting St Thomas Aquinas's requirements for beauty and recording a series of unofficial and unhallowed epiphanies. He is at once an Ibsenite, a classicist, an aesthete, and a poet storing up a treasure-house of words. All these attitudes may be found in *Dubliners* and yet the result is not one of incongruous variety or fluctuating uncertainty but of a subtle and substantial artistic achievement. *Dubliners* is a work of its time which owes much to the established conventions of late nineteenth-century short fiction. Nevertheless, in this youthful work Joyce outstripped his immediate competitors to produce a new type of short story, which was as intricate and carefully crafted as a lyric poem.

He was categorical enough in the statements he made about the book in letters between 1904 and 1906, when the bulk of the stories were completed. To Constantine Curran in 1904 he observed that 'I am writing a series of epicleti — ten — for a paper. I call the series "Dubliners" to betray the soul of that hemiplegia or paralysis which many consider a city'.[1] To Grant Richards, his prospective London publisher, he initially wrote that 'From time to time I see in publishers' lists announcements of books on Irish subjects, so that I think people might be willing to pay for the special odour of corruption which, I hope, floats over my stories' (*SL* 79). When Richards wrote back to say that the printer had objected to certain passages, Joyce retreated from this *épater-les-bourgeois* stance to a firmly self-righteous position. 'My intention was to write a chapter in the moral history of my country and I chose Dublin for the scene because that city seemed to me the centre of paralysis. . . . I have written it for the most part in a style of scrupulous meanness and with the conviction that he is a very bold man who dares to alter in the presentment, still more to deform, whatever he has seen and heard. I cannot do any more than this. I cannot alter what I have written' (*SL* 83).

Were these stories, then, 'epicleti' – invocations, epiphanic structures, scientific diagnoses which also set out to 'betray the soul' or reveal the confessional secrets of Dublin life? Or were they fictions written for the market, stories commissioned by a paper (AE's *The Irish Homestead*) and which the English reading public might be willing to pay for? Numbers of critics have set out to prove that the stories of *Dubliners* are 'epiphanies of paralysis', and it is true that the volume begins with a priest who has succumbed to physical paralysis, and with a narrator who lingers feelingly over the word itself ('It had always sounded strangely in my ears, like the word gnomon in the Euclid and the word simony in the Catechism', *D* 7). The volume ends with a story giving a broad view of Dublin's musical life, past and present, under the title 'The Dead'. Nevertheless, the final impression left by the book is not of a series of cold-hearted studies in spiritual paralysis, prominent though the motif may be. Neither is it true, as is often assumed, that Joyce refuses all authorial comment on the significance of his Dubliners' lives. The air of impersonality in the narration is itself a mask, and *Dubliners* uses a richly complex technique to convey a set of strongly ambivalent feelings towards Dublin life and people.

In the 1890s – H. G. Wells later recalled – short stories 'broke out everywhere'. Writers of all kinds responded to the new demand, and 'the sixpenny popular magazines had still to deaden down the conception of what a short story might be to the imaginative limitation of the common reader'.[2] 'Serious' and 'popular' writers alike found a market in the newspapers and magazines of the period. Though many of these writers may be loosely described as 'neo-romantics', specializing in adventure tales, in marvellous and uncanny incidents or in crime and detection, others introduced the sobriety, objectivity, and irony of French naturalism into English prose. The naturalist school in France claimed to have brought the scientific spirit into fiction by means of the accurate, carefully-documented and deliberately impartial portrayal of social conditions and psychological states. The naturalistic writers were materialists, holding that humanity was part of the biological kingdom and was subject to the universal laws of heredity and environment. The artist's role was that of a scrupulously accurate recording instrument, or 'court stenographer'. Zola was the ideologist of naturalism, while Flaubert and Maupassant – though standing at some distance from the more doctrinaire 'scientific' claims of the movement – were its leading practitioners in the short story. Joyce's most influential early admirers, including Pound and Edmund Wilson, saw *Dubliners* as a work in the naturalist tradition. In Wilson's view it differed from the work of Maupassant mainly by virtue of the graceful musicality of Joyce's prose.[3]

Zola's great novel-series *Les Rougon-Macquart*, following Balzac's less systematic series *La Comédie humaine*, had set out to make a representative sociological and psychological study of modern France. *Dubliners* belongs to a group of short-story collections with topographical titles, published around the turn of the century, which also claim to offer a composite portrait of a particular culture. Yet, by contrast with the massive novel-sequences, the 'portrait' they provide can only be a series of sketches or impressions. The popularity of this form and its techniques owes something to the advent of impressionist painting, which had drastically altered the relationship between the visual artist and his subject-matter. The subjects of the impressionists were 'found' *en plein air* rather than being elaborately designed and reconstructed in the studio. Established rules of pictorial composition were ignored and the paintings were executed deftly and rapidly, so as to capture the 'impression' before it was lost. The literary equivalent of the impressionists' concern with capturing the moment was the so-called 'slice of life' story which attempted to recreate a particular emotional 'atmosphere'. In France Maupassant was regarded as the master of this form of short fiction; but Joyce, as we shall see, took it further than Maupassant had done.

The genre to which *Dubliners* at first sight belonged was that defined by the urban realism of Arthur Morrison's *Tales of Mean Streets* (1894), Arnold Bennett's *Tales of the Five Towns* (1905) and, a little later, Sherwood Anderson's *Winesburg, Ohio* (1917). In Irish writing Joyce's predecessor and rival was George Moore, whose collection *The Untilled Field* – its title symbolizing an Ireland in which 'Nothing thrives . . . but the celibate, the priest, the nun and the ox'[4] – appeared in 1903. Moore's stories are, for the most part, bleak tales of the west of Ireland peasantry. Moore, however, uses the frame-story of a pair of Irish artists to present, in dialogue form, his own attitudes to the national culture. *Dubliners* betrays fewer illusions about Ireland and Joyce's manner is rigorously detached and impartial. He is a naturalist to the extent that he allows the paralysis of Dublin society to 'betray' itself, rather than analysing or denouncing it openly. None of his characters strikes us as primarily a mouthpiece. Eveline, Maria, Bob Doran, Tom Kernan, Gabriel Conroy and the others must convince us of their reality before we see them as exemplifying a thesis. Joyce took great care, too, that his settings should be utterly authentic. He admired the knowledge of India that Kipling had shown in *Plain Tales from the Hills* (1888) and, amusingly enough, he attacked Moore for showing a suburban lady looking up the times of trains on the Dublin–Bray commuter line – a line with a frequent and regular service (*SL* 44, 142). In *Dubliners* a 'scientific' concern for authenticity is taken further, perhaps, than any previous writer had done.

The specificity of *Dubliners* inevitably conditions the reader's response. 'Two Gallants' takes place around St Stephen's Green; Mrs Sinico dies at Sydney Parade. Eighty years ago this was felt to be uncomfortably realistic. A more conventional writer would have changed some of the names, as Arthur Morrison changed the names of his haunts in the London slums and Arnold Bennett changed the names and number of the North Staffordshire pottery towns. Joyce's refusal to use invented names was one of the reasons why *Dubliners*, which was completed in 1905 and revised and expanded a year or two later, did not appear until 1914. George Roberts of Maunsel & Co., a Dublin publisher, cited the naming of actual shops and pubs as one of his reasons for backing out of his agreement with Joyce. (Another reason was a disrespectful reference by one of the characters to King Edward VII; the English publisher Grant Richards, on the other hand, took these things in his stride but was upset by the word 'bloody'.) Why, one might ask, was Joyce so obdurate about details such as these? It is as if he had discovered in the physical actuality of Dublin, as well as in its speech, his essential and lasting subject-matter. To the modern reader of Joyce the city delineated in *Dubliners* is frequently enriched and overlaid by later impressions; for example, the Magazine Hill in Phoenix Park, from which Mr Duffy in 'A Painful Case' spied on couples lying in the grass, is the 'Magicscene' of an act of voyeurism which resounds throughout *Finnegans Wake*. Yet the activity of Joyce's writing is never confined to the single function of evoking a sense of place. Often – disconcertingly – the very phrases in which he evokes the presence of place have the effect of casting radical doubt on that presence. Take, for example, the opening sentence of 'A Painful Case': 'Mr James Duffy lived in Chapelizod because he wished to live as far as possible from the city of which he was a citizen and because he found all the other suburbs of Dublin mean, modern and pretentious' (*D* 119). Does such a sentence convey useful information or misinformation about Chapelizod? The boorish recluse Mr Duffy is scarcely someone we can accept on trust as an urban historian. The narrator, characteristically, offers no opinion on this matter, and the reader is left to make his own mind up.

There is another device Joyce uses to suggest that his narrator is an invisible recorder of Dublin itself − not the author of a prepackaged, 'fictionalized' view of the city. This is his insertion of what appears to be actual documentary material − shop-signs, canvassing cards and so on − into the narrative. The effect is rather like a Cubist *collage*. Once re-presented in fiction, the signs and notices lose their purely instrumental function and can be appreciated simply as items of language. The protagonist of *Stephen Hero* makes a similar discovery, finding 'words for his treasure-house . . . at haphazard in the shops, on advertisements, in the mouths of the plodding public. He kept repeating them to himself till they lost all instantaneous meaning for him and became wonderful vocables' (*SH* 36). Some of these words are on display in the opening story of *Dubliners*, 'The Sisters':

It was an unassuming shop, registered under the vague name of *Drapery*. The drapery consisted mainly of children's bootees and umbrellas; and on ordinary days a notice used to hang in the window, saying: *Umbrellas Re-covered*. (*D* 10)

The narrator reaches the door, but instead of reading the umbrella notice he reads another, and so do we:

1st July, 1895
The Rev. James Flynn (formerly of S. Catherine's Church,
Meath Street), aged sixty-five years.
R.I.P. (*D* 10)

The narrator is a child, by whom signs are still taken for wonders. Later, he will be tricked by a cynical and meretricious use of language − the use of the exotic word 'Araby' to glamorize a charity bazaar. Shop-signs are also reproduced in 'Araby', and in 'Two Gallants'. Later stories include such cultural source-materials as the verse of 'I Dreamt that I Dwelt' that Maria sings twice (in 'Clay'), and the canvassing cards and text of Joe Hynes's ode on the death of Parnell (in 'Ivy Day in the Committee Room'). Most remarkably, there is the newspaper report of Mrs Sinico's inquest which takes up about fifteen per cent of the length of 'A Painful Case'. In all these instances Joyce's documentation goes conspicuously beyond what was usual even in the annals of naturalism. There are several reasons for this: hints towards an interior view of those characters in whose minds the various documents are unforgettably lodged; the 'silence' or interruption of authorial discourse in the text which such documents provide; and, not least, simple authentication of the incidents Joyce describes. Like his use of proper names, the fictive documents assert that it is an actual city and not a mere figment of the artist's imagination that is portrayed in *Dubliners*.

The naturalistic novelists tended to show their characters as helpless victims of the 'fate' constituted by the forces of heredity and environment. Where the earlier nineteenth-century novel portrayed processes of moral, social and historical causation, by the end of the century the naturalists had come to understand character-development in increasingly brutal, biological terms. Julien Sorel, in Stendhal's *Le Rouge et le noir* (1831) was an ambitious boy born into a generation in which social advancement could only be bought at the price of hypocrisy. In 1800 he could have found preferment in the army; twenty years later, he must seek it through the church. George Eliot's Lydgate similarly lets himself get entangled in a restricting web of social circumstances not of his own making. In each case the character must take moral responsibility for his actions. When we come to Zola, however, we find characters whose lives are in theory closed to moral judgment since the author does his best to show that they could not do other than what they did. Joyce showed the same reductive impulse in choosing a medical term, paralysis, to sum up the spiritual condition of Dublin. Occasionally we meet with a phrase in his early work which comes straight out of the vocabulary of turn-of-the-century naturalistic clichés. Thus Eveline, unable to respond to her lover's entreaties, 'set her white face to him, passive, like a helpless animal' (*D* 43). Such a phrase makes a pretence at scientific impassivity but expresses a mixed attitude of authorial pity and disdain. Occasionally − despite the generally impersonal tone − Joyce permits himself a narrative comment wielding irony at the character's expense. Mrs Mooney, we are told in 'The Boarding House', 'dealt with moral problems as a cleaver deals with meat' (*D* 68). Appropriately enough, she is descended from a family of butchers.

In the 'slice of life' story pioneered by Maupassant, character is neither analysed at length (in the way that George Eliot does), nor is it unfolded (as in Zola) through a long-drawn-out action leading to an inevitable fate. Instead, it is sketched or sampled at a particular moment. Nevertheless, a typical Maupassant story revolves around an exceptional event and incorporates, as part of its narrative development, a biographical summary of the past life of the main character. The same is true of many of the *Dubliners* stories — notably 'A Painful Case' and 'The Dead' — but not all. 'Clay', for example is an impressionist sketch which, adapting the title of a 1960s film by Agnès Varda, we might call 'Maria from 5 to 10'. Its 'plot' involves nothing more startling than the loss of a slice of cake. 'Ivy Day in the Committee Room' also lacks any sort of recognizable plot. These are stories of a kind which might have been dismissed as 'mere anecdotes'. (As Wells recalled, 'The short story was Maupassant; the anecdote was damnable'.[5]) Yet, in their humble way, they are anticipations of *Ulysses* where the 'slice of life' extends across eighteen hours in the lives of three main characters with a huge supporting cast. It is no accident that *Ulysses* began as a project for an additional story in *Dubliners*.

The 'slice of life' story replaces extended description with the suggestive evocation of 'atmospheres'. 'Atmosphere' was a favourite book-reviewers' term of the period, although Joyce himself decidedly preferred the word 'odour'. He wrote to Grant Richards of the 'odour of corruption which, I hope, floats over my stories'. In 'Eveline' we meet — strategically placed in the opening paragraph, and later repeated — the phrase 'odour of dusty cretonne'. This gives an impression of Eveline's entanglement in drab and dingy circumstances, stated with an obviousness not found in the later stories in the book. Descriptive repetition, however, features elsewhere in *Dubliners*, and has often been misunderstood by critics unconcerned with the literary context in which Joyce was writing. Magalaner and Kain, for example, detect a 'heavily weighted structure of Hell symbolism' in 'Ivy Day in the Committee Room':

It seems inconceivable that so disciplined a writer as Joyce would mention maybe a score of times the fire, smoke, cinders and flames on the hearth of the committee room simply to tell the reader that the room contained a fire.[6]

Joyce, here, is creating an 'atmosphere'. The fire in 'Ivy Day' is a beneficent fire, warming the shabby crew of canvassers, lighting their cigarettes and popping the corks on their bottles of stout. Whatever Dantesque overtones readers may find, this is a vividly-rendered impressionistic background to a story which deserves better than to be reduced to trite Christian allegory.

Still more striking than Joyce's treatment of external atmosphere is

his use of the free indirect style to create a narrative coloured by his
characters' internal impressions or mental landscapes. 'Free indirect
style' is a form of third-person narrative which mimics the vocabulary
and idioms of a particular character. It aims to convey a mode of
thinking and feeling informally and 'from the inside', without resorting
to the explicitness of direct speech, reported speech, or authorial
summary. Once again it is a naturalistic technique, working through
'impressions' rather than analysis, and pioneered by the French. 'Clay'
– a boldly experimental story which has had much less than its due –
exemplifies Joyce's use of free indirect style. The opening paragraph
offers such brazen narrative clichés as 'spick and span' and 'nice and
bright'. The second paragraph coyly describes the heroine as 'a very,
very small person indeed'. As the story proceeds the distance between
Maria's self-protective version of events and the reality insinuated
between the lines is a source of gentle comedy:

What a nice evening they would have, all the children singing! Only she hoped
that Joe wouldn't come in drunk. He was so different when he took any drink.
   Often he had wanted her to go and live with them; but she would have felt
herself in the way (though Joe's wife was ever so nice with her) and she had
become accustomed to the life of the laundry. Joe was a good fellow. She had
nursed him and Alphy too; and Joe used often say:
   — Mamma is mamma but Maria is my proper mother.   (*D* 111)

To Maria this has all come to seem a very natural state of affairs. The
narrator appears at first glance to be neutrally recording her views. Yet
lurking beneath the surface is not only an awareness of the banality of
Maria's idiom ('in the way', 'ever so nice') but a realization of the
travesty that, in this environment, passes for conventional family life.
What caused the absence or dereliction of Maria's mother? We are
never told. What is it that drives Irish husbands and fathers to the
bottle? Here we are verging on the major theme of *Dubliners* – the
tribulations of manhood, womanhood and family life in a society that
Joyce knew intimately.
   The free indirect style is a stage in Joyce's development towards a
fully-fledged 'stream-of-consciousness' method such as he employs in
the early chapters of *Ulysses*. Its use of colloquialism, cliché and
euphemism draws attention to the uncertain distance between narrator
and character. The narrator's implicit attitude wavers between
sympathy and ironic superiority. If irony separates him from his
characters, it links him to his potential readers or addressees. Who are
the implied readers of *Dubliners*, and what is involved in Joyce's appeal

to them? The 'two or three unfortunate wretches', mentioned in discussion with Stanislaus, who 'may eventually read' this chapter in the moral history of their country are, in fact, a type of audience whose existence had been attested in other countries by many earlier nineteenth-century writers. Stendhal, for example, addressed himself to the 'HAPPY FEW'; Flaubert, to those superior enough to their surroundings to savour a *Dictionnaire des idées reçues*. Such audiences form a self-selected elite which prides itself on an inner detachment, not merely from particular classes of 'received ideas', but from the whole mode of discourse in which society at large exchanges ideas. Joyce's ironies in *Dubliners* often imply that sort of negativity. They are unearned, in the sense that they make no attempt to explain or justify the feelings they evoke or the prejudices to which they appeal; the reader is simply given a set of coded instructions, on pain of exclusion from the 'happy few' if he cannot interpret them correctly.

To what extent, for example, is Maria a simpleton or Eveline a 'helpless animal'? What should we make of the complacent wisdom of Mr Duffy, who, after a brief contact with an Irish socialist group, concludes that 'No social revolution . . . would be likely to strike Dublin for some centuries' (*D* 123)? In a sense (and this is what Joyce meant by the 'scrupulous meanness' of his writing) such questions are left to the reader. That does not mean that they are unanswerable. The answer is subtle and difficult to be sure of, but it does exist. In general the tone of *Dubliners* is harsher, the author's assumption of superiority over hapless humanity is more palpable, than in his later work. It is the 'moral history' of his country as seen by a somewhat embittered young writer. Some of the stories (especially 'Eveline', 'The Boarding House', 'Counterparts' and 'A Mother') have crudely cynical touches; none could be described as over-indulgent. It is significant that 'The Dead' was composed later than the other stories, and that it was preceded by the following confession in one of Joyce's letters to his brother:

Sometimes thinking of Ireland it seems to me that I have been unnecessarily harsh. I have reproduced (in *Dubliners* at least) none of the attractions of the city for I have never felt at my ease in any city since I left it except Paris. I have not reproduced its ingenuous insularity and its hospitality. The latter 'virtue' so far as I can see does not exist elsewhere in Europe. . . . And yet I know how useless these reflections are.   (*SL* 109–10)

Significant, too, is the difficulty we may find in decoding the later part of the *Portrait of the Artist*, where Joyce's irony is turned against his own earlier artistic ambitions.

If a work is difficult the suspicion arises that it is esoteric – that the reader is missing some arcane or hidden level of meaning, which would provide the key to full comprehension. Hence the inscrutability of Joyce's irony in parts of *Dubliners* inevitably leads to the question of symbolism. For many years symbol-hunting of various sorts has made the running in the criticism of Joyce's short stories. Yet it is far from clear that the occult correspondences fetched up by scholars have actually made the book more readable. A technique of retrospective interpretation, in which devices of multiple identification and symbolic association appropriate to *Finnegans Wake* are read back into the earlier Joyce regardless of the difference in fictional conventions, may actually lead to the delusion that *Dubliners* is *more* difficult (because ostensibly more simple) than anything that followed it. Yet, if symbolic interpretations of *Dubliners* have often been very wide of the mark, the dilemma they address is a real one. Joyce's earliest readers, once they had been alerted to the possibility of unseen depths in the stories, found themselves assailed by dark suspicions that all was not as it seemed. The publisher George Roberts (as Joyce recorded in a letter written from Dublin in 1912) 'asked me very narrowly was there sodomy also in *The Sisters* and what was "simony" and if the priest was suspended only for the breaking of the chalice. He asked me also was there more in *The Dead* than appeared'.[7]

Symbolism was described by Arthur Symons in 1899 as 'a form of expression, at the best but approximate, . . . for an unseen reality apprehended by the consciousness'.[8] Like naturalism, the symbolist movement in literature was a late nineteenth-century import from France. The theory of epiphanies described in the previous chapter is indebted to both naturalist and symbolist doctrines. Joyce's readers, however, did not encounter this theory until 1944, when *Stephen Hero* was published. The same year saw the publication of a scholarly article offering – I believe for the first time – an esoteric interpretation of *Dubliners*. Richard Levin and Charles Shattuck argued in 'First Flight to Ithaca' that *Dubliners*, like *Ulysses*, incorporated an elaborate structure of allusions to Homer's *Odyssey*.[9] The Homeric allusions made up a consistent layer of meaning which, they claimed, no earlier reader had spotted. This theory has been received, for the most part, in stunned silence. For one thing, it can neither be proved nor refuted. Seamus Deane, speaking in general terms, has written that 'Many of the coincidences that surround Joyce's work seem entirely accidental'.[10] But who knows which are and which aren't? A later symbolic interpretation of 'Clay', by Marvin Magalaner, drew the fire of no less formidable an enemy than Stanislaus Joyce. 'I am in a position to state definitely that my brother had no such subtleties in mind when he wrote the story', Stanislaus pronounced.[11] I cannot resist quoting Magalaner's reply, a little gem of scholarly self-importance:

This type of personal-acquaintance criticism is understandably dangerous. What family of a deceased writer has not felt that blood relationship and lifelong closeness afforded deeper insight into the writer's work than detached criticism could? This is a natural and healthy family tendency; ... at the same time, one may suspect critical judgments enunciated by such sources as the last word on, say, literary symbolism.[12]

It might equally be asked if there are any known cases of symbolic interpretations of literary works being withdrawn as a result of criticism. But nobody in this largely conjectural area will ever have the last word. Even Stanislaus Joyce accepted the presence of parodic allusions to Dante's *Divine Comedy* in 'Grace', because his brother told him they were there.[13]

Symbolism was a topical and widely discussed literary technique when Joyce was writing *Dubliners*. Yeats had been acclaimed by Arthur Symons as the leading English symbolist. Baudelaire's famous poem 'Correspondences', with its evocation of Nature as a temple filled with 'forests of symbols', had first appeared fifty years earlier. Baudelaire had been followed by the *symboliste* school of poets expounded by Symons, and also by a school of symbolist painters. Wilde's statement in the preface to *Dorian Gray* — 'All literature is both surface and symbol' — had done much to familiarize the concept. Later historians such as Edmund Wilson would regard symbolism and naturalism as opposing tendencies, thanks to their polemical association with the doctrines of spiritualism and materialism respectively. Yet Flaubert and Zola are inveterately symbolic novelists, and Ibsen pioneered both naturalism and symbolism in the theatre. Ibsen's symbolic mode is a crucial presence behind Joyce's story 'The Dead' (to be discussed later in this chapter).

Symbolic interpretation is an aid to understanding *Dubliners* so long as it is not pursued in isolation from other modes of reading. Just as Stephen Dedalus rested his theory of beauty on the epiphany or spiritual manifestation, each of the *Dubliners* stories works towards an intuitive and unparaphraseable insight into reality. Sometimes — as in 'A Painful Case' and 'The Dead' — these are elaborately presented, in a heightened and consciously poetic prose. But far more often the story ends on an understated and anticlimactic note. The presentation of Maria's song at the end of the Hallowe'en party in 'Clay' is a good example:

She sang *I Dreamt that I Dwelt*, and when she came to the second verse she sang again:

> I dreamt that I dwelt in marble halls
> With vassals and serfs at my side
> And of all who assembled within those walls
> That I was the hope and pride.
>
> I had riches too great to count, could boast
> Of a high ancestral name,
> But I also dreamt, which pleased me most,
> That you loved me still the same.

But no one tried to show her her mistake; and when she had ended her song Joe was very much moved. He said that there was no time like the long ago and no music for him like poor old Balfe, whatever other people might say; and his eyes filled up so much with tears that he could not find what he was looking for and in the end he had to ask his wife to tell him where the corkscrew was.   (*D* 118)

Only a three- or fourfold reading will begin to do justice to this passage. Joyce's naturalism enables him to present a wholly convincing picture of a lower-class Dublin family party. The popular song is written out in full as Maria performs it. Joe is all too clearly 'given away' by his final words and actions. We might (though Joyce doesn't) draw morals from this about the cultural functions of music and drink in turn-of-the-century Dublin. In fact Joyce distracts our attention from such incipient moralizing by the other layers of his technique. Impressionism dictates that our reaction to the song will be mediated entirely through Joe and that the story will close abruptly, on an ironic note, with the party still in progress though rapidly deteriorating. The irony leaves us hesitating whether to take Joe's nostalgia as a feeling of substance, or whether to dismiss him as a mere sentimentalist, a maudlin drunkard groping for the corkscrew. A symbolic reading, however, must start with Maria's mistake; at a symbolic level (Freudian or otherwise) no mistake is innocent or accidental. The verse that she has left out describes the young heiress as besieged by suitors. This will connect for us with earlier incidents, each of which involves shame and the deliberate suppression of instinctive feelings. There is the unexplained loss of the plumcake; we deduce that Maria was so flustered by her conversation with the elderly gentleman as to have left it on the tram. There is also Maria's choice of the clay and the prayer-book (and not the ring) when she is blindfolded in the Hallowe'en game – the clay from the garden has been brought in for a prank by 'one of the next-door girls' (*D* 117). A detailed knowledge of Irish Hallowe'en customs is the key to these enigmatic incidents.[14] Such knowledge, however, can only bring us back to the poignant human situation which can be appreciated without any special study of folklore. Maria is shown undergoing a painful if minor ordeal, and she nearly cries over her loss of the plumcake. Joe actually does cry at the end, with the result that 'he could not find what he was looking for'. In one sense he is a buffoon whose miniature farce contrasts with what, for Maria, is a genuine miniature tragedy. (In the Hallowe'en games the rebuffs she has received signify spinsterhood and death.) But Joe also stands for the reader who – not having been told why Maria omitted the second verse, or what happened to the plumcake, or that the stuff in one of the saucers was 'Clay' – equally has difficulty in finding what he is looking for. The ending is not only realistic, moving, and ironic, but also delicately self-referential. Joyce's story is very like a bottle for which someone has hidden the corkscrew. The homely metaphor suggests all those features of *Dubliners* which have prompted ingenious and learned critics to 'hunt the symbol'. Yet it should be remembered that in 'Ivy Day in the Committee Room' Joyce shows an alternative method of opening a bottle of stout, for which no corkscrew is needed. This method simply requires patience and warmth.

Signs of paralysis

Joyce's 'scrupulous meanness' of expression sets up a certain resistance to discussing the themes of his stories. Can we approach them thematically without violating the restraints and ignoring the indirectness which the author has so meticulously imposed upon himself? Joyce himself did so, by describing their burden as one of 'paralysis'. Paralysis, as a metaphor for the doomed and self-defeating life of Dublin, is most starkly seen in the story of Patrick Morkan's horse, as told in 'The Dead'. The horse, having been employed for years to drive a treadmill, was unable to master any other mode of locomotion. One day Mr Morkan decided to harness him to a trap and go for an outing in the park. The journey came to an end when the horse reached King Billy's statue, and began to walk round and round it. The horse, a creature of habit going round in circles, was a true Dubliner. Or is it that the story is a true Dublin story?

Central in *Dubliners*, as in all his work, is Joyce's handling of sexual and family relationships. Though the first three stories may have some autobiographical basis, the child in them is an orphan, living with his uncle and aunt. In other stories the family – especially the father – displays all the signs of paralysis. Fathers in *Dubliners* tend to be drunken, quarrelsome, inadequate at work and ineffectual in the home. They are bullies who take out their frustrations on their wives and children. Mothers are less uniformly selfish, but they too fall far short of what is desirable. Eveline thinks of her mother's 'life of commonplace sacrifices closing in final craziness' (*D* 41). The mother of Joe and Maria was mysteriously absent. Mrs Sinico takes to the bottle. Little Chandler's baby is caught between a weak-minded father and an over-protective mother. Farrington's wife, and the mother of his five children, is 'a little sharp-faced woman who bullied her husband when he was sober and was bullied by him when he was drunk' (*D* 108). Beside the squalid families of *Dubliners* the Blooms in *Ulysses* are paragons of mutual consideration and family happiness.

Joyce shows us the unfortunate courtships which lead to marriages like these. Lenehan in 'Two Gallants' dreams of having 'a warm fire to sit by and a good dinner to sit down to'. He could live happily 'if he could only come across some good simple-minded girl with a little of the ready' (*D* 62). His friend Corley has found such a girl, but has no intention of marrying her. In 'The Boarding House' marriage is forced on the unwilling Bob Doran by a determined mother-in-law. His bride, Polly Mooney, is nineteen. Bob Doran is around thirty-five. Mrs Kearney in 'A Mother' got married 'out of spite'. Before marriage 'the young men whom she met were ordinary and she gave them no encouragement, trying to console her romantic desires by eating a great deal of Turkish Delight in secret' (*D* 153). She also settled in the end for a much older man.

Florence L. Walzl has recently argued that, sordid though it may be, Joyce's portrayal of Dublin family life has an uncomfortable sociological accuracy. It reflects the position of early twentieth-century Ireland as one of the poorest countries in the civilized world, with a population depleted by the Great Famine and by mass emigration. 'For over a century following 1841, Ireland had the lowest marriage and birth rates in the civilized world. As a natural concomitant, it also had the highest rate of unmarried men and women in the world'.[15] Irish labour brought far more prosperity to London, Liverpool, Belfast, New York, Boston, and Chicago than it did to Dublin. Mr Henchy in 'Ivy Day in the Committee Room' laments the lack of industrial investment in the Irish capital, and other stories reflect the prevalence of arranged marriages, fruitless courtships, and wary bachelors. Gabriel and Gretta are the only married couple represented at the Misses Morkan's annual dance. Lily, the caretaker's daughter, is bitterly resentful of the opposite sex, and Freddy Malins, a middle-aged soak, is represented as an eligible 'young man of about forty' (*D* 210). Measured by the middle-class norms of more prosperous countries, most of the relationships in *Dubliners* are degenerate.

The opening story, 'The Sisters', is explicitly concerned with 'paralysis' and links it to the theme of degenerate fatherhood. The priest is addressed as 'Father', and embodies some of the moral authority lacking in the actual fathers Joyce portrays; moreover, Father Flynn has taken a paternal interest in the narrator, who is an orphan. Father Flynn has died of paralysis (also known as paresis, a consequence of tertiary syphilis).[16] To the boy the name of the disease is 'like the name of some maleficent and sinful being. It filled me with fear, and yet I longed to be nearer to it and to look upon its deadly work' (*D* 7). The details of the boy's relationship with the priest are left vague, yet he is aware that it is a source of adult disapproval. His curiosity is whetted by his uncle's friend Cotter, who has his own theory about Father Flynn, but won't say what it is. Cotter saw something 'uncanny' and 'queer' about the priest; something to be kept away from the young. The boy dreams that the priest is confessing something to him from beyond the grave. The dream is an 'out of the body' experience in which 'I felt my soul receding into some pleasant and vicious region' (*D* 9) – something that will occur also to Gabriel Conroy in 'The Dead'. Next day, his aunt takes him to pay his respects to the dead man. Downstairs, over a glass of sherry, a few details of the priest's guilt and mental collapse slowly emerge from among the conversational pieties. Earlier he had enthralled the boy with his descriptions of the mysterious rituals of the Church and the secrecy of the confessional. After he broke the chalice he himself was found one night 'sitting up by himself in the dark in his confession-box, wide-awake and laughing-like softly to himself' (*D* 17). The priest's sister's account has the effect of confirming what the boy sensed in his dream

– that Father Flynn had something on his mind he would have liked to confess. The delicacy of Joyce's telling consists in what is left unspoken as the boy encounters for the first time the world's corrupt and shameful mysteries. He feels liberated by the old priest's death, but it is an open question whether or not that feeling is an illusion. Will he in turn inherit, or discover in himself, the guilt and solitude which he still does not fully understand? Will he fall victim to physical or mental paralysis?

'The Sisters' is unusual in *Dubliners* in that it shows a penitent figure – the old priest in his confession-box, his mind unhinged – without making it clear what he has to confess (though a clue is provided by the word *simony*). Many of the other stories end with an act of formal penitence, but their subject-matter is the drama of rebellion or thwarted escape. 'An Encounter' and 'Araby' explore the schoolboy attractions of the Wild West and the mysterious East respectively. 'An Encounter' opens racily and describes a day spent wandering the streets and playing truant. Finally the boy attracts the attentions of another degenerate father-figure – a paedophile with sadistic interests. The man's obsession is a form of mental and emotional paralysis, a circuit of feelings from which, like Father Flynn, he cannot escape:

He gave me the impression that he was repeating something which he had learned by heart or that, magnetized by some words of his own speech, his mind was slowly circling round and round in the same orbit. . . . He began to speak on the subject of chastising boys. His mind, as if magnetized again by his speech, seemed to circle slowly round and round its new centre.
(*D* 26–7)

Both here and in 'The Sisters' Joyce was probing unpleasant (and at that time little written about) aspects of the relationship between adult and child. The stories are deliberately disturbing. The child's imaginative alertness and taste for the unorthodox leads, in the end, to a deeply disillusioning encounter. Both priest and paedophile have an 'elaborate mystery' (*D* 28) to unfold; the mystery is corrupt and repellent and yet undeniably human. Both men exert a powerful, tacit claim on his sympathies. In the final paragraph, the boy feels ashamed of calling to his companion for help, and 'penitent' for having earlier despised him. His shame and penitence strike deeper than the ostensible reasons he gives for them. These emotions suggest that the boy is learning to take on himself the guilt of the adult world, and also the circularity of a system of feeling in which 'sin' is forever being chased by 'penitence'.

'Araby' shows an intimacy with the narrator's experience, and a poetic intensity, such as Joyce perfected in *A Portrait of the Artist*. The boy has now reached adolescence, but the themes explored are entirely consistent with the two preceding stories. In his dream in 'The Sisters' he found himself in a strange oriental land, perhaps Persia. Now he is captivated by the magic of the name 'Araby', which is not only a charity bazaar but a symbol of his infatuation for Mangan's sister. (Her name – not to be defiled as the name 'Araby' is by the end of the story – is kept secret even from the reader.) The boy has moved into a house where a priest has just died. In 'The Sisters' we left Father Flynn in his coffin, 'solemn and truculent in death, an idle chalice on his breast' (*D* 17). In 'Araby' the narrator is a solemn adolescent who bears his imaginary 'chalice' (the worship of Mangan's sister) 'safely through a throng of foes' (*D* 31). He enters the room where the priest died and prays to Love instead of to God. The boy himself has become an idolatrous priest, but his sacramental visit to the bazaar (where he hopes to buy his beloved a gift) turns into a squalid farce. Delayed by his drunken and negligent uncle, he arrives only in time to hear the chink of coins and the banter as the stallholders shut up for the night. He sees himself as a 'creature driven and derided by vanity' (*D* 36). His 'anguish and anger' might have been directed at the adult world which has thwarted his dreams; instead, it is turned inwards, in an act of self-mortifying penitence. In worldly terms this is no very disastrous development; it will probably send the narrator back to his schoolwork. Put together with the other stories, however, it shows the operation of a culture which forces both adults and children into an intimate acquaintance with defeat.

The formula of escape leading to penitence occurs in many of the succeeding stories. At the end of 'After the Race' Jimmy 'knew that he would regret in the morning' (*D* 51); the heroine of 'Eveline' no doubt is in the same predicament. Bob Doran in 'The Boarding House' is ready to marry Polly Mooney since both he and his future mother-in-law agree that he owes 'reparation' for the 'sin' of making love to her. Chandler's revolt in 'A Little Cloud' ends in 'tears of remorse' (*D* 94). Mr Duffy is haunted by his cruelty to Mrs Sinico. 'Grace' ends with Tom Kernan's formal act of penitence, and Gabriel feels shame near the end of 'The Dead'. These acts of penitence are often morally suspect – most of all that in 'Grace', which is sanctioned by the explicit authority of the Church. Tom Kernan's drunkenness is an act of transgression which – like the other miniature escapes and rebellions in *Dubliners* — seems to express both a positive inner need and a self-destructive urge. The Church's role is to represent such actions as sins — sources of guilt, that is, for which reparation must be made. The priest hearing the confessions in 'Grace' is there to 'wash the pot', a circular process of cleansing and pollution which gives the communicant a fresh start so that he can sin again. Tom Kernan's wife, we are told, 'accepted his frequent intemperance as part of the climate' (*D* 93). Though Mr Kernan ends the story in a state of grace, there is no reason to suppose that the climate has changed.

'Grace' satirizes a whole range of Irish absurdities. There are the pompous opinions of Mr Kernan's gentlemen-friends, who come to his sickbed; the 'climate' in which men drink themselves insensible and beat up their wives, only to be nursed as invalids and fed with beef-tea; and, above all, there is the Church which adds social cement with its businessmen's retreat, at which Father Purdon presents himself as a 'spiritual accountant' (*D* 96) and speaks to his flock 'as a man of the world speaking to his fellow-men' (*D* 95). A less explicit, though equally potent, anticlericalism is to be found in a much earlier *Dubliners* story, 'Eveline'.

Eveline Hill, a frustrated and deprived young woman, is a version of the conventional naturalistic heroine pioneered by Flaubert in *Madame Bovary*. She dreams of escaping from her drab and dingy life, but at the crucial moment when escape is within her grasp, she is powerless to act. Eveline is not an inspiring figure, and the condescension that most readers feel towards her is perhaps merited. She is in love with a sailor, a 'kind, manly, open-hearted' (*D* 39) figure called Frank, who has promised her marriage and a home in Buenos Aires. Eveline's father suggests that Frank is not what he seems, and at least one critic, Hugh Kenner, agrees with him.[17] On the quayside waiting for the steamship, Eveline prays for guidance; the result is that she is pinned to the spot and lets Frank go off without her. The ship, Kenner maintains, would not have been bound directly for Buenos Aires, but for Liverpool. Has Eveline, thanks to divine intervention, just avoided a 'fate worse than death'? And if she has, would such a life be worse than the life her own mother was condemned to in Ireland? Her father was a drunkard, a bully and a wife-beater; her mother eventually went mad. Joyce himself had successfully wooed Nora Barnacle with promises which must have seemed no less far-fetched than those Frank makes to Eveline. Indeed, I would suggest that Nora's existence, and her willingness to leave for Europe without a marriage certificate and with a young man she had only known for a few weeks, is the standard against which Eveline's faint-heartedness ought to be measured. Curiously, one of the two or three major English naturalistic novels, Arnold Bennett's *The Old Wives' Tale* (1908), tackles a similar problem through its contrast of two sisters, Constance and Sophia Baines – the one a stay-at-home, the other a runaway. Joyce's impressionistic sketch leaves various questions unanswered; its tone, however, falls well short of Bennett's compassionate fair-mindedness. We leave Eveline seized by physical paralysis, 'like a helpless animal'.

At her moment of crisis she 'prayed to God to direct her, to show her what was her duty' (*D* 56). There is more to this than the circularity of escapism followed by penitence. Eveline is a young girl, facing the first great challenge of adulthood. She is trying to defy the will of her father, but her defeat comes, not in a direct confrontation with parental authority, but through an inner struggle resolved by her prayer. What Joyce shows repeatedly in *Dubliners* is not just the direct workings of repression – parental, sexual, religious – but its reproduction and internalization. Eveline is stopped, not by external restraints, but because she has learnt a self-restraint which cuts off her capacity for action and wipes out the adult personality she was struggling to establish.

A simple and, indeed, crude illustration of the reproduction of repression is the story 'Counterparts'. Here Farrington rebels against the tedious drudgery of his job, and is given the choice of making an abject apology or getting the sack. Humiliated at the office, he has a few drinks after work and goes home to bully his son. Home is the one place where he can exercise power over others. His wife is at the chapel, otherwise she too would (no doubt) have to bear the brunt of his rage. Tom, the son, instinctively relapses into pious whimperings as he is beaten:

– O, pa! he cried. Don't beat me, pa! And I'll . . . I'll say a *Hail Mary* for you. . . . I'll say a *Hail Mary* for you, pa, if you don't beat me. . . . I'll say a *Hail Mary*. . . . (*D* 109)

Where there is repression, there too is the Church with its message of mercy and forgiveness. Yet the Church, in Joyce's eyes, represents a humaner and more subtle system of repression. Each character in 'Counterparts' – even poor Tom as he tries to strike a bargain with a 'Hail Mary' – resorts to some form of power in a vain attempt to wipe out his subjection to forces not of his own making. The circuit of subjection continues.

The anticlericalism of *Dubliners* is a quality it shares with Moore's *The Untilled Field*. In Moore's collection the opening story ('In the Clay') sets up a schematic opposition between the priest and the artist. Rodney, an Irish sculptor, wants to work from the nude and finds a willing sixteen-year-old model. Her father sends for the priest and, as a result, the girl is forbidden to sit and Rodney finds his studio broken into and his work smashed to pieces. He leaves Dublin in disgust for Paris while Lucy the model (like many other characters in *The Untilled Field*) eventually goes off to settle in America. Moore's allegory here is not difficult to read: the deep bond between the Irish artist and the Irish people, thwarted by the Church, is nevertheless affirmed by their mutual resort to emigration, even though in practice that emigration takes them in different directions. Though Joyce disliked the melodrama and sentimentality of *The Untilled Field*, such a parable was clearly not lost on him. He, too, shows the 'paralysis' of Irish life opposed by people of a certain artistic bent. Little Chandler, Mr Duffy, and Gabriel Conroy in *Dubliners* are internal exiles, semi-alienated from their surroundings, yet lacking the talent and force of character to make a genuine bid for independence. Their role in the book is to be defeated, though in the case of Gabriel Conroy (and perhaps of Mr Duffy) there is some glory in defeat. Chandler, in 'A Little Cloud', is a would-be minor poet whose pathetic shallowness is evidenced by his admiration for his friend Ignatius Gallaher – a journalist who has escaped from Dublin only to become the vulgarest of cosmopolitans. Mr Duffy, author (like Joyce) of an unpublished translation of Hauptmann's *Michael Kramer*, is a fastidious recluse who nevertheless finds himself implicated in the most commonplace of sentimental tragedies. Gabriel, another lonely and sensitive man with literary tastes, tries to fulfil the social responsibilities thrust upon him by his aunts; but his self-respect is sorely tried by the need to be agreeable to people whose 'grade of culture differed from his' (*D* 203). In all three cases the artist's relationship with ordinary people – as in Moore – is the underlying burden of the story. But Joyce's way of exploring that relationship is entirely his own. He does so by creating halfway or partially alienated characters, rather than the stock Bohemian representatives of the artistic 'type'. The awkwardness of their participation in society is highlighted through their suspicion of its language.

The rich and mysterious potential of language has been seen in two of the childhood stories, 'The Sisters' and 'Araby'. In a story like 'Two

Gallants' the style of narrative description has a confusing richness:

The grey warm evening of August had descended upon the city and a mild warm air, a memory of summer, circulated in the streets. The streets, shuttered for the repose of Sunday, swarmed with a gaily coloured crowd. Like illumined pearls the lamps shone from the summits of their tall poles upon the living texture below which, changing shape and hue unceasingly, sent up into the warm grey evening air an unchanging unceasing murmur. (*D* 52)

'Fine writing', we might think, and pass on, were it not that the three sentences of this opening paragraph come progressively closer to paradox. It is August yet the air is only a 'memory of summer'. The streets are at once swarming and in repose. The crowd is both unceasingly changing and 'unchanging unceasing'. Here the narrator is dandyishly trying out his own virtuosity while his two actual dandies, Corley and Lenehan, betray the shallow and mercenary nature of their thoughts the moment they open their mouths. Lenehan's ponderous expansion of a cliché – 'That takes the solitary, unique, and, if I may so call it, *recherché* biscuit!' (*D* 53) – is the nearest they come to vitality of expression. The first sign of paralysis is a paralysed language.

It is language, again, which establishes the essential absurdity of Chandler's admiration for Gallaher. The pub conversation in which Gallaher shows off his worldliness and patronizes his friend is a prize collection of clichés. For Chandler to go home wondering 'Was it too late for him to try to live bravely like Gallaher?' (*D* 92) exposes his ludicrous self-deception; after this, we might feel, the little solicitor's clerk deserves all he gets. Joyce's satire is rather crude here. Mr Duffy and Gabriel, by contrast, establish some of their credentials in the reader's view by their fastidiousness about the words they use. Mr Duffy 'had an odd autobiographical habit which led him to compose in his mind from time to time a short sentence about himself containing a subject in the third person and a predicate in the past tense' (*D* 120). His friendship with Mrs Sinico ripens until one night 'he heard the strange impersonal voice which he recognized as his own, insisting on the soul's incurable loneliness' (*D* 124). Mrs Sinico seizes hold of his hand and presses it to her cheek – a linguistic error or failure of understanding which destroys their relationship: 'Her interpretation of his words disillusioned him'.

Mr Duffy is so alienated that he has no language in which to share his feelings with anyone. Gabriel, however, is anxious to find the right level of language and avoid a 'wrong tone' (*D* 204). He is faintly embarrassed at the literary phrase he has coined, 'a thought-tormented age'; nevertheless he uses it in his after-dinner speech, though omitting the quotation from Browning which he 'feared . . . would be above the heads of his hearers' (*D* 203). In the event his speech successfully blends personal feeling with the banalities expected on a festive occasion; his success, however, does nothing to appease his consciousness of himself as a 'nervous well-meaning sentimentalist, orating to vulgarians and idealizing his own clownish lusts' (*D* 251). Like Mr Duffy, he experiences his alienation from other people as a gulf between his private language, and public language.

Frequently in *Dubliners* Joyce turns a half-ironic, half-approving scrutiny on the public language of festive and social occasions. We hear Gabriel's speech, Maria's song and Joe Hynes's ode on the death of Parnell. Though irony is present, such moments do much to redeem the impression of drabness, degeneration, and failure that is otherwise so prevalent in the book. In his 1906 letter to Stanislaus (quoted above) Joyce wondered whether he had done justice to Irish hospitality. The book, as it happens, is full of hospitable and festive occasions. Where in later works he shows the comradeship of pubs and bars, *Dubliners* conveys the sense of community through a succession of private parties. Even in 'The Sisters' the boy's visit to the house of mourning is an occasion for cream crackers and the glass of sherry which is perhaps what gets the sisters talking. 'After the Race', one of the slightest stories in the book, is the story of an evening's high living among a group of cosmopolitan young men. They drink 'Ireland, England, France, Hungary, the United States of America' (*D* 50), and then settle down to play cards. The story is a political and economic allegory in which the game of cards stands for the 'great game' (*D* 51) of European diplomacy and high finance. The American foots the bill, and the outcome lies between the French and the English. Jimmy Doyle, the Irishman, gets cleaned out. Jimmy's doomed but sporting attempt to engage on level terms with the representatives of the great powers is Joyce's comment on Irish aspirations to nationhood. The Hungarian finally announces the new day, however, because Arthur Griffith, the founder of Sinn Fein, had taken Hungary's resistance to Austrian domination as an emblem of Ireland's struggle.

Jimmy Doyle's night of folly is succeeded by the Hallowe'en party in 'Clay', the political anniversary of 'Ivy Day in the Committee Room', and the bedside gathering in 'Grace'. All three are thoroughly Irish occasions, with bottles of stout well in evidence. Even while remaining detached from them the Joycean narrator shows them as occasions for jokes and sentiment, for poetry and song. These festivities bring out an underlying tension between local attachments and Irish pride, and the international culture of the modern bourgeois world. On the one side are the Hallowe'en customs, the Parnellite tradition and respect for the Irish priesthood, which is said in 'Grace' to be 'honoured all the world over' (*D* 185). On the other side are the 'two masters', London and Rome – not to mention the plutocracy of wealth and the internationalism of culture. Politics in 'Ivy Day in the Committee Room' are dominated by material interests; Parnell's memory has no place in a Nationalist party that is happy to accept Conservative support in the municipal elections to secure the defeat of Labour. Will the Nationalists endorse an address of welcome to be presented to the English King on his visit to Dublin? The signs are that they will. Mr Henchy's belief in enticing capital to Ireland seems to be carrying the day. Militant patriotism, which in 1904 was not yet a political force to be reckoned with, can be dismissed as a matter for 'hillsiders and fenians' (*D* 139). If political rule comes from London, religious authority, as we see in 'Grace', is invested in the Vatican and the doctrine of papal infallibility. Leo XIII, Mr Power says in reverential tones, was 'one of the most intellectual men in Europe, . . . I mean apart from his being Pope' (*D* 189). These political and cultural tensions are dramatically heightened in 'The Dead'. On one level, the dance held on the Feast of the Epiphany is almost disrupted by the intransigence of Miss Ivors, representing the resurgence of cultural nationalism, who accuses Gabriel of being a 'West Briton' and then walks out. At another level, however, a true cosmopolitanism is affirmed through the medium of musical culture. The good feeling at the Morkans's is in clear contrast to the acrimony of the Irish Language Society's concert, which Joyce satirizes in 'A Mother'. At the Morkans's Italian opera, the waltz, Mary Jane's Academy piece, and at the last moment an Irish folk-song (*The lass of Aughrim*) all contribute to the festivity. In a minor key the same cosmopolitanism is present in earlier stories. For example, the music of Balfe – a Dublin-born composer who began his career with the Italian Opera before settling and making his fortune in England – is present in 'Eveline' and 'Clay'. The much-travelled Frank takes Eveline to see *The Bohemian Girl*, and – after the Irish Hallowe'en rituals – Joe and Maria become sentimental over 'I Dreamt that I Dwelt'. Much later in his life Joyce was to rebuke his friend Arthur Power, who said that he was 'tired of nationality' and that he wished to write like the French, not the Irish, since 'all great writers were international'. Joyce's reply was 'Yes – but they were national first – if you are sufficiently national you will be international'.[18] Music in *Dubliners* seems to bear out this paradox. It is a positive expression of the bourgeois culture that, in other ways, Joyce was condemning for its 'paralysis'. Where there is music – with the dreadful exception of the semi-professional, semi-amateur concerts portrayed in 'A Mother' – there is also spontaneity, joy, and animation. It is here that we glimpse such zest and resilience as Joyce's Dubliners possess.

Visions of the outcast: 'A Painful Case' and 'The Dead'

Mr Duffy in 'A Painful Case' comes to feel that he is 'outcast from life's feast' (*D* 131). He too has been a music-lover, whose 'only dissipations' (*D* 121) resulted from his liking for Mozart. He is an utterly solitary man whose abortive friendship with the middle-aged Mrs Sinico could well have been the material of melodrama. A lesser novelist might have been tempted to show Mr Duffy coming across the dead body of his jilted lady on the railway line, or at least catching sight of her under the influence of drink. Joyce, however, conveys her degeneration only through the flat-footed prose of a newspaper report. He shows Mr Duffy rejecting all voluntary bonds of relationship both with an individual ('every bond . . . is a bond of sorrow', he tells Mrs Sinico, *D* 124) and with society at large. He lives far from the city and soon loses interest in the socialist party whose meetings he once attended. In fact, he languishes in the state of inert and purposeless disconnection which the French sociologist Emile Durkheim diagnosed as *anomie*. *Anomie*, a state of mind in which the individual feels no solidarity with his fellow-men and is free of all social restraints, is both a typical modern urban phenomenon and a contributing cause of suicide. Mr Duffy lacks the self-destructive impulse of Mrs Sinico and at the end, when he feels his 'moral nature falling to pieces' (*D* 130), we cannot say for certain that he is a suicidal figure. What he does experience, at a level of visionary intensity, is an awareness of the life he has missed by standing aloof.

His first impression after reading the report of Mrs Sinico's inquest (described by the Coroner as a 'most painful case', *D* 128) is one of revulsion: 'He saw the squalid tract of her vice, miserable and malodorous. His soul's companion!' (*D* 128). Her death is an illustration of the struggle for existence and it seems to justify his own ruthless instinct of self-preservation: 'Evidently she had been unfit to live, without any strength of purpose, an easy prey to habits, one of the wrecks on which civilisation has been reared' (*D* 129). Mr Duffy here sees civilization in Darwinian terms as a competitive, predatory struggle in which he at least does not intend to be among the victims. When the evening draws on and he walks out into the park, however, his repressed feelings and emotions seem to rebel against him. He is haunted by the sense of Mrs Sinico's presence. In his hallucinatory state 'he seemed to feel her voice touch his ear, her hand touch his' (*D* 130): she has risen from the grave, as it were, like the priest in the narrator's dream in 'The Sisters'. He finds himself envying the 'venal and furtive' sexual transactions taking place under the park wall. Finally the vision dies away:

He turned his eyes to the grey gleaming river, winding along towards Dublin. Beyond the river he saw a goods train winding out of Kingsbridge Station, like a worm with a fiery head winding through the darkness, obstinately and laboriously. It passed slowly out of sight; but still he heard in his ears the laborious drone of the engine, reiterating the syllables of her name.

He turned back the way he had come, the rhythm of the engine pounding in his ears. He began to doubt the reality of what memory told him. He halted under a tree and allowed the rhythm to die away. He could not feel her near him in the darkness nor her voice touch his ear. He waited for some minutes listening. He could hear nothing: the night was perfectly silent. He listened again: perfectly silent. He felt that he was alone. (*D* 131)

The goods train, like a 'worm with a fiery head', is a powerfully suggestive piece of symbolism. The passage both describes the rhythm of the engine and perfectly conveys the rhythm of Mr Duffy's feeling. It describes an uncanny experience, a hallucination — the engine reiterating 'Emily Sinico, Emily Sinico' picks up the earlier suggestion that she is somehow present and haunting the landscape — but the realistic control never falters and we are not inclined to view this as more than a momentary mental aberration. Joyce's achievement here was to create a prose style capable of fully rendering the private despair of a lonely, sensitive man. Earlier we heard that Mr Duffy was in the habit of composing short sentences about himself, with a subject in the third person and a predicate in the past tense. He is Joyce's creation and these are his sentences.

In 'A Painful Case' — for the first time in *Dubliners* since the opening stories of childhood — we sense a close identification (though the identification is balanced by revulsion) between Joyce and his protagonist. (His brother Stanislaus, as it happens, was an acknowledged model for Mr Duffy.) A still greater sense of sympathy and identification is felt towards Gabriel Conroy in 'The Dead'. Gabriel, who like Joyce has fallen in love with a country girl from Galway, is probably a fantasy-projection of the novelist as he might have been had his talent failed him and had he lived on to become a man of settled habits in his native city. The story is the longest and most substantial in *Dubliners*, and the last to be written. In it, however, Joyce abandons some of the technical innovations he had introduced in earlier, more impressionistic stories.

'The Dead', unlike 'Ivy Day in the Committee Room', has a plot. Both its dramatic structure and its symbolism testify to a revival on Joyce's part of his undergraduate passion for Ibsen. Ibsen's favourite tragic form is one in which the complacent, accommodating surface of bourgeois life is shattered by a long-delayed revelation of decisive events in the past. Much the same thing happens in 'The Dead', where Gabriel's self-complacency is destroyed by the discovery that his wife once loved another man whose name, Michael Furey, signifies the passionate nature that Gabriel lacks. The title of the story not only implies haunting but echoes Ibsen's *Ghosts* and *When We Dead Awaken*. The deathly appearance of some of Joyce's characters, such as Aunt Julia, and the spiritual deadness of others recall Mrs Alving's famous outburst which is responsible for the title of the former play:

I am half inclined to think we are all ghosts, Mr Manders. It is not only what we have inherited from our fathers and mothers that exists again in us, but all sorts of old dead ideas and all kinds of old dead beliefs and things of that kind. They are not actually alive in us; but there they are dormant, all the same, and we can never be rid of them. Whenever I take up a newspaper and read it, I fancy I see ghosts creeping between the lines.[19]

If *Ghosts* is an attack on the deadness of bourgeois society, *When We Dead Awaken* holds out the promise of a new life of self-liberation. Rubek, the hero, is a sculptor whose masterpiece was a tableau of the Resurrection. Years later, at a health resort in the mountains, he meets the woman who had served as a model for the central figure in his sculpture. Neither has remained faithful to the vision that sustained them in that earlier time, but now they resolve to break with the bourgeois world and 'resurrect' their lives. They disappear into the snowfields, and the play ends with the sound of the avalanche that engulfs them.

Joyce had written an attentive précis of *When We Dead Awaken*, published as 'Ibsen's New Drama' in the *Fortnightly Review* in 1900 (*CW* 47–67). Thirty-four years later he was to write a burlesque of *Ghosts*, in the form of a verse epilogue spoken by the ghost of the dissolute husband of Mrs Alving (*CW* 271–3). The general theme of paralysis in *Dubliners* is an extension of Ibsen's diagnosis of social death or *rigor mortis*. In 'The Dead' Gabriel, as we have seen, is not a great artist but a less exceptional and only partially alienated figure. He is not the man to make a grand gesture of self-immolation like that of Rubek and Irene. Yet, in the visionary passage at the end of the story, he has an 'out of the body' experience in which he travels in spirit to the region of the dead, and then westward across the snow-covered Irish landscape. Finally his soul 'swooned slowly' amid the snowfall. This experience – which may be no more than the wanderings of a mind falling asleep – is Joyce's way of rehandling the material of Ibsen's dramatic catastrophe.

Ibsen's dramatic symbolism serves to evoke an 'unseen reality' determining the action and yet excluded by the four walls of the bourgeois drawing-rooms in which his middle-period naturalistic plays are set. This excluded world may be evoked though verbal imagery, as in *Ghosts*, or by a physical representation on stage as in *The Wild Duck*. The snow-landscape which symbolizes Gabriel's fantasies of escape from the social world is presented in a similarly tentative, yet insistent way; at no point do we see Gabriel actually lost in a snowy wilderness. His preoccupation with snow is opposed to the fire-symbolism associated with the 'boy in the gasworks' (*D* 251), Michael Furey. There have been endless explications of the symbolism of the story, thanks to the complexity of Joyce's interweaving of themes and his use of stories within stories. There is a strong subsidiary geopolitical theme, which opposes Dublin (the centre of English influence where Gabriel writes for the *Daily Express*) to the Gaeltácht or Gaelic hinterland. The stories within the story include those of Michael Furey, of Gabriel's visit to the glassworks, of the old Italian opera companies and of Patrick Morkan's horse. Yet throughout 'The Dead' Joyce's symbolism, like that of Ibsen's naturalistic plays, is in the service of a realistic dramatization of social life and individual emotional dilemmas. In it Joyce demonstrated his mastery not just of 'visionary' writing but of a rich and crowded social scene.

'The Dead' shows his intimate knowledge of the musical culture of Dublin, and it also relies tacitly on our awareness of another art, which appropriately is that of theatre and 'stage-management'. Theatricality

and 'putting on an act' play a prominent part in several earlier stories:
the boys of 'An Encounter' adopting false names and mimicking a
Wild West adventure, the self-dramatization of Corley and Gallaher,
the backstage manoeuvrings of 'A Mother' and (for that matter) of
Polly's betrothal in 'The Boarding House'. In 'The Dead' the Misses
Morkans's dance is a well-rehearsed affair in which Gabriel is a key
figure both as behind-the-scenes manager (Freddy Malins in particular
needs to be 'managed', *D* 200) and as a principal actor with a carefully
scripted speech who nevertheless suffers badly from stage-fright. From
the moment of his arrival his over-hearty salutations betray him as
acting a role. One of his last actions at the party − pacing round the
hall in his goloshes in imitation of Patrick Morkan's horse − is still
more unmistakably theatrical. Yet it is immediately after that, when
he catches sight of his wife listening to Bartell D'Arcy's singing − a
prospect which at first makes him think of a third art, that of symbolist
or impressionist painting − that the theatrical continuity is shattered.
There is nothing staged about Gretta's emotion. Back at the hotel,
listening to her story and seeing himself as a 'pitiable fatuous fellow'
(*D* 251) in the mirror, Gabriel is like an actor with his greasepaint off.

A remarkable feature of 'The Dead' is the new understanding which
Joyce brings to his central woman character. In several of the earlier
stories the women are unsympathetic and shadowy figures. ('Clay' and
'Eveline' do not suffice to correct the prevailing impression.) In the last
section of 'The Boarding House' we find Joyce trying, but not wholly
succeeding, to show Polly Mooney's thoughts as she waits upstairs for
the outcome of the interview between her mother and the lodger.
Though her marital fate hangs on this she is neither frightened (once
she has recovered from a bout of tears), nor calculating, nor penitent.
Unlike her lover she feels no shame about her situation. Instead she
becomes lost in reverie, achieving a moment of mental freedom which
is precarious and measurable, almost, against the clock. When her
mother calls her there is a split second before she remembers that she
is in the middle of a crisis. All this is admirable, yet beyond references
to her 'hopes and visions' and 'secret amiable memories' (*D* 75) Joyce
gives very little idea of what might be going on in her mind. He shows
that she is not, like so many of his other characters, overburdened by
a conviction of sin; but he cannot make her interesting.

Gretta Conroy in 'The Dead' has suddenly recalled an old lover, of
whom she has never spoken and who moved her passions more deeply
than her husband has done. After the dance she confesses as much to

Gabriel, yet she too is remarkably free of shame, penitence, or the desire to apologize. Her love for Michael Furey, in fact, stands alone in *Dubliners* for its mutual passion (though we should remember that Gretta observed the social conventions and allowed herself to be sent away to a convent). At their last meeting Furey stood outside her bedroom window on a wet winter night and told her he 'did not want to live' (*D* 253). He died a week later, presumably of consumption. Gretta re-lives the agony of her loss but there is no sign that she blames herself for the course her life has taken. Has her immature passion for Michael Furey been succeeded by a mature love for Gabriel? Joyce does not say so openly, but we do sense that the humiliation Gabriel feels as a result of her confession is an exaggerated, over-dramatized first response. Later he calmly accepts the situation and this is what leads to the visionary state evoked at the end of the story.

Like the boy in 'The Sisters' and 'An Encounter', Gabriel is the involuntary recipient of a confession. Unlike the boy, however, he is able to hear the confession out and to receive it with full and generous sympathy. Though he fails to achieve the sexual intimacy with Gretta for which he had been hoping, he overcomes his purely selfish disappointment and achieves, in the last lines, a curiously passive liberation of the spirit:

Generous tears filled Gabriel's eyes. He had never felt like that himself towards any woman but he knew that such a feeling must be love. The tears gathered more thickly in his eyes and in the partial darkness he imagined he saw the form of a young man standing under a dripping tree. Other forms were near. His soul had approached that region where dwell the vast hosts of the dead. He was conscious of, but could not apprehend, their wayward and flickering existence. His own identity was fading out into a grey impalpable world: the solid world itself which these dead had one time reared and lived in was dissolving and dwindling.

A few light taps upon the pane made him turn to the window. It had begun to snow again. He watched sleepily the flakes, silver and dark, falling obliquely against the lamplight. The time had come for him to set out on his journey westward. Yes, the newspapers were right: snow was general all over Ireland. It was falling on every part of the dark central plain, on the treeless hills, falling softly upon the Bog of Allen and, farther westward, softly falling into the dark mutinous Shannon waves, It was falling, too, upon every part of the lonely churchyard on the hill where Michael Furey lay buried. It lay thickly drifted on the crooked crosses and headstones, on the spears of the little gate, on the barren thorns. His soul swooned slowly as he heard the snow falling faintly through the universe and faintly falling, like the descent of their last end, upon all the living and the dead. (*D* 255–6)

For all its undoubted beauty this passage has a little the air of an exercise

— the conscious perfection of Joyce's 'epiphanic' technique. The epiphany ends with a dying fall. 'Falling' is echoed seven times, with one 'descent'. 'Their last end' picks up an earlier reference to the monks of Mount Melleray who sleep in their coffins (*D* 230). As in 'A Painful Case', the passage describes a vision or hallucination which is nevertheless easily believable; the mind is drifting between waking and sleep. Gabriel's deathly 'swoon', like Rubek's last gesture in *When We Dead Awaken*, suggests both death as the end of everything (which is one meaning of 'his journey westward'), and death as a release from the false animation around him into a genuine spiritual life. Gabriel's soul, however, is not that of a Christian but of a would-be artist, a man of sensitivity and compassion who stands at a certain distance both from the festivities of ordinary life and from the 'feast' of passionate love. What he lacks compared with other men of a different 'grade of culture' he makes up for in his capacity for vision. While the first story of *Dubliners* shows the death and 'paralysis' of a priest, the conclusion to the volume thus points towards the transcendence of death through the artistic imagination. Yet if Gabriel, his soul swooning slowly, seems to have given up the struggle of life in this world, there is a remarkable emotional dissonance between this ending and the tone of Joyce's later works. A ribald defiance of death would take over, in *Ulysses*, from this reverent intensity of feeling. Its intensity and deliberate beauty help to account for the ease with which we may find ourselves detaching the ending of 'The Dead' from the rest of *Dubliners*. To do so, however, is to upset the balance of attraction and repulsion towards the common life of Dublin which makes Joyce's stories, for all their impressionism and 'scrupulous meanness', a 'chapter in the moral history of my country'.

4 *A Portrait of the Artist* and *Exiles*

The portrait and the artist

The text of *A Portrait of the Artist as a Young Man* is dated 'Dublin 1904 / Trieste 1914'. 1904 was the year in which *Stephen Hero* was written and Joyce left Dublin with Nora Barnacle to become a language teacher on the Adriatic. Ten years later, after some vicissitudes, he was still there. His life was about to be transformed, thanks to the First World War (which would force him to move to neutral Switzerland), and to a chance letter from Ezra Pound in December 1913, which marked the beginnings of his literary celebrity.[1] Pound arranged for serial publication of the *Portrait* to begin in the *Egoist*, a small avant-garde literary and political magazine, in February 1914; in June of the same year the London publisher Grant Richards at last brought out *Dubliners*.

The writing of the *Portrait* thus spans ten years during which Joyce kept rigorously to Stephen Dedalus's programme of 'silence exile and cunning'. His literary silence was broken only by *Chamber Music* and by a small quantity of essays and journalism, some of it written in Italian.[2] His exile, at first only temporary, was confirmed by his unhappy experiences in revisiting Ireland in 1909 and 1912. Cunning is evident in the far-reaching revisions with which he transformed *Stephen Hero*, a raw apprentice-work, into the *Portrait* with its eloquence of style and fastidious pursuit of artistic impersonality. Joyce makes Stephen Dedalus echo the famous passage in Flaubert's *Letters* which declares that the writer should stand aloof from his work: 'The artist must stand to his work as God to his creation, invisible and all powerful; he must be everywhere felt but nowhere seen'.[3] The *Portrait of the Artist* brings the doctrine of impersonality to bear in an area which Flaubert himself had never attempted. It sets out to be an impersonal or ironic autobiography.

The irony consists in Joyce's balancing of the different points of view it is possible to adopt towards the young Stephen. Stephen himself comes to believe he is following a predestined course, and unfolds a fervently idealistic artistic creed. Through him Joyce is able both to affirm the romantic myth of artistic genius, and to partially dissociate himself from the arrogance and self-conceit which follows from that myth. Irony is always implicit in the narrative, yet it cannot be too heavily underlined or it will destroy the basis of Joyce's − not merely Stephen's − claims for his writing. The book is uncertainly poised between mature reservation and an almost intoxicating sympathy with Stephen's experience. Finally, it may be, the artist-myth in the *Portrait* taken on its own was too powerful, and Joyce's attempt to re-live it burst the bounds of mature detachment. He then had to create a disillusioned sequel to his autobiographical novel, in the parts of *Ulysses* centred on Stephen.

Joyce started off, as few if any novelists before him had done, by sticking scrupulously to the ostensible facts of his own life. His rewriting of the main events of his life is as nothing compared with the melodramatic inventions to be found in even the most 'confessional' of earlier novels. This is the main point of difference between the *Portrait* and the *Bildungsromane* and *Künstlerromane* ('novels of education' and 'artist-hero' novels) of the nineteenth century. The *Portrait* is less close to books like *Wilhelm Meister, David Copperfield*, or Gissing's *New Grub Street* than it is to the genre of literary autobiography and memoirs. The pattern of destiny which Stephen discovers in the events of his own life suggests that one crucial source is the tradition of spiritual apology or confession, from St Augustine to Newman. Stephen's destiny, however, bears witness to the religion of Art rather than of Christianity, and it is in the field of artistic memoirs and autobiographical sketches that we shall find the closest analogues to the *Portrait*. One such memoir by an older contemporary − George Moore's *Confessions of a Young Man* (1888) − no doubt influenced Joyce's title.

Stephen's belief in the priestly role of the artist and his duty to 'forge in the smithy of my soul the uncreated conscience of my race' (*P* 253) has its roots in the high romanticism of Wordsworth and Shelley. The *Portrait* transmutes the stuff of actual experience into artistic myth as thoroughly as Wordsworth had done. In addition, it serves as a 'prelude' in the Wordsworthian sense to the more comprehensive edifices of *Ulysses* and *Finnegans Wake*. Nevertheless, the *Portrait* is not a straightforwardly romantic work. While Stephen remains ultimately committed to the Shelleyan notion of the artist as unacknowledged legislator of the world, his attention – unlike that of the Wordsworthian or Shelleyan hero – is devoted to disentangling himself from the external world and exploring the secrets and intricacies of his own art. His preoccupation with art as a sacred mystery links him to the Aesthetic and Decadent movements of the late nineteenth century. The reverence that the Aesthetes and Decadents felt for their romantic predecessors was tinged by the melancholy conviction that these poets had sought in the external world for 'what is there in no satisfying measure or not at all' (*CW* 78). (These words, borrowed from Walter Pater, were used by Joyce himself in his essay on the Dublin romantic poet James Clarence Mangan.) The artist now turned, not to unspoilt nature, but in on himself to find a truly satisfying richness and beauty. Oscar Wilde went so far as to suggest that all artists are solipsists, whether they know it or not: 'every portrait that is painted with feeling is a portrait of the artist', we read in *The Picture of Dorian Gray*.[4] It may have been a similar conviction that led Joyce to turn to autobiographical fiction in the first place.

Stephen Hero is written in the naturalistic manner and portrays Stephen, during his student years, as an Ibsenite. Early in 1904, however, Joyce had written a short essay called 'A Portrait of the Artist' which contrasts sharply with *Stephen Hero* even though Joyce incorporated some passages from it into his novel. The 'Portrait of the Artist' was – understandably – rejected by the editors of *Dana* as incomprehensible. Far from presenting the artist as a free-standing fictional character, through realistic description and dramatized dialogue, Joyce had written a tortuous, allusive and contemplative essay modelled on the Walter Pater of *Imaginary Portraits* (1887). Such a portrait was, as he expressed it, 'not an identificative paper but rather the curve of an emotion'.[5] The artist portrayed is one who turns aside from his contemporaries to seek the 'image of beauty'[6] in the byways of esoteric and occult learning. Though the essay concludes with a Shelleyan vision of social revolution, there is no suggestion here (as there was in the 'epiphany' passage in *Stephen Hero*) that the artist might find beauty in the 'commonest object' or amongst the people around him. Instead, 'To those multitudes not as yet in the wombs of humanity but surely engenderable there, he would give the word'.[7]

The artist, if he is to 'give the word' to future humanity, must follow the image of beauty and free himself of all servitude to the words of

those alien to him. That is equally the message of the 1904 'Portrait'
and of its 1916 counterpart. In the mature *Portrait* the words of others
are dramatized as external and internal voices. The book begins with
the voice of Stephen's father and ends with Stephen's departure for the
continent at the behest of imaginary voices clamouring 'We are your
kinsmen' (*P* 252). At this point he has rejected his father's voice in
favour of voices he believes to be more 'authentic', more 'internal'.
They are at once the Sibylline voices of inspiration and prophecy and
the voices of his fellow-artists in the literary tradition. Nevertheless,
Stephen's ability to discover such authentic voices remains unproven,
since only in his career as a writer, which he has yet to begin, can he
break his self-imposed silence and show that he, too, has it in him to
'give the word'. The proof of the oracle would be found in the writing.

Voice, memory, and discontinuity

'The past assuredly implies a fluid succession of presents, the
development of an entity of which our actual present is a phase only',
Joyce had declared in his 1904 essay.[8] The 'actual presents' out of
which his successive attempts at autobiographical fiction were written
included, of necessity, a strong autobiographical urge. The same urge
is present at least incipiently in every earlier stage of Stephen's
childhood and youth. We see him not only learning about and reacting
to his environment, but creating a sense of identity based on
accumulated experience and feelings. His sense of identity is intimately
connected with memory, and the *Portrait* begins, effectively, at the
point where Stephen as an infant first exercises his powers as a
memoirist. The description of him as 'retaining nothing of all he read
save that which seemed to him an echo or prophecy of his own state'
(*P* 155) belongs to a particular phase of adolescence, yet it is also deeply
characteristic of Stephen from the beginning. His inner knowledge of
his own identity is ratified by his discovery of a series of prophecies,
signs of a predestined outcome to his story, of which the principal one
is his own name. The oddity of the name Dedalus is foregrounded very
early in the *Portrait*: eventually he realizes it is 'a prophecy of the end
he had been born to serve' (*P* 169), in other words of artisthood. Joyce
uses the twin themes of predestination and habitual autobiography to
persuade us of the inevitability of Stephen's emergence as a writer, a
career towards which he is seen to be innately predisposed. And, as an

embryo writer, he is ceaselessly rewriting the 'book of himself' (*U* 187).

The narrative structure of the *Portrait* is a 'fluid succession of presents' (though each present is narrated in the past tense) linked by an evolutionary process, which shows the development of Stephen's identity and his accumulated memory. Each phase in the 'succession of presents' is a tightly constructed narrative unit which may seem sharply discontinuous with what comes before and after it. The discontinuity is textual and generic as well as temporal; in the *Portrait*, as in *Ulysses*, Joyce's method amounts to 'one style per episode'. Linking the episodes is a series of evolutionary chains of images and themes. It is helpful to enumerate these, and I shall do so in unsystematic fashion beginning with Stephen's understanding of his surname.

The epigraph of the *Portrait* is from Ovid and denotes the Dedalian theme: 'And he set his mind to work upon unknown arts' (*Et ignotas animum dimittit in artes*). Nasty Roche commences hostilities with his famous question to Stephen in the first Clongowes episode – 'What kind of a name is that?' (*P* 9). The oddity of his name is further noticed by Athy, and, much later, by Stephen's fellow-student Davin who asks whether it is Irish. Stephen's reply, offering to show Davin his family tree in the Office of Arms (*P* 201), is a brazen attempt by Joyce to naturalize the palpably fictional.[9] Earlier we have listened to Stephen trying out his name as it would look if he joined the priesthood – 'The Reverend Stephen Dedalus, S.J.' (*P* 161) – and finding it does not fit. His eventual discovery that the name Dedalus is emblematic of the artist, and that it betokens the artist's means of escape from the island of his birth and imprisonment, comes pat like the solution to a detective story which has been kept hidden by simply diverting the reader's attention.

Stephen's discovery of the significance of his name comes about as a result of his increasingly specialized involvement with language. The very first game that he plays is a language-game, in which he turns Dante's proverbial (and rhyming) threat about eagles into a symmetrical pair of verses:

> Pull out his eyes,
> Apologise,
> Apologise,
> Pull out his eyes. . . .   (*P* 8)

At Clongowes, the formal process of learning has begun and Stephen
spontaneously extends this to learning about language. He is fascinated
by the different meanings of such 'queer words' (*P* 11) as *belt* and *suck*,
as well as by the correspondence between words and things which
allows cold and hot water to come out of taps marked cold and hot. In
adolescence the secrets of his awakening sexuality and of his difference
from his father are summed up in the shock of the word '*Foetus*'
scratched on a desk. In the recognition scene on Dollymount beach
there is a famous (if slightly obscure) passage in which Stephen becomes
conscious of his obsession with words:

He drew forth a phrase from his treasure and spoke it softly to himself:
    – A day of dappled seaborne clouds.
    The phrase and the day and the scene harmonised in a chord. Words. Was
it their colours? He allowed them to glow and fade, hue after hue: sunrise gold,
the russet and green of apple orchards, azure of waves, the greyfringed fleece
of clouds. No, it was not their colours: it was the poise and balance of the period
itself. Did he then love the rhythmic rise and fall of words better than their
associations of legend and colour? Or was it that, being as weak of sight as he
was shy of mind, he drew less pleasure from the reflection of the glowing
sensible world through the prism of a language manycoloured and richly storied
than from the contemplation of an inner world of individual emotions mirrored
perfectly in a lucid supple periodic prose?   (*P* 166–7)

The passage is at once argument and evocation. To the extent that it
presents genuinely alternative views of language, they are the major
doctrines held by nineteenth- and early twentieth-century romantic
poets, spelt out one by one. Stephen appears to be rejecting Keatsian
verbal associationism, 'Pure Sound' and Paterian or Conradian
impressionism in favour of an expressionist model of language as the
precise representation of an 'inner world' of individual emotions, a
view which should have found favour with T. S. Eliot. Language,
moulded by the genius of the artist, has then become a 'perfect mirror'.
If this is the ideal toward which the young Stephen aspires, the fifth
section of the *Portrait* suggests the sort of resistance in language he may
be destined to encounter. For Stephen is a poet, the author of a
villanelle full of 'coloured' words, and not yet capable of 'lucid supple
periodic prose' such as we find in *Dubliners*. Moreover, the vocabulary
which surrounds him is not individual or authentic but secondhand.
Debating the word 'tundish' with the dean of studies, he reflects:

How different are the words *home, Christ, ale, master*, on his lips and on mine!
I cannot speak or write these words without unrest of spirit. His language, so
familiar and so foreign, will always be for me an acquired speech. I

have not made or accepted its words. My voice holds them at bay. My soul frets in the shadow of his language.   (*P* 189)

Stephen in the *Portrait* is searching for an authentic language which he can voice. It is a typically romantic quest, inherited by the symbolists and Decadents of the late nineteenth century and passed on to the early modernists. Arthur Symons's words in the peroration to *The Symbolist Movement in Literature* (1899) are representative:

> Here, then, in this revolt against exteriority, against rhetoric, against a materialistic tradition; in this endeavour to disengage the ultimate essence, the soul, of whatever exists and can be realised by the consciousness; in this dutiful waiting upon every symbol by which the soul of things can be made visible; literature, bowed down by so many burdens, may at last attain liberty, and its authentic speech.[10]

Stephen, as poet and aesthetic theorist, should have been in full agreement with Symons's exhortation. Symons's vocabulary is close to the *Portrait* and, moreover, he had dedicated his book to Yeats, whose verses from *The Countess Cathleen* are echoed by Stephen. But that is not the whole story. It is fairly clear what direction a young Irish romantic, attracted by the Decadence and chafing against the 'acquired speech' of his British rulers, might have been expected to take around 1900. Among the leaders of the 1916 Easter Rising were at least two published poets, Pearse and MacDonagh. It is the Irish nationalist in Stephen which makes him reflect, of *home, Christ, ale* and *master*, that 'I cannot speak or write these words without unrest of spirit'. Yet he is too honest to suppose that Gaelic, for him, would be any less of an acquired and secondhand speech. As he became an international writer Joyce tended more and more to represent the state of not being at home in one's language as a universal condition, the fate of fallen man after Babel rather than a product of the power-structure of the British Empire. In *Finnegans Wake* there is no 'authentic speech', since everything comes at secondhand; the 'voices' Joyce creates emerge from his mental 'word-processor' and are in no sense prior to, or more authentic than, the actual writing. In the *Portrait* there are one or two anticipations of Joyce's later comic sense of the use, and inevitability, of borrowed speech. Stephen takes over words and phrases of the Elizabethans, for example, to serve as an erotic shorthand (*P* 176, 233). Cranly's absurd dog-Latin does a good deal to enliven the dialogues of the final section. Joyce's later work implies that all modern literary language is bastardized and cut adrift from its roots — that language, in fact, has become grotesque. The world thus demands an art which reconciles Stephen's quest for a unique language with Cranly's ebullient philistinism.

Two further developing themes in the *Portrait* have already been mentioned: voices and memory. To see how words, voice and memory are intertwined we need only consider the cry which issues from Stephen's lips as, possessed by the demon of lust, he wanders into the red-light district of Dublin for the first time:

It broke from him like a wail of despair from a hell of sufferers and died in a wail of furious entreaty, a cry for an iniquitous abandonment, a cry which was but the echo of an obscene scrawl which he had read on the oozing wall of a urinal.   (*P* 100)

Words inscribed on a urinal wall (comparable, no doubt, to the word '*Foetus*' scratched on a desk) and then imprinted on his memory are 'echoed' in a cry. Stephen's whole development could be expressed in terms of a vocal metabolism in which words and voices enter into his consciousness and are digested by the memory, before issuing forth as emotional statements of which the simplest form is the cry. The disjunction between outer and inner, between voices and cries, becomes obvious to Stephen in adolescence, when he feels it at first as a sickness interrupting normal digestion:

His very brain was sick and powerless. He could scarcely interpret the letters of the signboards of the shops. By his monstrous way of life he seemed to have put himself beyond the limits of reality. Nothing moved him or spoke to him from the real world unless he heard in it an echo of the infuriated cries within him. He could respond to no earthly or human appeal, dumb and insensible to the call of summer and gladness and companionship, wearied and dejected by his father's voice.   (*P* 92)

Though it may weary him at this moment, his father's voice plays a crucial part in the novel. The *Portrait* begins (as we have seen) with his father's words and ends with a cry addressed to an imaginary father. Stephen's father's voice triumphs over Dante's voice in the Christmas dinner scene, though both are etched into the young boy's consciousness. When in adolescence he wearies of his actual father's voice, he is all the more vulnerable to those of the 'spiritual fathers', the priests. Joyce, indeed, introduces a startling innovation which amounts to a scandalous breach of the rules of modern fictional construction. In the third chapter the priest's voice takes over and dominates the *Portrait*, through the series of sermons which occupies nearly thirty pages of text or almost one-eighth of the whole book. After the priest's voice, it is the turn of the voices of nature and the imagination, which Stephen hears on the beach as he decides that his destiny is to be an artist. Once that decision is made he is again haunted by the voices of his social environment, which are raised against him in reproach. Leaving his house on the way to the university, he hears the screech of a mad nun but 'shook the sound out of his ears by an angry toss of his head':

His father's whistle, his mother's mutterings, the screech of an unseen maniac were to him now so many voices offending and threatening to humble the pride of his youth.   (*P* 175–6)

Stephen 'drove their echoes even out of his heart with an execration', but they are not to be dismissed so easily. Davin puts the claims of nationality, language and religion to him. His mother's voice is emphasized towards the end of the novel, pleading with him not to desert his religion and praying, Stephen reports, 'that I may learn in my own life and away from home and friends what the heart is and what it feels' (*P* 252). Nevertheless, he can summon up imaginary voices which assure him he is right. Just before his final walk with Cranly he gains strength in his fight with his mother from the cries of swallows returning from migration. 'The inhuman clamour soothed his ears in which his mother's sobs and reproaches murmured insistently' (*P* 224); the birds, as Stephen tells himself by means of pedantic references to Swedenborg and Cornelius Agrippa, are age-old vehicles of augury. The final picture of Stephen is of one who is stubborn enough, by and large, to make the voices around him tell him what he wants to hear. But it is not always so, and in *Ulysses* the circumstances surrounding his mother's death will stretch his ability to rationalize the path he has taken to the utmost.

The role of memory in the *Portrait* has already been touched upon. Unlike most protagonists in autobiography, Stephen's memory is active and is foregrounded even in childhood. In one respect this may seem no more than a compositional strategy: Stephen's first days at Clongowes are not narrated chronologically but by means of a series of flashbacks which betray the onset of fever, preventing him from routine absorption in such activities as the game of football. The term 'flashback' suggests an automatic process, like that which goes on in the cutting-room of a film studio. But Stephen's memory is not only episodic and repetitive but creative. For example, the train of references to the 'square ditch' with its rats and cold slimy water in the first few pages helps to determine the kind of person Stephen becomes. Wells's action in shouldering him into the ditch is probably the cause of his lifelong aquaphobia, seen in the beach episode ('how his flesh dreaded the cold infrahuman odour of the sea', *P* 167) and again in *Ulysses*. Memories of water at Clongowes − the ditch, the turf-coloured bathwater, the 'wettish' air − are so indelible that they can eventually be classed as instinctual and shown to influence the crucial decisions of his life. When Stephen is tempted to join the priesthood, memories of Clongowes cause his soul to revolt at the thought of collegiate life:

He wondered how he would pass the first night in the novitiate and with what dismay he would wake the first morning in the dormitory. The troubling odour of the long corridors of Clongowes came back to him and he heard the discreet murmur of the burning gasflames. At once from every part of his being unrest began to irradiate. A feverish quickening of his pulses followed and a din of meaningless words drove his reasoned thoughts hither and thither confusedly. His lungs dilated and sank as if he were inhaling a warm moist unsustaining air and he smelt again the warm moist air which hung in the bath in Clongowes above the sluggish turfcoloured water.
   Some instinct, waking at these memories, stronger than education or piety, quickened within him at every near approach to that life, an instinct subtle and hostile, and armed him against acquiescence.   (*P* 160–1)

Its reliance on 'instinct' rather than reason makes this a remarkably original passage. Any nineteenth-century novelist could have shown Stephen arguing with himself over the pros and cons of the priestly life, but Joyce does not do this. The question is settled at a level of feeling 'stronger than education or piety' and therefore prior to argument. Indeed, Stephen's decision is a bodily as much as a mental event. He is not conscious at this moment of the alternatives to a career in the Church; he is not yet ready to devote himself to art or to opt to go to university. He rejects the priesthood not because he wants to do something else, but because he knows he *is* something else; and that is the sum of his accumulated and remembered experiences which 'quickens' within him as if it were life itself. Towards the end of the *Portrait* the workings of Stephen's memory begin to be overshadowed by his maturing intellect and imagination. To trace the growth of intellect, imagination and memory together would be to describe the *Portrait of the Artist* as a whole.

The *Portrait* is unified not only by the workings of its protagonist's memory, but by an 'unconscious' textual memory or series of repetitions, which are most easily traced at the level of imagery. Hugh Kenner, in a 1948 article, pointed out that in the *Portrait* 'the first two pages, terminated by a row of asterisks, enact the entire action in microcosm'.[11] From the first two pages we can trace 'verbal leitmotivs' or image-sets which recur throughout the narrative. Stephen's impressions in infancy can be broken down (with some complications) into a series of binary oppositions. Thematically the most important of these may be tabulated as follows:

father	vs.	mother
father and mother		baby
his father and mother		Eileen's father and mother
telling stories		playing the piano
storytelling and playing the piano		singing and dancing
the Michael Davitt brush (maroon)		the Parnell brush (green)
Dante's rewards (the cachous)		Dante's punishments (the eagles)

In addition to these thematic oppositions, there are others which seem purely imagistic:

wild rose blossoms	vs.	*green wothe botheth*
warm urine		cold urine
hiding under the table		the coming of the eagles
living next door to the Vances		

It is open to any reader to trace these oppositions through the book. Stephen's class at Clongowes is divided into rival teams, York and Lancaster (the white rose and the red rose). He reflects that you 'could not have a green rose. But perhaps somewhere in the world you could' (*P* 12). Maroon and green are the colours of Davitt and Parnell, so that the red and green of Christmas (holly and ivy, or the 'great fire, banked high and red' and the ivy, *P* 20, 27) betoken a political schism. When Stephen becomes pious, the rosaries he says 'transformed themselves into coronals of flowers of such vague unearthly texture that they seemed to him as hueless and odourless as they were nameless' (*P* 148). The blankness and inanition of the religious life, 'a heart of white rose' (*P* 145), is then contrasted with the red rose of passion and art, embodied both in the lotus-like apparition Stephen sees at the end of the beach episode and in the 'roselike glow' (*P* 217) he senses as he writes his villanelle. The lotus speaks to him of 'some new world, fantastic, dim, uncertain as under sea, traversed by cloudy shapes and beings. A world, a glimmer, or a flower?' Yet Stephen's imaginary green rose retains a recognizable connection with Ireland and Parnell. The one place where you could have a green rose is, of course, in the *Portrait of the Artist*.

Image-analysis of this sort will take us some way (though certainly not all the way) into Joyce's novel. It is not always clear that he exerts a very precise control over his images – often the repetitions elude any unforced critical explanation by their very frequency and diversity. For example, the Dedalian leitmotiv of flight is represented by various images of birds and bats that crop up in Stephen's consciousness. Plainly his interest in flight connects with his fear of water (aquaphobia). During his adolescent religious phase he feels himself 'standing far away from the flood [of sexual desire] on a dry shore' (*P* 152). Stephen is not deeply attracted by the dryness of asceticism as manifested in the 'pale loveless eyes' (*P* 186) of the Jesuit priest; he wants to feel superior to the element of water, rather than just safely dryshod. Images of birds abound in the *Portrait*, but it is only in the beach scene and the scene on the steps of the National Library that the bird-images appear portentous or symbolic. The ancient hero whom Stephen adopts as his spiritual father is a 'hawklike man flying sunward above the sea', and the cry that rises to Stephen's lips in this moment is the 'cry of a hawk or eagle on high' (*P* 169). Girls and women, also, are compared to flying creatures. Stephen's girl on the beach 'seemed like one whom magic had changed into the likeness of a strange and beautiful seabird' (*P* 171). Emma's life, he thinks, might be 'simple and strange as a bird's life' (*P* 216). The birdlike girl is thus a transfigured version of the shadowy Emma, Stephen's 'beloved', but in the final chapter there is added a rather different, though equally idealized image of womanhood. Davin, the clean-limbed Irish nationalist and Gaelic sports enthusiast, tells Stephen of the pregnant countrywoman who invited him to her bed. To Stephen such guileless sexuality stands for the awakening soul of Ireland, 'a type of her race and his own, a batlike soul waking to the consciousness of itself in darkness and secrecy and loneliness' (*P* 183). (Why batlike? Presumably because bats are the quietest and most furtive of flying creatures.) The batlike soul is an image of much more than merely sexual promise; indeed it is as it were abstracted from sex. Davin's woman is made to stand for Stephen's potential audience, the type of person for whom he is to go out and 'forge in the smithy of my soul the uncreated conscience of my race'.

The danger of the symbolic or imagistic reading of the *Portrait* is that it overlooks, of necessity, the discontinuities, shifts of perspective and changes of focus which fissure the narrative. When Mr Dedalus describes the betrayers of Parnell as 'rats in a sewer' (*P* 34), the alert symbolic reader will recall the rat that Stephen saw at Clongowes, and point to Stephen's identification with the victimized Irish leader. What we are witnessing, however, is a type of linguistic accident or coincidence in which the same semantic material has, in its new (and metaphorical) context, an utterly different value. Joyce himself was to become fascinated by such coincidences, but there is no sign that he gave deliberate attention to this particular example. The result of pursuing such chains of poetic association too far is to produce a *Portrait* very different from the one Joyce actually wrote.

The book is divided into five chapters, which exhibit a clear chronological, aetiological and stylistic progression. At the same time, each chapter roughly exhibits the same pattern of development. According to Kenner, the pattern is one of 'dream nourished in contempt of reality, put into practice, and dashed by reality'.[12] Kenner describes the movement of the *Portrait* as a sort of vicious spiral, since 'each chapter closes with a synthesis of triumph which in turn feeds the sausage-machine set up in the next chapter'. The 'synthesis of triumph', we might add, is in each case an approximation to the cry Stephen finally utters at the end of the book: 'Welcome, O life!' Near the end of Chapter 4 he exclaims, 'To live, to err, to fall, to triumph, to recreate life out of life!' (*P* 172). Chapter 3 ends with 'Another life! A life of grace and virtue and happiness!' (*P* 146); Chapter 2 with Stephen's first kiss which is a new awakening and an image of life; and Chapter 1 with his successful appeal against injustice which leaves him feeling 'happy and free' and hearing the sound of cricket bats 'like drops of water in a fountain falling softly in the brimming bowl' (*P* 59) – an image of plenty which is reminiscent of the Psalmist's 'My cup runneth over'. When Stephen at the end of the book announces that he is going 'to encounter for the millionth time the reality of experience' (*P* 252–3), it is (the structure implies) already the fifth in an exhilarating sequence of new starts.

This repeated rhythm in the *Portrait* should not, however, be allowed to obscure the sense of disjointedness that the book conveys, especially on close reading. The surviving portion of *Stephen Hero* presents a much more conventional, continuous progression than the finished version, which moves by leaps and jerks. It would be naive to pretend that Joyce's artistic control, as he revised his manuscript, was total or that the end-product is altogether seamless. Stephen's younger brother Maurice, an important character in the earlier version, has been eliminated from the *Portrait* – except that he does make a single un-explained appearance in Chapter 2. (' – O, Holy Paul, I forgot about

Maurice, said Mr Dedalus' (*P* 71) — words which Joyce might have
echoed.) When we read at the beginning of the Cork episode that
'Stephen was once again seated beside his father in the corner of a
railway carriage at Kingsbridge', and a moment later find him recalling
'his childish wonder of years before and every event of his first day at
Clongowes' (*P* 86), it is not difficult to make out that Stephen's parents
took him to Clongowes by train. The momentary flashback must refer
to an earlier version of the *Portrait* which — as Joyce told his brother
on 15 December 1907 — 'began at a railway station like most college
stories'.[13] Joyce left traces of this beginning only in Stephen's memory
— or did he, rather, forget to remove them?

The effect of the *Portrait*'s many narrative suppressions is not only
to highlight the faculty of memory but to produce a book that has to
be negotiated warily. When Stephen felt sick and feverish in the
refectory at Clongowes,

He leaned his elbows on the table and shut and opened the flaps of his ears. Then
he heard the noise of the refectory every time he opened the flaps of his ears.
It made a roar like a train at night. And when he closed the flaps the roar was
shut off like a train going into a tunnel. That night at Dalkey the train had
roared like that and then, when it went into the tunnel, the roar stopped. He
closed his eyes and the train went on, roaring and then stopping; roaring again,
stopping.   (*P* 13)

This passage once again feeds speculation about Stephen's first train
journey, the source of the 'childish wonder' he will eventually recall.
Later that evening he imagines going home for the holidays in a 'long
long chocolate train with cream facings' (*P* 20) — an amusing phrase
in its own right, but also one which supports the conclusion that he went
to Clongowes by train. Here, however, we have an evening journey
passing through Dalkey on the line from Bray (where the Dedalus
family lives) to Dublin. A few pages later we see Stephen again
remembering the tunnel, and at the same time learning to manipulate
metaphor:

First came the vacation and then the next term and then vacation again and then
again another term and then again the vacation. It was like a train going in and
out of tunnels and that was like the noise of the boys eating in the refectory when
you opened and closed the flaps of the ears. Term, vacation; tunnel, out; noise,
stop.   (*P* 17)

This charming passage shows Stephen learning to understand his
experience, by reducing it to a kind of imaginative order. The in and
out of the tunnel, however, may serve as a metaphor for further
alternations in the opening chapter, which Stephen cannot perceive;

these are the alternations of narrative genre and of narrative units. The first two pages of infantile consciousness have a poetic, not a chronological form. (Chronologically they have no beginning or end, though there could be no stronger poetic beginning than 'Once upon a time'.) They give the effect of memories reassembled at a later date. The first Clongowes episode, however, shows Stephen actively using his imagination and memory, cut off as he is by fever from unreflecting participation in the life around him. This abruptly gives way to the Christmas dinner scene, a dramatized episode in which Stephen's time for reflection is reduced to a minimum. The second Clongowes episode is balanced between external event and inner reflection. Stephen, having broken his glasses, is set somewhat apart, though not as severely as when he was ill. His sensations of pain and fear as the pandybat hits him are described with extraordinary vividness. His inner consciousness remains paramount as he nerves himself up to complain to the rector, and walks alone through the 'low dark narrow corridor' not unlike a tunnel. Strengthened by the legend of the Irish patriot Hamilton Rowan (who outwitted his pursuers in the same place), Stephen emerges from this narrative tunnel into the lucidity of his interview with the rector. These four discontinuous episodes make up Chapter 1 of the *Portrait*. Joyce's suppression of linking passages in the narrative has become commonplace in twentieth-century fictional technique, though it was not so when he was writing. The result is a compromise between the linked collection of impressionistic stories or sketches (such as the first three stories in *Dubliners*) and the discursive continuity of the nineteenth-century novel.

As we read on in the *Portrait* there are further marked discontinuities. The sermons in the third chapter, the extended rhapsody on the beach in the fourth, and the aesthetic dialogues and journal entries of the fifth are all an affront to conventional narrative decorum. Thanks to Joyce's extensive use of free indirect style, the book's vocabulary, syntax and cadence tend to become more complex as Stephen grows older. The *Portrait* for this reason is not a 'well-made' novel in the nineteenth-century or the Jamesian sense, though it has often been acclaimed as an example, in Mark Schorer's phrase, of 'technique as discovery'.[14] The changes in technique reflect the stages in Stephen's mental evolution, the growth of his soul. Alternatively, we may wish to see the discontinuities of the *Portrait* as an index of the changing pattern of voices surrounding and defining Stephen.

Phases of an identity

Who is 'Stephen'? The earliest episodes of the *Portrait* show him learning the identity that is given him by family and school. In each case, there are indications of a primal unity which has already given place to division. Soon, with the repercussions of Parnell's fall, the larger divisions of church and state will forcibly enter his own history.

When in the fifth chapter Cranly tries to persuade Stephen to make his Easter duty, he tells him that 'Whatever else is unsure in this stinking dunghill of a world a mother's love is not' (*P* 241–2). Stephen first knows his mother as someone with a nice smell, who plays the piano so that he can dance. Yet even in the brief opening section she is present at a mysterious incident when he has done something wrong, and is required to apologize. Why did he hide under the table? Was it perhaps because he had expressed a wish to marry Eileen, the next-door girl whose family were Protestants? We do not know, but we do know that Stephen is conscious of estrangement from his mother very soon after this, as a result of being sent to boarding school. (Would Cranly have been so certain of a mother's love if *he* had been sent to boarding school?) The *Portrait* ends with Stephen saying goodbye to his mother and getting good advice from her; but the same thing also happens very close to the beginning. Even as a small child he has learnt the importance of a stiff upper lip on these occasions – 'he had pretended not to see that she was going to cry. She was a nice mother but she was not so nice when she cried' (*P* 9). That Stephen is adaptable enough to think of Clongowes as his home is emphasized by the deeply satisfying entry on the flyleaf of his geography book:

> *Stephen Dedalus*
> *Class of Elements*
> *Clongowes Wood College*
> *Sallins*
> *County Kildare*
> *Ireland*
> *Europe*
> *The World*
> *The Universe*   (*P* 15)

This is followed by a verse written by his schoolfellow Fleming 'for a cod':

> *Stephen Dedalus is my name,*
> *Ireland is my nation,*

> *Clongowes is my dwellingplace*
> *And heaven my expectation.* (*P* 16)

Clongowes, unfortunately, is not the cosy place in a unified world that
these inscriptions describe. Rody Kickham, the boy's-school-story
hero, ignores Stephen; Wells and Nasty Roche subject him to
unpleasant inquisitions; and Wells has impulsively shouldered him into
the ditch. Wells wants to know if he kisses his mother, while Roche tries
to convict him of social inferiority by asking who his father is. The
other boys' fathers, or some of them, are country gentry and
magistrates; Mr Dedalus's decision to send his son to Clongowes,
however, is an act of social pretension he will be unable to maintain for
long. When Stephen, in the sickbay, fantasizes about going home for
Christmas, one of his most telling pieces of wish-fulfilment is that 'His
father was a marshal now: higher than a magistrate' (*P* 20). Stephen
wants to go one better than the other boys, not merely to be like them.
The only 'marshal' he has encountered is a former inhabitant of the
house at Clongowes, whose ghost still haunts the stairs. Soon Stephen
is feeling sorry for his father, pitying him for not having reached the
magistracy. He remembers his father's reasons for sending him to
Clongowes – 'his father had told him that he would be no stranger
there because his grand-uncle had presented an address to the liberator
there fifty years before' (*P* 26) – and perhaps dimly recognizes his
family's doomed attempt to live up to past glories.

In dreaming that his father had become a marshal, Stephen is
beginning that quest for a new and better father that will culminate in
the *Portrait* in his idolization of the Greek hero Daedalus – though
Daedalus in turn will be discarded, and Stephen will continue his quest
for a spiritual father in *Ulysses*. Stephen's search originates as a psychic
manifestation of the kind which Freud termed a 'family romance'. In
a family romance, Freud wrote, 'the child's imagination becomes
engaged in the task of getting free from the parents, of whom he has
a low opinion, and of replacing them by others who, as a rule, are of
higher social standing'.[15] Stephen's family romance begins with the
fantasy that his father's social standing has miraculously risen. Later
he will come to the point of mentally disowning his family altogether:
'He felt that he was hardly of the one blood with them but stood to them
rather in the mystical kinship of fosterage, fosterchild and
fosterbrother' (*P* 98). In an extended sense, the family romance with
its burden of fantasy-compensation for the inadequacies of the actual
family is a pervading theme throughout Joyce's later work.

At home for Christmas, Stephen has been promoted from the nursery to the dignity of the family dining-table for the first time. The famous Christmas-dinner scene shows all pretence of family unity being shattered and, with it, Stephen's trust and confidence in his parents. The fall of Parnell, the Irish parliamentary leader, after the O'Shea divorce case in 1890 would have had legendary status in Irish history had Joyce never written; but the *Portrait* is a powerful addition to the legend. Stephen is 'for Ireland and Parnell and so was his father' (*P* 37). Parnell's fall coincides with a reversal in Simon Dedalus's fortunes, just as it did in the case of Joyce's own father. Simon invokes the authority of his ancestors, including a grandfather who was condemned to death as a 'whiteboy' or rural insurrectionary; all these men, he claims, would have supported Parnell against the treacherous priests. The Catholic priests have betrayed Ireland before, reneging on Irish independence soon after the British government had passed the Catholic Emancipation Act of 1829. Simon encourages the blasphemies of his friend Mr Casey and declares that 'We are an unfortunate priestridden race and always were and always will be till the end of the chapter' (*P* 37). His attitude scandalizes Dante Riordan and opens a bitter conflict between the 'patriarchy' and the 'matriarchy' in Stephen's family.

The Christmas dinner is a powerfully dramatized episode in which we only intermittently share Stephen's thoughts. It is a miniature tragedy, carefully orchestrated by Joyce to include echoes of both Ibsen and Aristotle. At the end Mrs Riordan sweeps out, slamming the door and leaving the menfolk prostrated behind her rather like Nora Helmer in *A Doll's House*. Then there is an Aristotelian catharsis of pity and fear as Stephen raises his 'terrorstricken face' and sees that 'his father's eyes were full of tears' (*P* 39). We must assume that the revolt of Dante, and his mother's ineffectual attempts as a peacemaker, leave Stephen's sympathies torn in two. He knows Mrs Riordan was a Parnellite until recently. Simon moreover, is clearly to blame for letting the quarrel get out of hand and spoil the Christmas dinner. Stephen is shocked by his father's coarse and self-indulgent anticlerical outburst – after all, it is his father who has sent him to Clongowes, to be taught by the priests. Though he recognizes that Parnell is the victim of injustice, Stephen cannot yet understand how injustice can be laid at the door of the Church. However, the next episode, in which he is brutally punished by Father Dolan for accidentally breaking his glasses, will speed up his education a little on this point.

The final Clongowes section replaces political and family tragedy with a tragicomic episode which might have been modelled on the plot of the conventional boarding-school story. The episode begins and ends with the 'pick, pack, pock, puck' (*P* 41, 59) of ball on cricket bat, and within it we hear another all-too-familiar sound, that of corporal punishment. It is a measure of the extent to which both his father and the priests have fallen in his eyes that, by the end of this section, Stephen has become his own romantic hero. He is egged on by the indignant and mutinous voices of his schoolmates, but, in deciding to complain to the rector about his unjust punishment, he is essentially on his own. His imagination calls up a whole series of mentors and father figures to sustain him in his resolve. Why did the prefect of studies have to ask twice what his name was? 'The great men in history had names like that and nobody made fun of them' (*P* 55). As he passes along the deserted corridor leading to the rector's room he is aware of the ghosts of the Jesuit saints, of the old marshal and of the patriot Hamilton Rowan (1751–1834), who escaped from the redcoats in this very house. Rowan and the marshal make an implicit link between the great men of history and the patriarchal tradition of the Dedalus family; we remember the grand-uncle who presented an address to the liberator (Daniel O'Connell, the hero of Catholic Emancipation) at Clongowes. History repeats itself, on a miniature scale. 'The senate and the Roman people declared that Dedalus had been wrongly punished' (*P* 53), as another boy puts it. As he comes back from the rector's office he is cheered by his schoolmates in triumph. His naive trust in family and school have been shaken, but he has learnt to believe in himself and has discovered, in the rector's magnanimity, a confirmation of the government of human life by an impartial court of appeal.

Stephen, however, is taken away from Clongowes, as his father cannot afford the fees. At the beginning of the second chapter he is back in the patriarchal world in which Uncle Charles and his father rehearse the family legends. Feminine influence on Stephen seems to have departed once Mrs Riordan abandoned the Christmas dinner-table and swept out of the door. His mother means little to Stephen and we see him as segregated from women, whether on his days with Uncle Charles, at his new school, Belvedere College (where boys take the female parts in the school play), or on his visit with his father to Cork. However, the male mentors who dominate this chapter come to seem both inadequate and fraudulent. Uncle Charles grows senile, Vincent Heron (Stephen's friend and rival at Belvedere) bullies him, and the rector of Clongowes comes down to earth so far as to share a joke with

Simon about his son's pandying. Stephen finds himself beset by the pious exhortations and badgerings of male voices:

While his mind had been pursuing its intangible phantoms and turning in irresolution from such pursuit he had heard about him the constant voices of his father and of his masters, urging him to be a gentleman above all things and urging him to be a good catholic above all things. These voices had now come to be hollowsounding in his ears. When the gymnasium had been opened he had heard another voice urging him to be strong and manly and healthy and when the movement towards national revival had begun to be felt in the college yet another voice had bidden him be true to his country and help to raise up her fallen language and tradition. In the profane world, as he foresaw, a worldly voice would bid him raise up his father's fallen state by his labours and, meanwhile, the voice of his school comrades urged him to be a decent fellow, to shield others from blame or to beg them off and to do his best to get free days for the school. And it was the din of all these hollowsounding voices that made him halt irresolutely in the pursuit of phantoms.   (*P* 83–4)

The 'phantoms' that beckon Stephen to turn aside from the male world are, increasingly, those of real and imaginary women. Throughout the chapter Stephen is beset by sex. 'He wanted to meet in the real world the unsubstantial image which his soul so constantly beheld' (*P* 65). The unsubstantial image is represented by Mercedes, the heroine of *The Count of Monte Cristo*, and Stephen's attempts to locate the image in the real world are seen in his two failed trysts with a girl of his own age called Emma, and later in his visit to a prostitute. The chapter balances the growth of imagination against the moral squalor Stephen detects in his family now that his father's fortunes are in decline. Simon's hypocrisy, which is extravagantly displayed on the visit to Cork to sell off his property there, destroys any remaining illusions Stephen has about his family and its traditions.

The property in Cork, which Simon has squandered in his attempts to keep up the family appearances, should have been Stephen's inheritance. Throughout the visit Simon superbly patronizes his son, as if he were indeed coming into an inheritance rather than being done out of one. Stephen needs all the detachment and bitter aloofness he can muster to cope with his father's incessant cock-and-bantam rivalry. A tongue-tied silence characterizes much of his behaviour on the visit to Cork – an episode of interminable paternal monologues to which he listens without sympathy. In what one critic has called an 'autobiography within an autobiography',[16] Simon is telling his son the story of his life and covering up present failure with nostalgia for his cavalier youth. But for Stephen his torrent of self-indulgence is overshadowed by a single word cut on a desk in Queen's College – the word '*Foetus*', which seems to express all the 'monstrous reveries' and 'monstrous images' of his awakening consciousness of the body. Masturbation guilt sweeps over him. Yet the shock of the word '*Foetus*', unloosing the 'infuriated cries within him' (*P* 92) and closing his ears to his father's wearisome voice, is a salutary one. The nameless and speechless foetus is a challenge to his own knowledge of origin and personal identity; and, in response to the challenge, Stephen speaks his name to himself:

– I am Stephen Dedalus. I am walking beside my father whose name is Simon Dedalus. We are in Cork, in Ireland. Cork is a city. Our room is in the Victoria Hotel. Victoria and Stephen and Simon. Simon and Stephen and Victoria. Names.   (*P* 92)

His memory of his childhood grows dim; all he can recall are the names. But then, cut off from the child that he once was, he begins to tell himself the story of that 'little boy in a grey belted suit'. For the space of a paragraph he becomes a deliberate autobiographer, recalling the geography lessons he had from Dante, his experiences at Clongowes and his impressions and sensations in the infirmary. Notably absent from this mini-autobiography is any mention of his immediate family. The omission makes his story that of one who, as Simon's friend Johnny Cashman hints, is 'not his father's son' (*P* 94) – a small ex-boarding school boy who was once a nameless foetus. In this mood he has, however, two new resources. One is a 'cold and cruel and loveless lust' (*P* 96). The other is literature. Stephen is able to salve his bitterness and despair by repeating some lines of Shelley. And so this disturbing episode ends by confirming his ability to oppose the written word (his own and others') to the hollowsounding voices around him.

Stephen, however, still has to cope with the explosion of consciousness represented by the word '*Foetus*'. In giving way to his sexual desires he is unloosing the 'cry that he had strangled for so long in his throat' (*P* 100). Degrading though it may be, his visit to the whore restores the human contact that he has missed ever since his knowledge of his father's failure began to impinge on his innocent days with Uncle Charles. Stephen is tongue-tied once again in the young woman's room, but it is her physical gestures more than her words – touching his arm, ruffling his hair, and undoing her gown – which bring him into a state of peace with his body. For the first time since childhood he becomes aware of speech, not as disembodied admonition but as a vehicle of empathy with another person. With her

kiss, he seems to pass beyond the world of 'hollowsounding voices' to
the root of speech:

> He closed his eyes, surrendering himself to her, body and mind, conscious of
> nothing in the world but the dark pressures of her softly parting lips. They
> pressed upon his brain as upon his lips as though they were the vehicle of a vague
> speech; and between them he felt an unknown and timid pressure, darker than
> the swoon of sin, softer than sound or odour.   (*P* 101)

Stephen has been segregated from female influence during his
adolescence; now the physical reality of the woman bursts on him like
a revelation. Such a blissful escape from the realms of socially
acceptable voice and speech cannot possibly be allowed to last.[17] He
feels he has transgressed the social order and that the 'squalor and
insincerity' (*P* 67) he had felt around him have taken possession of his
own mind. In a heightened version of the movement we have observed
in *Dubliners*, the rapture of the kiss is succeeded by the sense of sin and
the agonies of penitence. In the next chapter the whore's penetration
of Stephen's brain and soul is cauterized by Father Arnall's pungent
sermons. Father Arnall's is a paternal voice far more compelling in its
sway over the adolescent mind than that of Stephen's natural father.
Through his eloquence the text itself is pervaded by the crushing
authority of the Church.

Catholic and Protestant readers alike have responded to this chapter
in which Joyce – like such near-contemporaries as Dostoyevsky and
D. H. Lawrence – exposes traditional Christianity not as a religion of
love but one based on torture, fear and self-mortification. Stephen's
combination of imaginative power and newly-awakened sensuality
makes him an easy prey for the preacher's morbid evocation of physical
disgust. His early sexual experience was an attempt to appease a sort
of soul-hunger, a longing to escape from the banalities of existence
represented by his father and his schoolmates; but the Church is far
better qualified than the red-light district to offer a genuine 'other
world' beyond theirs. Stephen's first sexual rapture has long faded
when the retreat begins, and – echoing Shelley's fragment which he
voiced in the previous chapter – he is again subject to 'weariness' and
the solitude of an empty, chaotic universe. Catholicism repopulates the
universe with heaven and hell, reward and punishment, presided over
by the Virgin 'whose emblem is the morning star' (*P* 105). For Stephen,
this revelation of the imaginative depths of the religion he has been
brought up in since childhood is irresistible. There is nothing surprising
about his agonies of penitence.

Father Arnall's sermons are the product of the literary tradition of 'spiritual exercises' deriving from St Ignatius Loyola, the founder of the Jesuit order. Their authority over Stephen, however, owes everything to oral delivery and can best be described in the phrase Joyce used for the artist's endeavour in his essay 'A Portrait of the Artist': these are sermons which conclusively 'give the word'. Yet in writing them into his novel Joyce was embarking on a Swiftian or Voltairean philosophical exercise, designed to expose the contradictions and absurdity of the traditional view of the terrors of hell. In the measure that Stephen becomes enthralled by the voice of the priest, so should the reader become immune to it. Starting out from the commonplaces of Christian doctrine, the sermons tease out the implications of these doctrines with a literalness and realism which amount in the end to a grotesque perversion of reason. When Father Arnall discourses on eternity, for example, his purpose is to make the brain 'reel dizzily' (*P* 132), in fact to torture it. The more vivid the listener's imagination, the more he is likely to be stunned and – given the social authority vested in the Church – inoculated against any further questioning of the eternal verities. Would not such a questioner, a potential heretic, be like the little bird coming to the mountain, 'reaching from the earth to the farthest heavens' (*P* 132) for its grain of sand in the knowledge that the mountain will rise again and again even after his puny intellect has succeeded in demolishing it? Yet, from another point of view, the technique of the sermons is surprisingly crude and indiscriminate: for all their eloquence and ingenuity, in their resort to terrorizing the audience and in their deliberate confusion of literal and metaphorical statements they come close to absurdity. So far as terror and intimidation are concerned, they invite the response of the English master, in a brief respite between sermons:

 – I suppose he rubbed it into you well.
 – You bet he did. He put us all into a blue funk.
 – That's what you fellows want: and plenty of it to make you work. (*P* 125)

The master's healthy cynicism suggests that religion is no more than social cement, an 'opium of the people'. The priest's voice encourages the boys to get on with their work by discouraging idle speculation; it is an aversion therapy designed to make thinking for oneself seem painful and profitless. Stephen's reaction is an extreme example of such a conditioned reflex. Father Arnall says that, bad as are the physical punishments of the damned, their worst torments are mental and result from unappeasable remorse and from envy of the blessed from whose good fortune they are eternally excluded. Memory and imagination, the very faculties which distinguish Stephen from his fellows, thus become the most refined instruments of infernal torture.

Stephen confesses his sins, though not – significantly – to one of the priests at Belvedere College. Joyce uses the imagery of physical evacuation ('The last sins oozed forth, sluggish, filthy', *P* 144), but the sins sound paltry once they are put in words, and the 'old and weary voice' (*P* 145) of the Capuchin priest betrays that he is too worldly-wise to expect that the penitent will give up his sins – they will recur as inevitably as the body secretes fluids. This priest represents another face of the Church, not the inhuman rigour of 'spiritual exercises' but the promise of communion and spiritual peace in exchange for penitence and submission to authority.

As he went through the back streets of Dublin in search of the chapel where he could make his anonymous confession, Stephen felt a brief reverence for the poor people around him. His communion, however, is taken within the privileged circle of Belvedere College. He goes to Mass with the comfortable thought that a substantial breakfast awaits him at home. Earlier in the chapter this would have been a sign of gluttony, one of the deadly sins into which he has fallen; now it is taken as a sign of grace:

White pudding and eggs and sausages and cups of tea. How simple and beautiful was life after all!   (*P* 146)

So Joyce's irony undercuts Stephen's penitence. Purged of the cries of self-assertion that arose within him, he has rejoined the Church, and at the same time reestablished his right to enjoy his bourgeois comforts. He says Amen to the words of the service and – in an ending which parallels the kiss of the previous chapter – raises the host to his lips.

The fourth chapter begins with Stephen's display of religious piety which, far from appeasing his soul-hunger, leads to a 'sensation of spiritual dryness' (*P* 151). Since Joyce will end this chapter with an epiphany on Dollymount Beach, it is notable that he begins by showing Stephen metaphorically stranded and beached. The 'flood of temptation' (*P* 152) remains well away from his dry shore; but at the end of the chapter he will master his aquaphobia and walk out towards the passionate tides across the sands of Dublin Bay. He does so in obedience to a voice which is neither that of his father nor the Church – a voice which we do not, perhaps, need the authority of a quotation from Newman to identify as the '*voice of Nature*' (*P* 164).

Nature, his sense of what is innate to him, is Stephen's chief reason for refusing to train for the priesthood. The words of the subtle and urbane director of Belvedere are unable to inspire him with a sense of vocation, a sense that he has been 'called'. We see both the inevitability of Stephen's refusal and his own limited understanding of the step he has taken. His decision to try for university pleases his father but confirms an unspoken breach with his mother. What he does not know is that he is about to receive another 'call', and that his path will be determined by a spiritual experience as overwhelming as any call to the priesthood. The final section of the chapter is a sustained poetic rhapsody in which every prompting of the external world and of his own nature points towards his becoming an artist.

It is on Dollymount Beach that, as he would later put it, Stephen's 'soul is born' (*P* 203). Whatever its earlier stirrings, only now can he say that 'His soul had arisen from the grave of boyhood, spurning her graveclothes' (*P* 170). (The image is again reminiscent of Ibsen's *When We Dead Awaken*.) Joyce affirms the birth of the soul in a rich, vibrant and sonorous prose which marks the culmination of the romantic vision of artisthood expressed in the *Portrait*. The section contains many mingled strains of poetic imagery: evocations of the sands and the sea, of clouds and flight, and of noises and names are interwoven to create a rapturous and spellbinding symphony in words. The verbal symphony attempts to give sound and substance to the single inarticulate 'cry' which Stephen himself experiences – a cry which comes forth both from deep within himself and from the natural world around him:

His throat ached with a desire to cry aloud, the cry of a hawk or eagle on high, to cry piercingly of his deliverance to the winds. This was the call of life to his soul not the dull gross voice of the world of duties and despair, not the inhuman voice that had called him to the pale service of the altar. An instant of wild flight had delivered him and the cry of triumph which his lips withheld cleft his brain.
(*P* 169)

The references to voices in this extract are developed throughout the beach episode. The voice of the world of duties is represented by his father's 'shrill whistle' which he expects to call him back (*P* 164), by the tramping of the squad of Christian Brothers whose names Stephen hears (or imagines hearing) on the bridge, and by the banter of his bathing schoolfellows. Set against these outer voices is the inner music which resounds in Stephen himself: an 'elfin prelude' (*P* 165), a 'chord' (*P* 166), 'a confused music within him as of memories and names which

he was almost conscious of but could not capture even for an instant'
(*P* 167). The music, however, issues in words: 'He felt his cheeks aflame
and his throat throbbing with song' (*P* 170). Two symbols, the birdlike
girl and the hawklike man, express the communion between Stephen's
own nature and the wild nature around him. He is 'crying to greet the
advent of the life that had cried to him' (*P* 172), and his cry is summed
up in words which suggest a transferred religious ecstasy, a 'nature-
worship' such as is found in the novels of Meredith and D. H.
Lawrence:

> – Heavenly God! cried Stephen's soul, in an outburst of profane joy. (*P* 171)

Stephen has rejected the priesthood but has by no means dispensed with
broadly religious categories of experience.

The beach episode illustrates Matthew Arnold's influential contrast
of Hebraism and Hellenism – of Christian revelation and artistic
'sweetness and light' – and it is no accident that the voice of nature
speaks partly through Greek symbols and emblems. Stephen's fellow-
students unwittingly introduce the Hellenistic motif when they offer
back his name in a Greek form: ' – Stephanos Dedalos! Bous
Stephanoumenos! Bous Stephaneforos!' (*P* 168). Daedalus, the
inventor of flight, manifests the artist's ability to create 'a new soaring
impalpable imperishable being' (*P* 169), akin to the 'dappled seaborne
clouds' (*P* 166) which can travel in reality where Stephen can only go
in his imagination. The girl in midstream, who seems 'like one whom
magic had changed into the likeness of a strange and beautiful seabird'
(*P* 171), is both a secular angel and a manifestation of the Muse as she
would appear to the Daedalian or wingéd artist. The chastity of
Stephen's vision as he contemplates the girl in this annunciation-scene
is both wholly convincing and in sharp contrast to other visions of
beach-girls and girls with their skirts pinned up in Joyce: not only Gerty
MacDowell, the modern Nausicaa whose self-display is watched by the
tired businessman Leopold Bloom in *Ulysses*, but also the women
conjured up earlier in this chapter by the rector's joke about bicycling
priests (*P* 155).

Stephen at the end of the fourth chapter has, as it were, taken his
vows and become an artist. Artisthood for him appears as a vocation
or state, not as a process of achievement, so that he can glory in
possessing it long before he has produced any artistic works. To
artisthood as a vocation he transfers the dedication and religious
ardour that conventionally pertain to the priesthood. He has exchanged

the spiritual dryness of his days as a neophyte Christian for the spiritual (and possibly physical) state of 'dewy wetness' (*P* 217) in which he later prepares to compose his villanelle.

Stephen now tends to cast the Church as his enemy and rival. Particularly telling is his jealousy of Father Moran, the priest with whom he suspects his 'beloved' of flirting in the Irish language class in the fifth chapter. The priest, Stephen contemptuously tells himself, is 'but schooled in the discharging of a formal rite', whereas he, the artist, is a 'priest of eternal imagination, transmuting the daily bread of experience into the radiant body of everliving life' (*P* 221). This is a very transparent conception, which reveals a veneration of eternity reminiscent of Father Arnall and his sermon. The stage of self-liberation that Stephen has reached at the end of the *Portrait* (and the same may be said of Joyce at the age when he began to write) is that of staking everything on his sense of belonging to a heretical priesthood, the custodians of the 'religion of art'. At the same time he has begun the process of intellectual and emotional hardening destined to make him very different from the languorous *fin-de-siècle* poets who were his predecessors in turning art into an object of worship. The 'Villanelle of the Temptress' that is Stephen's principal literary composition in the fifth chapter marks his homage to the Decadent school. Many of the Decadent poets, as is well known, recanted their aesthetic heresies and ended their days back in the bosom of the Church. By the end of the *Portrait* we are beginning – but no more than beginning – to perceive that Stephen may be made of sterner stuff.

The third and fourth chapters have taken place largely in the theatre of Stephen's consciousness – a theatre, however, which echoes with a few commanding voices from outside, and notably the voice of Father Arnall. The presentation of Stephen's university life restores the sense of human variety and the breadth of social perspective which were absent from these chapters. For a time, Stephen listens acutely to the voices around him, though by the end he has withdrawn into diary-keeping, and listening has given place to writing. It is hard to do justice to the variety and rich modulations of this chapter, which introduces a number of characters with the greatest economy of gesture and contains some of Joyce's liveliest and most memorable dialogues. Much as he may despise his fellow-students Stephen tends to make them into larger-than-life figures, representatives of the major attitudes at work in the society around him. Of Davin, for example, Stephen reflects that 'The gossip of his fellowstudents which strove to render the flat life of the college significant at any cost loved to think of him as a young fenian' (*P* 181). Stephen is as adept as any of his fellows at giving a legendary quality to the flat life of the college, at least to the extent that it impinges on him. It is true that this portrait is an unflattering one, which did not please everybody. Maud Gonne, the Irish revolutionary, wrote in 1917 that 'Those who know the young students in Dublin, the intensity and vividness of their lives . . . would find it hard to recognise the uncouth nonentities presented by Joyce'.[18] Posterity, it must be confessed, tends to prefer Joyce's 'uncouth nonentities' to Maud Gonne's brand of high-minded zealots.

Stephen begins the chapter by driving the voices of his father, his mother, and the mad nun out of his heart with an execration. For the time being these are supplanted by a new set of voices: those of his friends, and also the silent voices ('silence' is a keyword in this chapter) of the literary tradition. Walking to college, he thinks in turn of the words of Gerhart Hauptmann, Newman, Cavalcanti, Ibsen and one of Ben Jonson's songs − in itself a remarkable display of intellectual precocity on Stephen's part. Beyond this there is the philosophical task he has given himself, that of deriving a theory of beauty from some sentences of Aristotle and Aquinas, even though their learning is 'held no higher by the age he lived in than the subtle and curious jargons of heraldry and falconry' (*P* 180).

If literature and philosophy are portals of discovery they can also serve as defence mechanisms, helping to shut out the noise of his environment. The same is true of his conspicuous adoption of the role of the poet: it forces him to justify himself, and at the same time protects him against the claims of the more assertive of his fellow-students. It is both amusing and, in the light of Ireland's subsequent history, deeply instructive to see how Stephen evades the challenges represented by three of these, MacCann, Davin and MacAlister, by playing off each against the others. MacCann is collecting signatures for a universal disarmament petition, '*Pax super totum sanguinarium globum*' (*P* 198) as Cranly mockingly puts it. Stephen's refusal to sign is characteristic and yet not easy to justify (Joyce, after all, never wavered in his detestation of militarism and violence). He discredits the petition by remarking that Davin, the 'fenian', has signed; Davin in his simplicity can find no contradiction between universal peace and armed rebellion in the cause of Ireland. Davin is the most likeable of the student ideologists, but Stephen exposes him (and with him a whole strain of Irish nationalism) as incorrigibly sentimental and given to self-deception. Davin's well-meant confusion reflects ironically on the idealism of MacCann, who believes that the petition is a step on the road to a new millennium of universal altruism. MacAlister, the Ulster Catholic, is the least sympathetic of the three characters under consideration. His attitude to knowledge is crassly utilitarian, he accuses Stephen of intellectual crankery, and (worst of all) he has a grating Belfast accent. Stephen is irritated by him to the point of 'bidding his mind think that the student's father would have done better had he sent his son to Belfast to study and have saved something on the train fare by so doing' (*P* 193). Another student, Moynihan, calls MacAlister 'a devil for his pound of flesh' (*P* 193); and it is perhaps the self-righteousness implicit in this remark which persuades Stephen to swallow his own irritation: 'Can you say with certitude by whom the soul of your race was bartered and its elect betrayed – by the questioner or by the mocker?' (*P* 193–4), he reflects.

Treachery, in Stephen's view, is an inescapable part of Ireland's heritage. The belief that the Irish invariably betray one another is one of his justifications for washing his hands of his native country. Later, the same belief sustained Joyce's own habitual cynicism about Irish politics. Parnell's fate, on this view, was both predictable in itself and a warning to all his potential successors. Moreover, the betrayers are not necessarily the utilitarian northerners, the West Britons or those most infected by English values. Sentimental, self-righteous southern Republicans also have a history of treachery. Whatever we think of Stephen's (and Joyce's) political disenchantment, he cannot be accused of being pro-English. H. G. Wells, reading the *Portrait* at much the same time as Maud Gonne (that is, within a year of the 1916 Easter Rising) noted that 'everyone in this story, every human being, accepts as a matter of course, as a thing in nature like the sky and the sea, that the English are to be hated'.[19] But Stephen's attitudes grow out of his experiences in childhood and youth which have taught him that the ideological voices of his fellow-students, like the earlier voices of duty and moral exhortation, are so many snares and nets. He says to Davin, 'You talk to me of nationality, language, religion. I shall try to fly by those nets' (*P* 203).

Stephen's search for spiritual freedom coexists with an extreme defensive anxiety to secure himself against the possibility of betrayal. This is the rationale behind his watchwords 'silence exile and cunning' and also, I suspect, behind his theory of aesthetic 'stasis' in which the mind is 'arrested and raised above desire and loathing' (*P* 205). The static work of art is by definition silent – eloquently silent, no doubt, like Keats's Grecian Urn – but still the opposite of a voice exhorting its hearer to take some action. Stephen's dedication to silence is not yet complete, since he still feels able to confess his feelings to friends such as Davin and Cranly. It is Cranly who first hears of his refusal to make his Easter duty, which opens a breach between him and his mother and is his first unequivocal act of rebellion. Cranly is a shrewd listener, telling Stephen how curiously his mind is 'supersaturated with the religion in which you say you disbelieve' (*P* 240). Beneath his hardboiled exterior he shows considerable affection for Stephen, and is vividly aware of the loneliness to which his rebellion will bring him. Yet Stephen also constructs an imaginary romance beween Cranly and Emma, the shadowy girl from his adolescence to whom he still feels emotionally drawn. It is as if he has singled out Cranly from the other students only to force him into the mould of the betrayer.

Is he, then, perfecting himself as an artist at the (necessary) expense of the human relationships Dublin could offer? If so, the exhilarating cry of 'Welcome, O life!' with which the *Portrait* ends must be read as a triumphant announcement that Stephen has fulfilled his artistic novitiate. This would imply that artisthood is indeed the noblest of vocations and that – as with the priesthood – the world is well lost for it. There is, however, another less exalted and religiose view of the artist which serves as an implicit corrective to Stephen's effusions, and as a source of irony. (The irony, of course, is very much more patent when we think of Stephen as he appears in *Ulysses*.) A priest is judged by what he is – by the state of his soul – but an artist must earn his title by what he creates or produces. Stephen takes it for granted that he commands the privileges of the artist, though his title to them rests on a distinctly meagre performance in the present, and an unknown promise for the future.

In accordance with this ironic perspective, Stephen's actual development as a writer in the *Portrait* is a mixture of real discoveries and false starts. In part we see him as an *epiphanist*, recording the manifestations of beauty he encounters. He collects a 'garner of slender sentences' (*P* 176) from Aristotle and Aquinas and some less exalted phrases from the Elizabethan lutanists. Instructed by his dabblings in theosophy he looks out for natural symbols, such as the returning swallows he sees and hears outside the National Library – creatures which are 'in the order of their life and have not perverted that order by reason' (*P* 225). These are Yeatsian sentiments, and in turn they evoke the death-speech from Yeats's play *The Countess Cathleen*, which Stephen has witnessed at the disastrous opening of the national theatre:

> *Bend down your faces, Oona and Aleel,*
> *I gaze upon them as the swallow gazes*
> *Upon the nest under the eave before*
> *He wander the loud waters.*

A soft liquid joy like the noise of many waters flowed over his memory and he felt in his heart the soft peace of silent spaces of fading tenuous sky above the waters, of oceanic silence, of swallows flying through the seadusk over the flowing waters. (*P* 225–6)

Like several other passages towards the end of the *Portrait*, this has the deliberate air of an epiphany. The 'soft liquid joy' – wetness – is reminiscent of the much more extended sequence in which he is inspired to compose the villanelle. At the same time the imagery is almost identical with that of Poem XXXV of *Chamber Music*:

> All day I hear the noise of waters
>   Making moan
> Sad as the seabird is when going
>   Forth alone
> He hears the winds cry to the waters'
>   Monotone.
>
> The grey winds, the cold winds are blowing
>   Where I go.
> I hear the noise of many waters
>   Far below.
> All day, all night, I hear them flowing
>   To and fro.

This fine lyric, severely modelled on a verse-form of Verlaine's, is a much more genuine achievement than the self-conscious 'symbol of departure or of loneliness' (*P* 226) in the *Portrait*. In it the poet *is* the seabird. In the prose passage, however, the lush word-painting comes close to absurdity. 'Oceanic silence' is an oxymoron, and the 'soft liquid joy' seems to be produced, in the end, by no more than Stephen's intoxicated contemplation of his own words: 'A soft liquid joy flowed through the words where the soft long vowels hurtled noiselessly and fell away, lapping and flowing back and ever shaking the white bells of their waves in mute chime and mute peal and soft low swooning cry' (*P* 226). But this is only one of the directions in which Stephen's precocious intelligence is turning.

Stephen's aesthetic theory both extends and distorts what has earlier been put forward in *Stephen Hero*. Once again Joyce sets it out with a curious blend of autobiography and fictional artifice. Speaking to Lynch, Stephen claims to be quoting from a 'book at home' in which he has written down a series of questions (*P* 214). These questions may be found in the 'Paris notebook' in which Joyce made signed and dated entries in 1903 – a year *after* his graduation from University College. In the *Portrait*, Stephen opposes 'kinetic' to 'static' art, redefines *integritas*, *consonantia* and *claritas*, and then distinguishes between the lyrical, epical and dramatic forms of art. Stephen's definition of *claritas* or radiance – the key to his theory of beauty – has a quite different emphasis to the one he offered in *Stephen Hero*. He starts by disavowing symbolism or idealism, in the ninetyish or Yeatsian sense of 'the supreme quality of beauty being a light from some other world'. That would, perhaps, be a too obviously mystical or religious view of art for Stephen to espouse. In its place, he offers a lyrical account of the experience of artistic inspiration. The supreme quality of beauty 'is felt by the artist when the esthetic image is first conceived in his imagination' (*P* 213). Shelley's comparison of the mind in creation to a fading coal, and the physiologist Galvani's description of a cardiac condition 'called the enchantment of the heart', are thrown in by way of elaboration. All this is profoundly evasive, a mystification of the artistic process which gives no indication of the sources of the all-important 'esthetic image'. Shelley, as a neoplatonist, *would* have believed that the image is a light from some other world. Aquinas likewise would argue that our ability to respond to earthly beauty is divinely inspired. Stephen can merely speak of an 'enchantment of the heart' without saying by whom or what the poet is made open to enchantment. The answer is implicit in the following episode – in which he composes the 'Villanelle of the Temptress' – but Stephen does not manage to formulate it theoretically. In the villanelle episode the poet is enchanted by the 'Temptress' or muse, and she in turn is a figment of his own brain. Because his brain is still supersaturated with the Catholic religion, the 'Temptress' is also the Virgin Mary.[20] For the same reason, Stephen in the *Portrait* is unable to evolve a satisfactory theory of artistic creation. One indication of its unsatisfactoriness is that he unceremoniously abandons it, in favour of a wholly different and much more materialistic approach, which he expounds (using Shakespeare as his text) in the Library chapter of *Ulysses*.

Stephen has more success in the *Portrait* as a theorist o
genres. Indeed, his distinction between the lyrical, epical, and
forms has possibly attracted as much comment as the rest of
put together. My interest at present is simply to read it as a commentary
on Stephen's (and Joyce's) artistic development, which is clearly a
progression from the lyrical to the dramatic. The lyrical form is 'the
simplest verbal vesture of an instant of emotion, a rhythmical cry such
as ages ago cheered on the man who pulled at the oar or dragged stones
up a slope. He who utters it is more conscious of the instant of emotion
than of himself as feeling emotion' (*P* 214). Stephen has uttered many
such cries in the course of his childhood and adolescence, and with the
composition of the villanelle he shows himself capable of a highly
sophisticated, verbally elaborate rhythmical cry. But also, 'the simplest
epical form is seen emerging out of lyrical literature when the artist
prolongs and broods upon himself as the centre of an epical event and
this form progresses till the centre of gravity is equidistant from the
artist himself and from others' (*P* 214–15). Stephen from childhood has
been shown constituting himself as an autobiographer, brooding upon
his own development as the centre of an epical event. The process
involves detachment of the 'personality of the artist', which 'passes into
the narration itself' and thus becomes separable from the character of
the hero, though not always unambiguously so. Stephen's emergence
as an autobiographical artist remains quite incomplete, since it can only
be fulfilled by the writing of the *Portrait* itself. The third stage – the
dramatic form which is realized when 'the vitality which has flowed and
eddied round each person fills every person with such vital force that
he or she assumes a proper and intangible esthetic life' (*P* 215) – is still
more a prophecy for the future.

Read in this way, Stephen's theory of literary genres serves to
rationalize Joyce's development, rendering a unique and perhaps
fortuitous process as classical and inevitable. The symbols and
prophecies which herald Stephen's emergence as an artist have the same
effect. The *Portrait* as a whole is the outcome of a long romantic
tradition of special pleading on behalf of the artist. Joyce's absorbing
and utterly convincing picture of Stephen's childhood and youth
persuades us of the inevitability and poetic justice of his later
specialization. At the same time, the *Portrait* cuts itself off from the
ideal of the fully rounded human personality. Karl Marx imagined a
non-alienated society in which the fulfilled man would be able to hunt
in the morning, fish in the afternoon, rear cattle in the evening and be

a critical critic after dinner. Such a life would be meaningless to Stephen, whose whole identity is founded on the idea of a predestined, priestlike vocation. It would, however, suit Leopold Bloom who already lives a bourgeois version of the all-round life. The *Portrait*, though one of the most brilliant of early twentieth-century novels, would seem distinctly one-sided did it not also serve as a prologue to *Ulysses*.

In the *Portrait* two views of the artist − the Dedalian view that he is born and the more conventional view that he must prove himself by what he makes − are held in a subtle dialectic. The latter view, though unstated, is the basis of the narrator's ironic detachment. There is, however, an implied resolution of the dialectic in the notion that Stephen is the future author of an achieved work of art, the *Portrait of the Artist*, which largely vindicates the high claims he has made. Or can it be that the formative experiences that would show him how to *write about* his childhood belong in the future, and are as yet unforeseen? The ending of the *Portrait* is delicately balanced between these two interpretations. The final pages are in the form of a writer's notebook. The first entry is dated March 20 and is a memorandum of a talk with Cranly, the dramatized version of which we have already read. Here the bridge between Stephen as protagonist and Stephen as autobiographer is deliberately crossed. The three concluding notebook entries form a coda terminating the novel in exquisitely musical fashion, in which the dialectic of 'voices' and 'cries' is brought to a triumphant resolution. The restraining voice of his mother, reminding him 'what the heart is and what it feels', is set against the 'spell of arms and voices' − those of imaginary kinsmen, like the temptress he has conjured up in his villanelle; siren voices beckoning him away from home with their 'tale of distant nations'. Stephen resolves the conflict with a final invocation of his 'Old father, old artificer' − primarily his adopted mentor Daedalus, but carrying an inevitable implied salute to the real father, whose stature has fallen steadily during the course of the narrative only to rise again, as the storyteller with whose voice it all began. 'In my end is my beginning' − for, to begin his task as autobiographer, Stephen will have to write an opening paragraph in which he adopts his father's voice.

Such an interpretation is momentarily satisfying, presenting the *Portrait* as a closed and circular narrative in the manner of *Finnegans Wake*. But it overlooks both the imminence of *Ulysses*, which in some respects is a genuine sequel to the *Portrait*, and also the actual texture of the last few pages of notebook entries. Most of these are disparate, inconsequential, and inharmonious. Stephen's tone is frequently brittle, posturing, and unstable. Far from knowing what he is looking for, he is setting down 'epiphanies' of a very varied kind which just might be worked up into something substantial. Is this the artist who is ready to 'forge in the smithy of my soul the uncreated conscience of my race'? The answer must be that he is still at the stage of life when his ambition outruns his capabilities. With Emma, for example, he makes 'a sudden gesture of a revolutionary nature. I must have looked like a fellow throwing a handful of peas into the air' (*P* 252). The gesture is premature and out of place – but at least Stephen himself can see the irony of it. Emma, it is clear, regards him as something of an exhibitionist rather than revering him as an artist. His chapter-ending cry of 'Welcome, O life!' – repeated, as we have seen, for the fifth time – does not of itself guarantee that Stephen will achieve the deliverance he seeks. In this sense the *Portrait* is open-ended. The young artist's rejection of family and friends will lead him not to assured international fame but to the Martello Tower and the voices he will hear in *Ulysses*.

Giacomo Joyce and *Exiles*

Two further autobiographical works came between the *Portrait* and *Ulysses*. *Giacomo Joyce* is an undated manuscript, posthumously edited by Richard Ellmann and composed in or before 1914. It consists of a series of brief prose epiphanies recording Joyce's infatuation with one of his Triestine students, set down with arch and mawkish literary self-consciousness. It is a much more refined and studied example of the sort of notebook sequence Stephen gives us at the end of the *Portrait*. The choice of the name 'Giacomo' for the protagonist – who is transparently James Joyce, or, as he is named in the text, Jamesy or Jim – conveys something of the text's affectation. Biographically, *Giacomo Joyce* is a nakedly confessional piece, and to the student of style it marks the transition between the interior descriptions and free indirect style of the *Portrait* and the soliloquies of *Ulysses*. At times the result is simply a record of imaginary conversations and things Joyce said to himself:

She says that, had *The Portrait of the Artist* been frank only for frankness' sake, she would have asked why I had given it to her to read. O you would, would you? A lady of letters.   (*GJ* 12)

A gentle creature. At midnight, after music, all the way up the via San Michele, these words were spoken softly. Easy now, Jamesy! Did you never walk the streets of Dublin at night sobbing another name?   (*GJ* 6)

The openly ironic, even sarcastic tone of these extracts is different from the *Portrait* where the irony so often consists in things left unsaid. *Giacomo Joyce* shows its author trying to strike a new, though no less precarious, sort of balance between sardonic detachment and passionate involvement. Quirks and spurts of grotesque humour puncture the poetic and emotional intensity of the piece. On a country outing with his beloved he notes her 'falsely smiling face' with 'streaks of eggyolk yellow on the moistened brow, rancid yellow humour lurking within the softened pulp of her eyes' (*GJ* 2). The sequence ends with an arch dismissal of the courtly ideal it has earlier struggled to sustain. 'Love me, love my umbrella' (*GJ* 16) is Joyce's parting shot.

Many of the carefully worked phrases and cadences of *Giacomo Joyce* ended up in *Ulysses* and in the fifth chapter of the *Portrait*, which Joyce revised in 1914. *Exiles*, a naturalistic stage play published in 1918, is a far more self-contained work, which stands alone in Joyce's oeuvre. Formally it is his most conventional text, an act of homage to Ibsen which lacks both the Norwegian's poetic texture and his vividness of social observation. The author's notes included in modern editions are overburdened with ideas which Joyce has not managed to embody in the dialogue, although the play consists entirely of analytical dialogue rather than action. An unsympathetic reader might conclude that even Joyce was human enough to take time off from writing *Ulysses* to compose a second-rate play. Yet *Exiles* is a notable contribution to Joyce's autobiographical process. Its exploration of marriage and adultery clearly indicates the sort of experience he was to draw on in *Ulysses*.

'Why the title *Exiles*?' Joyce wrote. 'A nation exacts a penance from those who dared to leave payable on their return' (*E* 164). The play is the portrait of a returning artist, Richard Rowan, who is accompanied by Bertha, the simple woman who has shared his exile, and their child. The protagonist's name alludes to Hamilton Rowan, the eighteenth-century Irish patriot whose exploits inspired the young Stephen Dedalus at Clongowes — although Richard (no doubt prudently if

Joyce ever had an Irish theatre audience in mind) claims not to be descended from his famous namesake. In what Joyce termed 'three cat and mouse acts' (*E* 172) the play explores Richard's relationships with Bertha and with the two old friends who greet his return to Ireland, Beatrice Justice and her cousin Robert Hand. Beatrice is in love with Richard; Robert would seduce Bertha if he could; Bertha reports all Robert's moves to Richard, who has a deep need to experience remorse and betrayal; and confessional têtes-à-tête between the characters abound.

Although some have argued otherwise,[21] it seems inescapable that Richard is the central figure of *Exiles*. Unfortunately, Joyce was unable to create a stage role commensurate with the intensity of suffering imputed to his protagonist. When at the end he confesses to Bertha that 'I have a deep, deep wound of doubt in my soul' (*E* 162) the reader is not moved to pity, as he should be. Richard is besieged both by the actual voices of his friends heard on stage and by the silent voices that inspire his writing. The play, however, can do little more than gesture towards these inner voices. Though Richard struggles each night in his study to give literary expression to the material of his own life, the play gives us no access to these struggles; it is set in a naturalistic drawing-room, not in the study or in the theatre of Richard's imagination. We see the fact of the artist's loneliness and yet barely glimpse the forces which impel that loneliness. Naturalistic drama, as it turns out, is a highly intractable form for Joyce's autobiographical obsessions.

Richard and Robert were once two gallants who spent 'wild nights' (*E* 53) of revelry in a cottage to which they brought wine, blasphemy and women. Since then Richard has gone away with Bertha, as well as becoming emotionally involved with Beatrice, a Protestant whom Robert associated with 'gloom, seriousness, righteousness' (*E* 37). Though not a conventional penitent, Richard lacks the defiant amorality of Robert and, in a different way, of Bertha, whose whole moral being lies in her dedication to the 'strange wild lover' (*E* 162) for whom she will go anywhere and submit to any indignity. Robert is one of the few people who understands how much she has willingly sacrificed to Richard's egotism. Robert is an attractive figure, possibly based on the more courtly, worldly (and dissolute) side of Joyce himself. He is also a writer, though the fruits of his late-night sittings are clever and cynically crafted newspaper articles. Still very much a gallant, he is hopelessly torn between idealized and debunking attitudes to women. The view of female beauty that he confides to Richard embodies a ruthless displacement of the classical by the grotesque:

Not those qualities which she has and other women have not but the qualities which she has in common with them. I mean . . . the commonest. [*Turning over the stone, he presses the other side to his forehead.*] I mean how her body develops heat when it is pressed, the movement of her blood, how quickly she changes by digestion what she eats into – what shall be nameless. [*Laughing.*] I am very common today.   (*E* 55)

Like Lynch in the *Portrait*, who wrote his name in pencil on the backside of the Venus of Praxiteles, Robert is cynically dismissive of the aesthetics of classical sculpture:

Once I made a little epigram about statues. All statues are of two kinds. [*He folds his arms across his chest.*] The statue which says: *How shall I get down?* and the other kind [*he unfolds his arms and extends his right arm, averting his head*] the statue which says: *In my time the dunghill was so high.* (*E* 56)

Robert's worldly cynicism – which owes something to Swift and something to Wilde – is the mark of an unstable and unbalanced character. The rivalry he feels with Richard over Bertha makes for the sort of triangular friendship that Ibsen had portrayed in *Hedda Gabler*. But where *Hedda Gabler* ends with an accidental shooting and a suicide, *Exiles* deliberately avoids any sort of melodramatic denouement. At most, Joyce uses the possibility of melodrama to create theatrical suspense. Robert pays court to Bertha in a Wagnerian, romantic vein, full of overblown roses and narcissistic fantasies of plunging to death 'listening to music and in the arms of the woman I love' (*E* 46). If we feel some pity for him it is because (as the play implies at two points) his talk of suicide may be genuine. Cut adrift from approved social and religious values, he is a dilettante who believes in nothing except (possibly) keeping up appearances.

   That Robert, a mere journalist, is the suicidal character – whilst Richard is a successful lover and family man who exerts a continuing fascination over both Robert and Beatrice – is indicative of Joyce's view of the mature artist. In stark contrast to many other leading twentieth-century writers, there is no evidence that Joyce's own thoughts ever turned towards suicide. However tortured and self-centred the artist may be (and *Exiles* is very revealing in this respect), he has a strength of inner vision and purpose that protects him from the self-destruction to which some of those around him are subject. Suicide or self-destruction in Joyce is the fate of Mrs Sinico not Mr Duffy, and of Rudolph Virag not Leopold Bloom; even protagonists with whom he sympathizes only partially seem to share the artist's own immunity. Richard has had a mother who disowned him because of his illicit union with Bertha, and a cavalier father, a 'smiling handsome' man who on his deathbed sent the fourteen-year-old boy off to hear *Carmen* with his blessing. Like Stephen in the *Portrait*, Richard has done his best to throw off these voices from the past; the result is a certain cold vanity and detachment which makes Bertha, who has suffered amply from it, accuse him of never even having loved his mother (*E* 72). Now the flattering offer of a professorship at the university tempts him to stay in Dublin permanently. But what Richard discovers – and what Stephen Dedalus did not know – is that the deliberate exile can never escape from the voices of his upbringing. Richard has thrown off moral restraints and got away with it; but deep down he cannot believe that Bertha's love is freely given and wants to see himself betrayed by his best friend, which would confirm all his self-doubts. What is more, he wants the shame and humiliation of confessing his longing. So he eagerly monitors Bertha's flirtation with Robert. It is as if he cannot help reproducing the teaching of the Church he has abandoned, that sexual desire is shameful and corrupting. He craves the humiliation of the penitent, though he believes in open relationships and rejects all the conventional occasions of penitence. His distorted sexuality contrasts with the impenitent frankness of Bertha, who kisses Robert and tells Richard – and then tells Robert that she has told Richard – and is still defiantly unashamed of her acts.

At the level of everyday relationships, *Exiles* can now be appreciated as a study in the paradoxes and double-binds of sexual permissiveness. But Richard is also an artist, protected against despair and able to justify his exploitation of other people's emotions because it is necessary to his vocation as a writer. We do not know what he writes, but we must assume that – as with Stephen in the *Portrait* and *Ulysses* – it owes something to his solitary walks on the strand and the voices he hears there:

RICHARD
[*Stands in the doorway, observing her for some moments.*] There are demons [*he points out towards the strand*] out there. I heard them jabbering since dawn.

BEATRICE
[*Starts to her feet.*] Mr Rowan!

RICHARD
I assure you. The isle is full of voices. Yours also, *Otherwise I could not see you,* it said. And her voice. But, I assure you, they are all demons. I made the

sign of the cross upside down and that silenced them.   (*E* 141)

And later:

ROBERT

Did you hear Bertha return?

RICHARD

No. I wrote all the night. And thought. [*Pointing to the study.*] In there. Before dawn I went out and walked the strand from end to end.

ROBERT

[*Shaking his head.*] Suffering. Torturing yourself.

RICHARD

Hearing voices about me. The voices of those who say they love me. (*E* 156–7)

What is remarkable is the immediate transposition from dramatic dialogue into the material of the inner voices: the words '*Otherwise I could not see you*', here spoken back at her, were Beatrice's own words in Act I. The 'demons' refer to Ibsen's *Ghosts* and, perhaps, to the siren voices that Stephen Dedalus heard. Robert Hand's newspaper article, which heralds Richard's return and flatteringly compares him to Swift, is one of them. Richard is cut off from Bertha — he has reduced her to simply another of 'those who say they love me' — and so all that he has with which to oppose the voices is the daemonic willpower (figured by the 'sign of the cross upside down') which sustains his writing. This may temporarily silence the voices, but no doubt they will return to plague him. Certainly they returned to plague Joyce. On 6 August 1937, nearly twenty years after the completion of *Exiles*, he wrote from Paris to Constantine Curran that 'Every day in every way I am walking along the streets of Dublin and along the strand. And "hearing voices" '.[22]

Exiles shows the artist as a haunted individual, cut off from other people by the 'deep wound of doubt' (*E* 162), which is the penance he has brought upon himself. The play ends, however, with the restatement of Bertha's love for him. The doubt and the haunting are in Richard's own mind. Bertha's passionate belief in the healing power of sexual fantasy stands as an affirmation of the 'joy of life' such as Ibsen had made in *Ghosts*:

RICHARD

And now I am tired for a while, Bertha. My wound tires me. [*He stretches himself out wearily along the lounge.* BERTHA *holds his hand, still speaking very softly.*]

BERTHA

Forget me, Dick. Forget me and love me again as you did the first time. I want my lover. To meet him, to go to him, to give myself to him. You, Dick. O, my strange wild lover, come back to me again!

[*She closes her eyes.*]   (*E* 162)

Bertha's capacity for joy is almost, but not quite, unique in this austere play. Archie, the Rowans' son, makes his first entry by scrambling through the window, and is deeply excited by an excursion on the milkcart to Booterstown. Though Richard finds the strand populated by voices and demons — figments of his inner conflict — the play also shows it as a source of unharnessed nature, beyond good and evil, to those who are able to appreciate it. Act I showed Robert caressing the cool, flat stone which Bertha had brought in from the shore (for him, predictably, it is like a 'woman's temple', *E* 54). In Act III there is the passing fishwoman shouting 'Fresh Dublin Bay herrings!' (*E* 153). These are Chekhovian interventions, momentary reminders of the broad concerns of life from which Richard and Robert, engrossed in their own feelings, have largely excluded themselves. Their final significance is entirely uncertain. Since Richard's 'wild nights' are now given over to writing, and his mornings to haunted walks along the strand, it may be that Bertha's last appeal will come to rejoin the clamouring voices of which, for him, the island is full. Richard is very much freer than Stephen Dedalus; yet his spiritual unrest and weariness suggest that the full liberation that Stephen sought is unattainable even by the successful artist.

Robert, still more than Richard, is in thrall to the Catholic religion and uses its terminology even though he disbelieves in it. For example, he describes his meeting with a divorcee in a nightclub as leading to 'what the subtle Duns Scotus calls a death of the spirit' (*E* 155). Only Bertha, alive to Robert's attractions yet devoted to Richard, is impervious to the 'voice of duty' and the circuit of sin and penitence. Bertha, tense and emotionally vulnerable like Gretta in 'The Dead', falls far short of the uninhibited physicality of her successor Molly Bloom. Joyce's notes to the play suggest the slightly portentous role he had in mind for his heroine. 'Europe is weary even of the Scandinavian women . . . whom the poetic genius of Ibsen created', he wrote; 'On what woman will the light of the poet's mind now shine? Perhaps at last on the Celt' (*E* 173–4). Very probably he had been more intent on outdoing Ibsen — though he hardly succeeds in this — than on creating a drama for the twentieth century. 'Hedda! Hedda Gabler!'

exclaims the writer of *Giacomo Joyce* (*GJ* 8). When we consider Joyce's reputation as a modernist it should be remembered that all his works up to and including *Exiles* invite comparison with nineteenth-century models and, at times, betray a certain nostalgia for them. But if *Dubliners*, the *Portrait* and to a lesser extent *Exiles* were substantial achievements, *Ulysses* was the stuff out of which literary revolutions are made.

PART II

Ulysses: List of episodes

I. *Telemachiad*

1.	Telemachus	The Martello Tower
2.	Nestor	Mr Deasy's School
3.	Proteus	Stephen on Sandymount strand

II. *Odyssey*

4.	Calypso	Breakfast at 7 Eccles St
5.	Lotos-Eaters	Bloom in the streets
6.	Hades	Dignam's funeral
7.	Aeolus	The newspaper office
8.	Lestrygonians	Bloom in the streets: lunchtime
9.	Scylla and Charybdis	The National Library
10.	Wandering Rocks	Dublin: afternoon streets
11.	Sirens	Ormond Restaurant
12.	Cyclops	Barney Kiernan's pub
13.	Nausicaa	Sandymount strand: Gerty MacDowell
14.	Oxen of the Sun	Maternity hospital, Holles St
15.	Circe	Nighttown

III. *Nostos ('return')*

16.	Eumaeus	The cabman's shelter
17.	Ithaca	7 Eccles St: Bloom and Stephen
18.	Penelope	Molly Bloom's monologue

NOTE. The names of the episodes given in the left-hand column are Joyce's working titles, which he chose to delete from the manuscript at the proof stage. These titles are invariably used by Joyce critics and scholars and should presumably be restored in some future critical edition of the text. Reference is made to them throughout the chapters that follow.

5   A Dublin *Peer Gynt*

Joyce first thought of the title 'Ulysses' in 1906, when he was projecting a number of additional stories for *Dubliners*. One of these was to recount a day in the life of a peripatetic Dublin Jew, Alfred Hunter. The other stories – 'The Last Supper', 'The Street', 'Vengeance', 'At Bay' and 'Catharsis' – were never written.[1] 'Ulysses' nearly met a similar fate. Early in 1907 Joyce was regretting that it 'never got any forrader than the title'.[2] A few months later he thought of working it up into a short book, which, as he told Stanislaus, would be a 'Dublin "Peer Gynt" '. Stanislaus added the following pregnant comment in his diary: 'I suggested that he should make a comedy out of it, but he won't'.[3]

The social world of *Ulysses* is continuous with the social world of *Dubliners*. Several characters reappear and Bloom himself, we are told, attended the funeral of the unhappy Mrs Sinico. Yet the crucial steps Joyce took in planning *Ulysses* were not so much his initial choice of Homer's *Odyssey* as a model, as his successive decisions to expand it in the *Peer Gynt* manner and then to join it with a sequel to the story of Stephen Dedalus – all the while preserving a time-span limited to a single day. *Ulysses*, that is, began as a complex hybrid, a union of the classical epic, the autobiographical novel, the modern short story and a picaresque poetic drama. Such a hybrid was always likely to turn into parody and burlesque, however solemn Joyce's original intentions may have been. Moreover, it proved to be almost indefinitely expansible. Joyce began writing his book at long last after completing the *Portrait* in 1914, but he could not then foresee the eventual result, and some of the familiar features of *Ulysses* were only added at the proof stage. The later episodes are far longer than the earlier ones. After 1918, Joyce seldom if ever spoke of his new book as a novel, preferring the more grandiose terms 'epic' and 'encyclopaedia'.[4] The individual episodes began increasingly to take on a life of their own. Some of the earlier chapters such as 'Telemachus' and 'Lotos-Eaters' have the economy and explicit poetic modelling of a short story; their successors, however, like 'Cyclops' and 'Circe', are 'chaffering allincluding most farraginous chronicles' (*U* 420) in themselves.

The dramatist J. M. Synge, in his preface to *The Playboy of the Western World* (1907), had spoken of the dilemma facing the urban writer at the beginning of the twentieth century:

> in countries where the imagination of the people, and the language they use, is rich and living, it is possible for a writer to be rich and copious in his words, and at the same time to give the reality, which is the root of all poetry, in a comprehensive and natural form. In the modern literature of towns, however, richness is found only in sonnets, or prose poems, or in one or two elaborate books that are far away from the profound and common interests of life. One has, on one side, Mallarmé and Huysmans producing this literature; and on the other, Ibsen and Zola dealing with the reality of life in joyless and pallid works.[5]

Joyce, of course, had never seen Ibsen's works as 'pallid', and Synge's solution, to seek poetic richness by imitating the language of uneducated peasants, was the very opposite of his. Both authors, however, were seeking to reconcile the false polarity of 'naturalist' and 'symbolist' writing. Joyce wished to be 'rich and copious in his words', yet he had no intention of abandoning the urban subject matter which had served him in *Dubliners*. Stephen Dedalus, in the theory of epiphanies, had suggested that beauty could be found in the 'commonest object' and in the 'vulgarity of speech or of gesture' (*SH* 218, 216). Joyce was also aware – as he makes George Russell say in *Ulysses* – that Ireland's 'national epic' had yet to be written (*U* 192). Ibsen in *Peer Gynt* had produced a national epic drama which relied (as Synge's plays would) on rural manners and traditional folklore for much of its inspiration. Yet *Peer Gynt* stood almost alone in the Ibsen canon as a sprawling, episodic, multi-generic play which transported its audience from Norway to the pyramids and filled the stage with peasants, trolls, lunatics, slaves, dancing-girls and international capitalists. As the idea of *Ulysses* took shape Joyce devised a fiction of similar variety; a 'comic epic poem in prose', with a large cast of Dubliners which would take in farce, satire, literary parody, and phantasmagoria as well as the traditional concerns of character and story. Joyce's modern Ulysses, like Peer Gynt, would be an 'Everyman' figure, but at the same time Joyce would abandon the conventional form of humanist drama inherited from the medieval Morality play – the form, that is, of the life-drama or character-biography. He would show his hero's life not as a series of significant stages but as an immanent experience, from minute to minute. Where *Peer Gynt* traces its hero's exploits across half a century, *Ulysses* is confined to a few hours.

First Joyce had to find his hero. The concept of a national epic implies, as Georg Lukács has put it, protagonists who are 'total individuals who magnificently concentrate within themselves what is otherwise dispersed in the national character'.[6] The rise of nationalism in the nineteenth century had led to the creation for symbolic propaganda purposes of such semi-official national heroes, or 'tribal gods', as Uncle Sam, John Bull, Britannia, Marianne, and Cathleen ni Houlihan. The 'cult of personality' in politics grew from the legend of Napoleon. Ibsen's *Peer Gynt* may be seen as a literary artist's attempt to create an alternative national hero or tribal god, who was utterly incapable of being reclaimed by the politicians. Gynt, the selfish, greedy, quick-witted scapegrace, was a subversive figure, a Falstaff or Sancho Panza whom people took to their hearts because he embodied the furtive underside of the national life. Writers in other countries have created characters with a broadly similar function: Dickens's Sam Weller, Mrs Gamp and the Artful Dodger, Wells's Mr Polly, and Synge's Christy Mahon are among those who inspire universal sneaking admiration rather than pompous patriotic pride. Yet perhaps only Jaroslav Hasek's Good Soldier Švejk — the first of whose adventures appeared in Czech in 1911 — is a subversive national symbol of the same order as Peer Gynt.

Joyce, however, chose to attempt something quite singular: a 'national epic' whose hero was not a native. Far from summing up the underside of Irish life, Leopold Bloom stands slightly on the margin of that life (which nevertheless is abundantly present in *Ulysses*) by virtue of his Jewishness. His roots are not in the provinces or the Irish people — the traditional soil out of which national heroes spring. Indeed, he has no roots in the usual sense at all. His grandfather came from Hungary, his father was a suicide, his wife grew up in Gibraltar, he is cut off from the Jewish as well as the Catholic faith, and he has only a 'theoretical' (*U* 609) knowledge of Hebrew. He defends himself against the chauvinists in Barney Kiernan's by reminding them that 'the Saviour was a Jew and his father was a Jew. Your God' (*U* 340). He astounds his hearers by his indifference to the mystique of nationhood. Bloom, by these actions, is clearly casting himself as an outsider.

His adventures are, of course, modelled on a pattern from Homer. Joyce had studied Charles Lamb's *Adventures of Ulysses* at school and, living in a seaport on the Adriatic, he became fascinated by modern theories of the *Odyssey*, particularly that of Victor Bérard who argued that the hidden subject of the poem was the travels, not of a Greek hero, but of the commercial Phoenicians. It is true that Joyce regarded Ulysses himself – wily, versatile, and irrepressibly inquisitive – as the one 'complete all-round character' in world literature.[7] Yet many aspects of Ulysses, the 'city-sacker', are alien to Bloom. Joyce's commercial traveller can claim lineal descent from Bérard's Phoenicians but, apart from that, he owes far more to the contemporary world than he does to his author's reverence for the classics. To write the adventures of a modern Ulysses was, at best, a worthy aim for a young artist. To make the modern Ulysses not only a 'cultured allroundman' (*U* 234) but a Jewish advertisement canvasser with an unfaithful wife was a bold stroke of genius. It was Joyce's way of registering the deracination and cosmopolitanism of bourgeois life, and of writing an epic which would be both essentially Irish and permeated through by the spirit of exile. If Bloom is the representative of a transient population, compelled to sink his roots in a shallow soil, his position in Ireland is no different from that of millions of Irishmen overseas. The common culture that he and his fellow-Dubliners share is, in Joyce's view, the international mass-culture of modern consumerism. Technological innovations such as the telegraph and telephone enable the Dubliners to follow the English cricket scores and to bet on the Ascot Gold Cup. Advertising slogans and jingles are part of their lives. The entertainments on offer in their city range from opera and music-hall to the forthcoming visit of a Midwestern evangelist and the brothel whose madam is sending her son to Oxford. Amid such excitements it is useless to lament the passing of an 'authentic' national life. The chauvinistic nationalism that Joyce portrays is also a product of modern conditions. It uses contemporary propaganda-techniques and is quick to adopt the latest weapons. When the Citizen attacks Bloom it is not a traditional spear or clod of turf that he hurls after him, but a Jacob's biscuit-tin.

Second only in importance to the choice of a hero was the allotted time-span of *Ulysses*. Eighteen hours is the time taken by a short story rather than by the action of any previous novel. A day in the life of Leopold Bloom, however dramatic its events, could only be a sample or 'slice' of his life; and Joyce was not planning to show any really dramatic events, only a funeral, a cuckolding, a meeting and a homecoming. Minute-to-minute experiences, rather than long perspectives and dramatic conflicts, were what must fill such a narrative. The reader would *hear* the characters, and see life as they saw it, with a precision and depth of understanding which no earlier novelist had been able to offer. At the same time, the 'meaning' of life would appear to recede; the epic sweep of the fiction was in danger of getting lost amid trivialities.

The notions of 'absolute realism' and of an epic treatment of everyday experience had been entertained by other writers besides Joyce. Here is Arnold Bennett, for example, writing in *Fame and Fiction* (1901):

> The spirit of the sublime dwells not only in the high and remote; it shines unperceived amid all the usual meannesses of our daily existence. To take the common grey things which people know and despise, and, without tampering, to disclose their epic significance, their essential grandeur − that is realism, as distinguished from idealism or romanticism.[8]

But Bennett, when he came to write his major novel *The Old Wives' Tale*, portrayed the whole life-span of his two heroines, as if he had not really meant what he said about 'daily existence'. An older novelist, George Gissing, had left it to one of his characters to advocate an 'absolute realism' which Gissing himself was far from exemplifying. Harold Biffen in *New Grub Street* (1891) wants to reproduce life 'verbatim, without one single impertinent suggestion of any point of view save that of honest reporting'. Reproducing the love-talk of an ordinary man and girl he had overheard by Regent's Park, he could produce 'such a love-scene as . . . has absolutely never been written down'; its only defect, which for Biffen was a guarantee of its truth, was that it would be 'unutterably tedious'.[9] To a novelist of a still earlier generation, Bennett's ideal of 'all-embracing compassion' and Biffen's ideal of reproducing life 'verbatim' threatened to produce not tedium but a meaningless cacophony of sounds:

> If we had a keen vision and feeling of all ordinary human life, it would be like hearing the grass grow and the squirrel's heart beat, and we should die of that roar which lies on the other side of silence.[10]

Joyce once conceded that 'absolute realism is impossible, of course'.[11] But he came much closer to it than Bennett, Gissing, or George Eliot had done. If his hero was an 'Everyman', then everything he experienced could be made interesting, he believed. Every aspect of the culture of a city such as Dublin, from its great literary and philosophical heritage to the results of the day's sporting events, was worth including. Following the principle of 'documentation' established in *Dubliners*, *Ulysses* would be full of jokes, speeches, slogans, letters, street-signs

and printed ephemera. The spoken and printed ephemera would sit side
by side with the evanescent stuff of consciousness, memories, fantasies,
and fleeting impressions.

But how was all this normally excluded material to be incorporated
into a narrative? Would not the result be – as H. G. Wells's narrator
says of *Tono-Bungay* (1909) – an 'agglomeration', 'a vast hotch-potch
of anecdotes and experiences'?[12] Or a book that – as Erich Auerbach
was to write of *Ulysses* – 'makes severe demands on the reader's
patience and learning by its dizzying whirl of motifs, wealth of words
and concepts, perpetual playing upon their countless associations, and
the ever rearoused but never satisfied doubt as to what order is
ultimately hidden behind so much apparent arbitrariness'?[13]
Auerbach, a great European scholar of the mid-century, failed to
anticipate the emergence of a school of 'post-structuralist' criticism
which would look upon the 'dizzying whirl', 'perpetual playing' and
'arbitrariness' of *Ulysses* and *Finnegans Wake* with unmitigated
enthusiasm. For Roland Barthes, Jacques Derrida and their admirers,
an 'ever rearoused but never satisfied doubt' is precisely what protects
writing from finite interpretation and ideological sterility. Yet ever
since *Ulysses* first appeared the dominant tradition of favourable
criticism has stressed, not its hotch-potch quality, but its order. Such
readers have found in it not the 'roar which lies on the other side of
silence', not a hubbub or cacophony, but an imaginatively congruent
pattern of voices.

When *Ulysses* was published in 1922 it was as a banned book, which
for many years could not be read in England, Ireland, or America
except by those with access to the copies smuggled in from Paris.
Nevertheless it caused a literary sensation. Of all the things written
about it in the early years perhaps the only essay of permanent value
was by T. S. Eliot. '*Ulysses*, Order and Myth' (1923) decisively rejected
any notion of chaos or arbitrariness in *Ulysses*. The chaos, instead,
belonged to 'contemporary history', which Joyce had found a way of
structuring and ordering. In Eliot's view Joyce's use of the Homeric
parallel was the key to his construction and had 'the importance of a
scientific discovery':

It is simply a way of controlling, of ordering, of giving a shape and significance
to the immense panorama of futility and anarchy which is contemporary
history. . . . Instead of narrative method, we may now use the mythical
method.[14]

Eliot, of course, was scarcely writing as an impartial witness. His reading implicitly links *Ulysses* to *The Waste Land*, a poem unified not by any narrative structure but by the interweaving of motifs from the contemporary anthropological study of myth. When he speaks of the 'mythical method' it is not, apparently, Joyce's imitation of a classical literary model – the *Odyssey* of Homer – that he has in mind; nobody could describe such a well-tried approach as having the importance of a scientific discovery. Joyce had followed the sequence of Homeric episodes (with some alterations) because, apart from the passing of time, there is almost no causal sequence of events in *Ulysses*. Bloom's peregrinations, and Stephen's, seem to be as much intended to fill the available time as to reach any definite goal. Both characters have an interest in avoiding, or at least postponing, the principal goal of the *Odyssey*, which is that of homecoming. The puzzling meaning of Joyce's imaginary voyage is quite unlike the translucency of Homer.

Eliot's 'scientific discovery', then, implies the existence in *Ulysses* of other levels beside that of epic storytelling. One of the book's determining features is its use of secondary mythic parallels to augment the basic parallelism between its characters and Homer's. Stephen is not only Telemachus but Hamlet, the Prodigal Son, Wagner's Siegfried, and so on; Bloom is Sinbad the Sailor, the Good Samaritan and the Wandering Jew. It was the publication of Stuart Gilbert's *James Joyce's 'Ulysses'* in 1930 which first fully revealed the encyclopaedic character of *Ulysses*, and the pedantic care which had gone into its making. Gilbert, a friend and disciple of Joyce, was the first of many critics to reproduce an authorial 'schema', showing each episode with its appropriate 'Art', 'Colour', 'Symbol', bodily organ, allegorical significance, and 'Technic' or style. Richard Ellmann in *Ulysses on the Liffey* discusses further variants of the Schema, with the relevant diagrams, but they are not reproduced in the present book since they no more offer a complete guide to *Ulysses* than does a wiring diagram to the systems propelling a motor car. (One of these systems is, of course, a driver.) The schematic, artificial skeleton around which *Ulysses* is constructed – its materials disposed from episode to episode as across a grid – is linked to the surface by means of innumerable sets of verbal markers, correspondences or leitmotivs, all of which the reader has to learn to carry in mind if he is to aspire towards an (unattainable) complete reading of the work. The parodic styles of the later sections show up the deceptiveness of the 'stream-of-consciousness' realism of the early episodes of *Ulysses* (see Chapter 8 below). Yet even the early episodes are incrusted with ornamental layers of meanings and images which cannot be grasped by the unaided first-time reader. At the same time *Ulysses*, like Eliot's poems, can be enjoyed for its poetic richness and suggestiveness long before it is fully and analytically understood.

Stuart Gilbert's critical study was closely vetted by Joyce himself; later, however, Vladimir Nabokov, who had challenged Joyce on the subject, recalled that he described his collaboration with Gilbert as an 'advertisement for the book' and a 'terrible mistake'.[15] For Gilbert was not content with throwing light on the laborious technique which had gone into the making of *Ulysses*. He offered a number of pronouncements on the frame of mind in which it should be read. 'It is impossible to grasp the meaning of *Ulysses*, its symbolism and the significance of its *leitmotifs* without an understanding of the esoteric theories which underlie the work', he wrote.[16] Readers who dared to criticize its details simply had not approached it in a sufficiently humble and reverential spirit:

Ulysses is a book of life, a microcosm which is a small-scale replica of the universe, and the methods which lead to an understanding of the latter will provide a solution of the obscurities in *Ulysses*. . . . Some critics of *Ulysses*, while accepting the work as a whole, accuse defects in this passage or that, in the technique of one episode or another, and blame the author for leading us round unnecessary detours; it is often . . . precisely in the offending passages that the text is at its most significant. For no passage, no phrase in *Ulysses* is irrelevant; in this grain of sand, this banal day in the life of an inglorious Dubliner, we have a complete picture of the human situation, and a clinical analysis of that skin-disease of Gaea Tellus (heroine of the concluding episode) which we call Life.[17]

Ulysses, in effect, was a sacred book, the work of a priest or prophet of eternal imagination who had finally and infallibly 'given the word'. Its text was as sacrosanct as the text of scripture.

Ulysses as Gilbert described it was the book that the humourless, priggish young Stephen Dedalus would like to have written. A 'complete picture of the human situation' recalls the *Summa Totius Theologiae* of St Thomas Aquinas, and a 'clinical analysis' recalls Aristotle as well as Stephen's own talk of paralysis and vivisection. Yet *Ulysses* is self-evidently neither of these things. Gilbert's book is best understood as a sanitary effort, an attempt to cleanse *Ulysses* once and for all of the unsavoury reputation it had gained as a piece of deliberate obscenity — a 'dirty book' written by a hater of Western (and especially English) civilization. Among many examples of the scurrilous abuse vented on *Ulysses* by people who should have known better, the views of Edmund Gosse may be taken as representative. Gosse, born in 1849, was a friend of Stevenson and Henry James and a highly respected elder statesman of English letters. Among his books was a biography of Ibsen. *Ulysses*, he wrote to Louis Gillet (who was preparing an article on Joyce for the *Revue des Deux Mondes*), was a 'cynical appeal to sheer indecency', 'an anarchical production, infamous in taste, in style, in everything'. Its author was 'the perfect type of the Irish *fumiste*, a hater of England, more than suspected of partiality for Germany, where he lived before the war' (*sic*).[18] Faced with such a wall of hostility and prejudice,[19] it was not surprising if Joyce's work attracted younger disciples who made exaggerated and even fanatical claims in its defence. With hindsight, however, it is clear that no critical assessment is satisfactory which simply glosses over the 'indecent' and 'anarchical' aspect of *Ulysses*. Joyce had laboured to give an air of sacredness to the most profane matter possible. His prodigious virtuosity, wit, and ingenuity had been expended in creating a burlesque scripture which was, in one of its aspects, simply a vast hoax or tall tale. When Gilbert spoke of the 'esoteric theories' underlying the book, he was referring no doubt to theosophy and other forms of occult speculation. But while Joyce dabbled in these matters, and used their frameworks when they proved helpful, he lacked one essential part of the equipment of the prophet or sage that Gilbert made him out to be; and that was a passionate belief in the truth of his own 'revelation'. Stephen, when asked if he really believes in his theory of Shakespeare, answers that he does not (*U* 213). One of Stephen's choicest pieces of profanity is reserved for the devotees of esoteric religion: 'Through spaces smaller than red globules of man's blood they creepy-crawl after Blake's buttocks into eternity of which this vegetable world is but a shadow'. Stephen's response, which is Joyce's, is to 'Hold to the now, the here, through which all future plunges to the past' (*U* 186).

Joyce's mockery and ridicule, in other words, have their own kind of moral justification. Though far from a 'complete picture of the human situation', *Ulysses* is an artist's challenge to the claims of orthodox religion and morality to pre-empt human value. A work of fiction masquerading as scripture, it appeals to readers who combine a sense of fun with a fascination with complexity. Where it is cryptic and esoteric its difficulty is as much that of a crossword puzzle or chess problem as of a genuinely religious excursion into the unknown. If it is a book of life, it is because its subversive vision has more hold over many modern readers than the doctrines of priests and prophets.

Ulysses, then, may be quite properly judged by the criteria of literary comparison and truth to experience. Its encyclopaedic claims can hardly be taken seriously if they are not subjected to such a test. Joyce's upside-down version of the 'Everyman' theme contains, inevitably, certain limitations and certain kinds of distortion. What these may be has been pertinently investigated by some of the Marxist critics of the work. Though Marxism in the 1920s and 30s threw up its quota of scurrilous attacks on *Ulysses*, the Communist critics were undoubtedly right to stress the consequences of Joyce's rejection of a teleological or end-directed narrative. The charge was expressed in *The Meaning of Contemporary Realism* (1956) by Georg Lukács:

The perpetually oscillating patterns of sense- and memory-data, their powerfully-charged — but aimless and directionless — fields of force, give rise to an epic structure which is *static*, reflecting a belief in the basically static character of events.[20]

The rejection of history is in itself a major theme of *Ulysses*. Stephen avows that 'History . . . is a nightmare from which I am trying to awake' (*U* 40). He says this in conversation with Mr Deasy, an Ulster Protestant whose view of history is quite as militant and messianic as that of orthodox Marxism:

– The ways of the Creator are not our ways, Mr Deasy said. All history moves towards one great goal, the manifestation of God.   (*U* 40)

Deasy will 'fight for the right to the end' (*U* 41), but the 'history' he expounds is pure ideology, a tissue of *canards* and plausible inventions. His interview with Stephen is interrupted by a shout from the playground. A goal has been scored:

Stephen jerked his thumb towards the window, saying:
– That is God.
Hooray! Ay! Whrrwhee!
– What? Mr Deasy asked.
– A shout in the street, Stephen answered, shrugging his shoulders. (*U* 40)

Stephen's gratuitous invention reveals what it is he means by waking from the 'nightmare of history'. In identifying God with a shout in the street, he himself is the creator. The act of creation — artistic or intellectual — is what he opposes to the deadweight of history. Yet, if such creation begins in irresponsibility, it ends in solipsism, as Stephen's theory of Shakespeare suggests:

We walk through ourselves, meeting robbers, ghosts, giants, old men, young men, wives, widows, brothers-in-love. But always meeting ourselves.(*U* 213)

Stephen on 16 June 1904 does not meet himself, however; he meets Leopold Bloom, whose views on the rights and duties of the artist and the 'importance of dietary and civic selfhelp' (*U* 587) are a timely corrective to Stephen's self-dramatizing solipsism. Bloom simply cannot understand him when he asserts that 'Ireland must be important because it belongs to me' (*U* 565). Yet Bloom, for all his sense of citizenship, is content to be distracted from the 'nightmare of history' by the freedom of his moment-to-moment experience and the urgencies of his private life. He is wholly lacking in the political awareness desiderated by Marxists and his life (apart from his somewhat leisurely business activities) is lived on the domestic rather than the public stage. Through Bloom the motifs of European cultural history are not only concentrated in an individual but diluted, as it were, for consumption in the home.

Amid the various literary backgrounds to *Ulysses* – Ibsen, Homer, Shakespeare, the models provided by sacred books and scriptures – we should never forget its pre- or sub-literary background in the urban culture which is epitomized by the modern newspaper. 'Writing for the newspapers', Bloom assures Stephen, 'is the readiest channel nowadays' (*U* 565). In a newspaper events are reported and features are juxtaposed in an order which, on the face of it, owes nothing to the priorities of historical narrative. The sense of history exhibited with some pomp on the editorial page is little in evidence elsewhere in the paper. *Ulysses* is full of parodies of newspaper language and reveals considerable insight into the nature of the press. At the same time, it too is a journal of a day's events which includes a number of simple news items. For example, we learn in the 'Cyclops' episode that Dublin Corporation voted on 16 June 1904 for the restitution of the Irish language (*U* 323). There is nothing in the rhetoric of the book to suggest that this small but significant moment in the political emergence of modern Ireland was any more epoch-making than other reported events of the day such as the Gold Cup race, Iremonger's century for Nottinghamshire (*U* 586), or the Viceregal procession. In most newspaper reporting a dim sense of the goals of history or of a particular nation persists but it is impossible to perceive much movement towards those goals on the basis of a single day's events. Much the same may be said of *Ulysses*. Where Joyce does (as Eliot said) give shape and significance to contemporary history is not in any publicly acceptable retrospective narrative but in his exploration of private consciousness and the informal and unofficial creation of meanings. As he walks along the beach in 'Proteus', Stephen suddenly reflects that 'These heavy sands are language tide and wind have silted here' (*U* 50). Like a good journalist, the Joyceian artist is something of a beachcomber as well as a meticulous designer. (It comes as no surprise to learn that Joyce possessed a book called *The Common Objects of the Sea-Shore*.[21]) At the Soviet Writers' Congress in 1934, at which Joyce was held up as the last word in bourgeois decadence, Karl Radek warned that 'trying to present a picture of revolution by the Joyce method would be like trying to catch a dreadnought with a shrimping net'.[22] Joyce, surely, would have taken this as a compliment. He shows no liking for dreadnoughts but an enormous gusto in scooping up the delicacies of everyday life into his net.

6   Stephen in *Ulysses*: the loveliest mummer

In Ireland in June 1904 the Abbey players are in rehearsal. Buck Mulligan and Haines, with whom Stephen is sharing the Martello Tower, have been along to see them:

> We went over to their playbox Haines and I, the plumbers' hall. Our players are creating a new art for Europe like the Greeks or M. Maeterlinck. Abbey theatre! I smell the public sweat of monks.   (*U* 215)

Theatricality is in the air and Mulligan provides an egregious example of it. His first act, and the book's opening gesture, is to impersonate a priest celebrating Holy Communion. Mulligan likes to organize his friends and his preferred role is that of impresario or master of ceremonies rather than simple mummer. From a generation that has 'grown out of Wilde and paradoxes' (*U* 24) he craves recognition as the latest and most outrageous of the Irish wits. In mockery of the new national theatre (and especially, one suspects, of J. M. Synge) he has 'conceived a play for the mummers', a 'national immorality in three orgasms' (*U* 216). He is provocative and patronizing towards Stephen, whom he addresses as 'Kinch, the loveliest mummer of them all' (*U* 11).

Stephen is like someone who has agreed to take part in a serious play and is disgusted to see it turn into farce. A year after being summoned back from Paris to his mother's deathbed, he has fallen in with Mulligan's proposal to set up house in the tower. Mulligan wants Stephen to help him 'do something for the island. Hellenise it' (*U* 13). Together, that is, they are to inhabit an avant-garde stronghold which will also be a beacon of aesthetic 'sweetness and light'. But it is a stone, not an ivory tower. Already Mulligan's promises have begun to look as chipped and battered as the sentence in which Stephen recalls them:

> To ourselves . . . new paganism . . . omphalos.   (*U* 13)

'To ourselves' – *Sinn féin*, the Irish political slogan of 1904 – implies the seclusion Stephen needs in which to find his voice as an artist. But Mulligan has broken their solitude by importing his Oxford friend Haines, a 'ponderous Saxon' (*U* 10) in love with the colourful Celts

127

and with the native culture which Stephen sees as a badge of Irish servitude. While no actor in his waking life, Haines terrifies Stephen by raving in his sleep about shooting a black panther. The prospects of achieving the 'new paganism', of becoming the omphalos or spiritual centre, are nullified by Haines's presence, and perhaps they were none too good anyway. Mulligan, after all, is a crude jester who will soon bestow the name 'omphalos' (the reference is to the navel-shaped stone at Delphi in Greece) on his projected 'national fertilising farm' of eager and serviceable women (*U* 399). Mulligan's avant-garde notions are simply a pose, and the Martello Tower scene – which he does his best to direct – is brittle, undergraduate theatre.

Mulligan, whom Joyce modelled with malice aforethought on his former associate Oliver Gogarty, is not a very pleasant figure. As a fictional character who can launch Joyce's odyssey with dramatic éclat, however, he is superb. His flamboyance and frivolity strike a note we shall hear throughout *Ulysses* with its wealth of parodies, burlesques and bawdy jokes. Joyce's initial concern is to establish the incompatibility of Mulligan and Stephen. The dramatic contrast of these two young men touches on many of the pervasive themes of *Ulysses*, and particularly the theme of the human body. Mulligan's robust, medical student's attitude to the body ('I see them pop off every day in the Mater and Richmond and cut up into tripes in the dissecting room', *U* 14) foreshadows the attitudes of Bloom and Molly. For Stephen, however, many aspects of physical life are taboo. He refused to pray at his dying mother's bedside and yet he was, and still is, deeply wounded by Mulligan's unceremonious description of her as '*beastly dead*' (*U* 14). Though an atheist Stephen, it seems, still adheres to the doctrine of the soul. The schema of *Ulysses* that Joyce drew up for Carlo Linati shows that, unlike all the subsequent episodes, the three opening chapters (the Telemachiad) have not been allotted a bodily organ since 'Telemachus does not yet bear a body'.[1]

Stephen, after much brooding, has come to see his mother's death in an intensely melodramatic light. This melodrama overshadows the air of casual, irresponsible farce that Buck Mulligan radiates. When the old woman comes up to the tower to deliver the milk, for example, Mulligan indulges in some mild badinage at her expense:

– That's a lovely morning, sir, she said. Glory be to God.
– To whom? Mulligan said, glancing at her. Ah, to be sure.
Stephen reached back and took the milkjug from the locker.

– The islanders, Mulligan said to Haines casually, speak frequently of the collector of prepuces.   (*U* 20)

To Stephen the old woman is a symbolic presence, 'maybe a messenger'. There is a messenger in Homer at this point but – with Irish theatre in mind – it may also be worth remembering Yeats's deadly messenger, the legendary old woman of his play *Cathleen ni Houlihan* (1902) who calls forth young men to die for Ireland. Stephen feels slighted by the old woman, but he himself has refused Ireland's call at its most sacrosanct, when his mother begged him 'with her last breath to kneel down and pray for her' (*U* 11). Now he is haunted by the scene, which is symbolized for him by the china bowl which held the results of his mother's vomiting. This, the 'bowl of bitter waters' (*U* 15), becomes the centre of a fervid cluster of images in his mind. A triple French pun (*la mère/la mer/l'amère*?) links the bowl to the 'ring of bay and skyline' (*U* 12), the seascape of Dublin Bay from Dalkey to Howth Head which he surveys from the top of the tower. Beyond this, the 'bowl of waters' signifies the shaving-bowl which Mulligan has held aloft in parody of the Mass, the 'boat of incense . . . at Clongowes' (*U* 17), and the Mediterranean sea which was crossed by Daedalus and Ulysses.

However brutal his methods, Mulligan is apparently sincere in wanting to free Stephen from his maternal obsession. Stephen spurns his help and influence, and yet there is a subtler sense in which he is being shaped by his friend and rival. Frank Budgen recalls that Joyce found himself losing interest in Stephen during the composition of *Ulysses*. 'He has a shape that can't be changed', was Joyce's remark.[2] This shape is established in the course of the Telemachiad, and not a little of it, in the reader's eyes, is formed by Buck Mulligan's tart observations:

You wouldn't kneel down to pray for your mother on her deathbed when she asked you. Why? Because you have the cursed jesuit strain in you, only it's injected the wrong way.   (*U* 14)

Buck Mulligan slung his towel stolewise round his neck and, bending in loose laughter, said to Stephen's ear:
– O, shade of Kinch the elder! Japhet in search of a father!   (*U* 24)

The first of these statements is an act of psychological unmasking, differing little from Cranly's observation that Stephen is 'super-saturated with the religion in which you say you disbelieve' (*P* 240). The second has the characteristic Mulligan tone of high camp, a parody of ham acting. It is this second pronouncement, with its self-conscious theatricality, which suggests the later rather than the earlier Joyce and points not so much to a psychological as to a scriptural or typological reading of *Ulysses*. *Japhet in Search of a Father* was the title of a once popular novel by Frederick Marryat (1836).[3] If Stephen is Japhet he is also Hamlet and Telemachus; he is every son who has lost a father in recorded history. It is at Mulligan's prompting that we begin to perceive *Ulysses* as a Freudian 'family romance' in which Stephen, disowned by his natural father, goes in search of a substitute father for whom he could feel some portion of reverence. We have already encountered the family romance theme in the *Portrait*, where Stephen first dreamed that his father had become a marshal and then claimed a 'real father' in the legendary Daedalus. His search for fathers in *Ulysses* begins with Mulligan himself – the 'stately, plump' father-confessor of the opening charade. The priest, however, is only the first item in the repertoire of 'Mercurial Malachi' (*U* 23). By the end of the 'Telemachus' episode he has played his part in ushering Stephen onto the fictional stage, and has provoked him moreover into a silent decision to leave the tower. Mulligan to Stephen is neither a father nor a potential stage-manager but a 'Usurper' (*U* 29). The final appearance of his 'sleek brown head' parting the waters as he takes his morning dip is that of a performing seal.

In the next episode, 'Nestor', Stephen himself is called upon to perform in public. His aloofness and morbid sensitivity make him a decidedly eccentric schoolmaster. The Latin lesson ends with him teasing his pupils with an obscure and baffling riddle:

> *The cock crew*
> *The sky was blue:*
> *The bells in heaven*
> *Were striking eleven.*
> *Tis time for this poor soul*
> *To go to heaven.*   (*U* 32)

The answer is 'The fox burying his grandmother under a hollybush' (*U* 33). Given the fox as the symbol of cunning – one of Stephen's watchwords at the end of the *Portrait* – this nonsense answer seems to intimate that Stephen killed his mother.[4] Mulligan – citing his aunt's opinion – has already suggested this (*U* 11, 12). Stephen's private remorse helps to account for his maverick performance in the classroom, and it is not surprising that Mr Deasy should anticipate his early resignation. For the time being, however, he is useful to an employer who relishes some contact with the literary world and enjoys imparting sententious advice. Mr Deasy, 'that old pelters' (*U* 133), is the second of Stephen's substitute fathers and, once again, he is a rank imposter.

'Telemachus' and 'Nestor' are dramatized episodes incorporating an intermittent representation of Stephen's unspoken thoughts. In the famous beach episode, 'Proteus', Stephen is taking a solitary walk and the narrative mode, according to the Linati schema, is one of uninterrupted 'soliloquy'. The word 'soliloquy' suggests a stage convention, but two other names are in common use for Joyce's method here – 'stream of consciousness' and 'interior monologue'.

Robert Humphrey defines stream-of-consciousness fiction as 'a type of fiction in which the basic emphasis is placed on exploration of the prespeech levels of consciousness for the purpose, primarily, of revealing the psychic being of the characters'.[5] The terms used here are not very precise. The idea of a 'stream of consciousness' derives from William James's attempt in *The Principles of Psychology* (1891) to describe the workings of consciousness as we experience it. James impressionistically defines the consciousness as a continuous succession of 'brain-states' (thoughts, feelings, impulses, emotions, and so on) which have not necessarily reached the stage of linguistic formulation. Stream-of-consciousness narrative, like the so-called 'automatic writing', derives some of its appeal from the illusory possibility of expressing the flow of 'brain-states' directly in the form of language.

In *The Nature of Narrative* (1966) Robert Scholes and Robert Kellogg set out to show that the literary stream of consciousness was organically related to a much older form of narrative, the interior monologue. Classical writers such as Apollonius, Virgil and Ovid used the interior monologue to give expression to the inner turmoil of a lovelorn heroine. The interior monologue – the narrative of a character's consecutive silent thoughts – is thus connected with the passivity and narcissism so often ascribed to female sexuality. Joyce's presentation of Molly Bloom is in the same tradition.[6] If this is true then Joyce's innovation was to extend the literary convention of passive narcissism to male characters such as Bloom and Stephen. In addition, the Joycean interior monologue is constructed according to the premises of modern empirical psychology.[7] The older monologues, based on rhetorical principles, were debates or arguments where the marshalling of the 'reasons of the heart' led in the end to some sort of resolution. Jane Austen has some fine examples of such unspoken debates. Stephen and Bloom, by contrast, are not shown as engaging in any sustained activity of disciplined or directed thinking. For much of the time their minds jump from one association to the next in the unpredictable, intuitive manner that Joyce had already represented in the *Portrait of the Artist*. Grammatically, the Joyceian monologue now adopts a form of 'direct speech' – which he claimed to have imitated from a forgotten French symbolist novel, Dujardin's *Les Lauriers sont coupés* (1887)[8] – in place of the indirect free style of the *Portrait*. Moreover, the narrative of 'Proteus' and succeeding episodes is filled with the daily detritus of consciousness, random and circumstantial to a degree undreamt of in earlier fiction.

In saying that the interior monologues are composed of 'associations' or 'detritus of consciousness' we must be careful not to take refuge in psychological jargon. The monologues of Stephen and Bloom are narrated, though not always obtrusively, in the third person. They reveal 'character' in the process of internal, unspoken action. In Stephen's case at least this action may be figured as a succession of presences and voices. As in the *Portrait*, Stephen is trying to chart his way through a terrain of conflicting voices and, like Richard in *Exiles*, he goes to the beach to hear those voices:

Ineluctable modality of the visible: at least that if no more, thought through my eyes. Signatures of all things I am here to read, seaspawn and seawrack, the nearing tide, that rusty boot. Snotgreen, bluesilver, rust: coloured signs. Limits of a diaphane. But he adds: in bodies. Then he was aware of them bodies before of them coloured. How? By knocking his sconce against them, sure. Go easy. Bald he was and a millionaire, *maestro di color che sanno*.   (*U* 42)

The episode begins on a high level of abstraction, and generations of readers have puzzled over the difficulty of phrases like these. What is most significant, however, is the extent to which these phrases (Weldon Thornton's *Allusions in 'Ulysses'* lists 'Ineluctable modality of the visible', 'signatures of all things', 'Limits of the diaphane. But he adds: in bodies', 'By knocking his sconce against them', 'Bald he was and a millionaire', and '*maestro di color che sanno*'[9]) either consist of or allude to the words of others. Abstract thinking, as Stephen practises it, is largely a process of recalling and rearranging the voices of philosophical and theological tradition. For the reader, the process of reading Stephen's mind is like that of scanning a linguistic collage. Decoding the chapter, we discover not only the vividness of his

memories and physical perceptions, but the richness and diversity of
his accumulation of thoughts.

'Proteus', then, offers a cacophony of voices, quotations and
idiolects speaking through Stephen. The reader (guided intermittently
by the narrator) must select from these in order to arrive at some
coherent view of the episode. Stephen has alighted from the bus or train
he must have taken from Dalkey and Sandymount, roughly halfway
to Dublin, with a vague intention of calling on his aunt Sara Goulding
who would be likely to offer him a bed for the night. The tide is out,
giving him the opportunity for a prolonged walk on the beach. The
nearer he gets to the Gouldings', the more distasteful seems his
projected visit. He imagines his uncle's patronizing bluster and his
'consubstantial father's' jeering voice, should the news of a stay at the
Gouldings' get out (*U* 44). He hears Mulligan's voice and reads once
again his father's telegram summoning him home. He is besieged by
memories of Paris, the writers he read there, the conversations he
heard. He remembers Kevin Egan, the ageing Fenian settled in Paris,
and his son Patrice, now a 'soldier of France' (*U* 49). Kevin Egan may
have taken a paternal interest in Stephen but, steeped in Irish
nationalist mythology, he could not help the young man to find the
identity he was seeking. It was Egan who told him, 'You're your
father's son. I know the voice' (*U* 48). Is Stephen his 'consubstantial
father's' son? Much of his behaviour on 16 June 1904 – his
squandering of his pay-packet, gathering drunkenness, and roistering
with the medical students – might suggest that he is. Like his father,
he has scant regard for the other members of his own family. Stephen's
brother gets as short shrift here as in the *Portrait*: a single reference
('My whetstone. Him, then Cranly, Mulligan'), followed by the
comment that 'A brother is as easily forgotten as an umbrella' (*U* 211).
In the 'Wandering Rocks' Stephen has a poignant encounter with his
undernourished sister, who has just spent a hard-earned penny to buy
a French primer. Stephen still has money left, but does not surmount
his aversion to his family who, he feels, would drown him in their bitter
waters:

She is drowning. Agenbite. Save her. Agenbite. All against us. She will drown
me with her, eyes and hair. Lank coils of seaweed hair around me, my heart,
my soul. Salt green death.   (*U* 242)

Stephen feels remorse ('Agenbite') but does nothing about it. He is
travelling down a moral slope that will end, late in the evening, with him
prostrate in the gutter. Yet there is someone at hand to save him from

drowning there. Though Stephen effectively denies any links of obligation towards his family, he is eventually forced to admit at least temporary dependence on the charity of a near-stranger, who (as others have been) is moved by paternal affection towards him.

As yet, however, Leopold Bloom has not made his appearance and Stephen remains obsessed by fears of drowning. He is a 'hydrophobe' (*U* 593) who has come to the beach with no intention of getting wet, his last bath having taken place the previous October. Earlier in the *Portrait* we saw him on Dollymount strand thinking that 'a voice from beyond the world was calling', and 'singing passionately to the tide'. Now the sea has a sinister aspect which owes much to its Swinburnian associations with his dead mother. It is bilious, 'snotgreen', 'scrotumtightening' (*U* 11). Stephen is haunted by the wasted body of his mother, by the corpse of the drowned man that may have been washed up, and by the 'bloated carcass of a dog' (*U* 50). Towards the end of 'Proteus', however, he is calmed by the Shakespearian notion of a 'sea-change' ('Seadeath, mildest of all deaths known to man', *U* 55–6), and it is sea-change, or change after death, which has produced the 'signatures' or deposits on the beach. In Stephen's mind the flotsam of his own past jostles with the collage of philosophical abstractions and, also, with his awareness of the rich and strange objects littering the tide-edge. Bladderwrack and 'eely oarweeds', porter-bottles and worm-eaten timbers all attest to the physical reality of the 'signatures' he reads. These beach-deposits lie on the sands like solid nodes of meaning – 'epiphanies', perhaps – embedded in the cacophony of voices and impressions in Stephen's mind. For, as he reflects, 'These heavy sands are language tide and wind have silted here' (*U* 50).

Amid this alluvial bed of language Stephen is searching for something equivalent to the *objets trouvés* on the beach: meanings and a voice which may be mysteriously 'found', like the stone in *Exiles*, but which he can handle and call his own. His intellectual precocity is a trying-on of voices, a virtuoso performance in which nothing is unambiguously his. One of these borrowed voices is the flippant, self-ironizing, self-patronizing tone he uses to comment on the naivety of his younger self ('You were going to do wonders, what?' *U* 47), but also on his present actions. When struck by an idea for a poem, he says to himself – 'putting on' a voice for the purpose – 'Here. Put a pin in that chap, will you? My tablets' (*U* 53). Yet Stephen's self-irony is born of a kind of nervousness here. He is still committed to artisthood as the discipline through which he is to find an authentic identity. He is not making much progress, however. In *Ulysses* we are given some specimens of his current artistic production, which is both meagre and jejune.

The poem that Stephen writes down in 'Proteus', on a torn-off slip of Mr Deasy's Letter to the Editor, is given to us in two versions. There is first a series of phrases appearing in his interior monologue, from which the completed poem would be difficult if not impossible to reconstruct:

Behold the handmaid of the moon. In sleep the wet sign calls her hour, bids her rise. Bridebed, childbed, bed of death, ghostcandled. *Omnis caro ad te veniet.* He comes, pale vampire, through storm his eyes, his bat sails bloodying the sea, mouth to her mouth's kiss.   (*U* 53)

When he turns to his 'Tablets' to write this down the impersonal narrator takes over. His next reported thought alludes to his lack of writing paper ('That's twice I forgot to take slips from the library counter'). The finished poem, however, is quoted in the 'Aeolus' episode, at the moment when Stephen hands over Mr Deasy's letter to the *Evening Telegraph*'s editor, Myles Crawford:

> On swift sail flaming
> From storm and south
> He comes, pale vampire,
> Mouth to my mouth.   *(U* 133)

The poem is more or less plagiarized from one of Douglas Hyde's *Love Songs of Connaught* (1904) – the volume that Haines was hoping to buy.[10] Both in Hyde and in the second version of Stephen's poem, the speaker is a woman. The 'pale vampire' is Stephen's invention. What does it signify?

Stephen's subject is what might be called a Black Annunciation. The pale vampire, is, literally, the angel of death, whose kiss sucks forth the victim's soul. The phrase 'behold the handmaid of the moon' alludes to the words of the angel to Mary in the Annunciation passage in Luke. The woman is one whose hour has come and who is found out on the 'bed of death'. The poem is not only death-ridden but (unsurprisingly) it clearly refers to Stephen's mother. The 'bat sails' might suggest the clumsy contraptions of an early airman – Daedalus or Icarus – crossing the sea. Stephen's poem thus cryptically argues that he came home, vampire-like, to administer to his mother the kiss of death. The vampire-kiss and his identification with the evil angel suggest the confused emotions of hatred, remorse and eroticism Stephen feels towards his mother. The poem is a Gothic outburst, a pinhead *Dracula* which betrays an aspect of Stephen's inner chaos that is hidden beneath the stream of interior monologue and can find no other means of coming to consciousness.

Proteus, the sea-god, appears to Stephen as a formless array of voices – a multitude of mental transformations. Yet the poem Stephen writes on the beach, however minute its scope, contrives to express his deeper psychic levels. In both of the later episodes in which he figures prominently – and before he finds a spiritual affinity with Leopold Bloom – Stephen engages in further acts of (oral) literary composition. The first of these gives rise to the 'Parable of the Plums', a ribald narrative with which he entertains Myles Crawford and Professor MacHugh in 'Aeolus'. Beside the vampire poem it seems unpromising material. Stephen tells how his protagonists, two elderly 'Dublin vestals', make an outing to Nelson's Pillar and sit down at the top of the monument to eat their bag of plums. In their comfortable simplicity they spit out the plumstones through the railings and onto the street below. Here is a vignette of Irish womanhood done with an almost Swiftian disgust. Nothing quite as sordid is to be found in *Dubliners*, which the 'Parable' otherwise anticipates. The journalists who applaud its cynical misogyny would be the first to ridicule or vilify an artist who seriously offered such morsels in print for public consumption. (Dublin theatre audiences rioted, and the press applauded their actions, for much less than this.) The story is thus throwaway material (like the plumstones) but it is joined to the riddle and the poem we have already analysed by its animus against elderly women. Professor MacHugh interprets it for the reader in a broader and more prophetic sense:

– You remind me of Antisthenes, the professor said, a disciple of Gorgias, the sophist. It is said of him that none could tell if he were bitterer against others or against himself. . . . And he wrote a book in which he took away the palm of beauty from Argive Helen and handed it to poor Penelope.   (*U* 149)

If this seems an anticipation of *Ulysses* and Molly Bloom, we should remember that there is nothing in the 'Parable of the Plums', the vampire poem, or the riddle of the fox burying his grandmother to suggest a capacity for appreciating the beauty of Penelope. There is much that suggests unresolved emotions and a Swiftian, neurotic fear of the flesh. If 'Paternity may be a legal fiction' (*U* 207), femininity for Stephen is a bowl of bitter waters, a mystery that appals and disgusts him yet which he cannot stop himself from morbidly contemplating. Such is the 'agenbite' of Stephen's remorse.

Stephen's theory of Shakespeare, which he expounds in 'Scylla and Charybdis', is also misogynistic and yet expresses a slightly happier side to his personality. Stephen is fumbling in the dark towards his own artistic identity. Yet he remains confident that a great artist such as Shakespeare does possess a consistent identity which it is given to the critic to perceive (though he will, of course, in the end disown his account of that identity). The identity is that of an exile:

The note of banishment, banishment from the heart, banishment from home, sounds uninterruptedly from *The Two Gentlemen of Verona* onward till Prospero breaks his staff, buries it certain fathoms in the earth and drowns his book. It doubles itself in the middle of his life, reflects itself in another, repeats itself, protasis, epitasis, catastasis, catastrophe.   (*U* 212)

Shakespeare 'found in the world without as actual what was in the world within as possible' (*U* 213). Stephen argues that those inner possibilities of Shakespeare's selfhood were, for all the infinite variety of his creation, nonetheless limited possibilities.

Stephen's theory forms part of his own search for self-definition in two ways. If we apply his theory reflexively, it should, like Shakespeare's plays, be capable of revealing the inner characteristics of its creator. Secondly, Stephen expounds his theory in public, for the benefit of a small but select audience to whom he is one of a number of young pretenders to the title of an Irish poet. In their eyes he is clever, and worth a hearing, but not as overwhelmingly clever as he thinks he is. He is 'the only contributor to *Dana* who asks for pieces of silver' (*U* 214). Joyce shows us Stephen's inner uncertainties and the vagaries of his consciousness as well as the rather mixed impression he makes on his hearers.

Joyce's depiction of a set of minor Dublin literati – Richard Best, John Eglinton, George Russell (AE) and the Quaker librarian – is one of the most telling studies in existence of the nature of Victorian and Edwardian bookishness. Stephen's listeners span a range of opinions – from the occultism of AE to the moral gravity of the Quaker librarian – but theirs is a common literary culture, founded upon reverence for artistic 'genius' and a humanistic belief in literature as individual expression. It was this late nineteenth-century obsession with personality in literature, together with the advent of scientific scholarship, which made it the great age of Shakespeare biography. Stephen's, or his hearers', acquaintance with this branch of writing may have begun early: biographies of Shakespeare were frequently given away as school prizes in those days. The lives of Shakespeare by

Edward Dowden, George Brandes, Sidney Lee, and Frank Harris provide much of the small change of the discussion. Stephen's own involvement with Shakespeare-theory brings to mind the Shakespeariana of earlier creative writers such as Goethe, Mallarmé and Wilde. His first care is to meet his listeners on their own ground. His theory, to all appearance, is yet another piece of humanistic literary history, and he tries to emulate and outdo his predecessors by a display of biographical erudition: 'Local colour. Work in all you know' (*U* 188) he admonishes himself. If he goes too far and evokes his hearers' dissent, it is in directions well trodden by his predecessors. AE expresses the modern concern with artistic impersonality when he deprecates 'this prying into the family life of a great man' (*U* 189). John Eglinton is unimpressed by Stephen's strident assertion that 'A man of genius makes no mistakes' (*U* 190). Even as a self-parody Stephen's theory is no innovation, since Oscar Wilde had written the classic send-up of theories of Shakespeare's sonnets, 'The Portrait of Mr W.H.', fifteen years previously. As the librarian says, with unintended irony, 'Mr Mulligan, I'll be bound, has his theory too of the play and of Shakespeare' (*U* 198). What aspiring wit — it seems to be implied — has not?

It was Goethe in *Wilhelm Meister* who pioneered the romantic view of *Hamlet* as a Shakespearian self-portrait. The early twentieth century returned to this view, which was now modified by the advent of psychoanalysis. Among Joyce's contemporaries T. S. Eliot (in 'Hamlet and His Problems') and D. H. Lawrence (in *Twilight in Italy*) indulged in speculation about the psychic determinants of Hamlet's display of sexual emotion. Stephen's approach is more systematic and more pedantic than theirs. For him, not only *Hamlet* but every one of Shakespeare's plays worries away at the emotional wound of the playwright's cuckoldry and exile. Stephen's rather startling premise is that, while *Hamlet* is a work of self-revelation, it is not the prince but the murdered father whose predicament mirrors Shakespeare's own. (Tradition has it that, when *Hamlet* was put on at the Globe Theatre, Shakespeare played the part of the Ghost.) The reconstruction of the great man's family life, beginning with his seduction by Ann Hathaway who then commits adultery with his brothers and presents him with a son named Hamnet, is crucial to the whole exposition. It is a neat, if wildly fanciful, theory amounting (as Eglinton roundly tells Stephen) to a 'French triangle' (*U* 213) or rather a series of triangles. These triangles reflect the three-cornered relationships between a mother, a set of possible fathers and a son:

Mother	*Possible fathers*	*Son*
Ann Hathaway	William Shakespeare/ Edmund and Richard Shakespeare	Hamnet Shakespeare
Gertrude	Hamlet senior/Claudius	Hamlet
Penelope	Odysseus/suitors	Telemachus
Mary	Joseph/angel/God the Father	Jesus
May Dedalus	Simon Dedalus/Daedalus?	Stephen Dedalus

Stephen's interest is in the least well-defined of these relationships — that of son and possible father — and his suggestion that not only all Shakespeare's works but also the *Odyssey* and the New Testament bear out the same pattern converts this pattern into a universal myth, an eternal statement of the uncertain and hence fictive nature of paternity. It is small wonder that Buck Mulligan, who has heard this theory before, is under no illusions about Stephen's own need for a substitute father.

What, then, is Stephen's putative relationship to Shakespeare? In a sense, if Stephen is Hamlet, and Shakespeare is the Ghost, it is one of spiritual sonship. Yet Stephen aspires to a higher status, which is that of a younger brother. The Quaker librarian sums up 'those priceless pages of *Wilhelm Meister*' as 'A great poet on a great brother poet' (*U* 184). Contemplating Shakespeare's seduction by Ann Hathaway, Stephen wistfully asks himself 'And my turn? When?' (*U* 191) — the typical younger brother's question. And, of course, there is a strong implicit suggestion that Stephen's desire to repeat the pattern of experience he has fathered upon Shakespeare is indeed prophetic. Shakespeare's supposed concerns with cuckoldry and exile are precisely the concerns of *Ulysses*, as revealed in the coming-together of Stephen and Bloom.

Early in 'Telemachus' Stephen has remembered a dream in which his dead mother appeared reproachfully before him:

In a dream, silently, she had come to him, her wasted body within its loose graveclothes giving off an odour of wax and rosewood, her breath bent over him with mute secret words, a faint odour of wetted ashes.

Her glazing eyes, staring out of death, to shake and bend my soul. On me alone. The ghostcandle to light her agony. Ghostly light on the tortured face. Her hoarse loud breath rattling in horror, while all prayed on their knees. Her eyes on me to strike me down.   (*U* 16)

The dream resembles the ghostly visitations experienced by Mr Duffy in 'A Painful Case' and by the boy in 'The Sisters'. Stephen knows he should put behind him his obsession with his mother ('No, mother. Let me be and let me live', *U* 16), but he lacks the power to do so. His dream returns in a lurid, dramatized form at the climax of the 'Circe' episode. Once again he refuses his mother's demands, then panics and smashes the chandelier of the brothel with his stick. The words of defiance that he calls out in his extremity are borrowed from others. '*Non serviam*', 'I will not serve', is the phrase attributed to Lucifer in the *Portrait* (*P* 117); *Nothung* was the name of Siegfried's sword in Wagner's *Ring* (*U* 517). Stephen, drowning in the bitter waters, lashes out violently and indiscriminately; he is at a dead end.

And yet, since the beginning of the day, he has been becoming part of another man's story. The reader's first intimation of this possibility comes also in a dream, which Stephen recalls in the 'Proteus' episode:

After he woke me last night some dream or was it? Wait. Open hallway. Street of harlots. Remember. Haroun al Raschid. I am almosting it. That man led me, spoke. I was not afraid. The melon he had he held against my face. Smiled: creamfruit smell. That was the rule, said. In. Come, Red carpet spread. You will see who. (*U* 52)

Leopold Bloom also has visions of 'awned streets', fragrant Eastern fruits and 'Mrs Moll' in red slippers and turkey trunks (*U* 59, 62, 394). The source of both his and Stephen's orientalism is the children's pantomime *Turko the Terrible*. Nevertheless, the man in the 'street of harlots' is unmistakably Bloom. He invites Stephen into his home. Holding a melon (symbol of Molly with her 'melonous' rump, *U* 656?) against Stephen's face, he is at once a pimp and a man who inspires instinctive trust. Stephen remembers this dream again when Bloom crosses his path in the National Library (*U* 217). He also recalls an actual meeting with Bloom, as he hurried home to his mother's deathbed; a casual, yet deeply significant meeting:

He knows your old fellow. . . .
　Hurrying to her squalid deathlair from gay Paris on the quayside I touched his hand. The voice, new warmth, speaking. Dr Bob Kenny is attending her. The eyes that wish me well. But do not know me. (*U* 207)

Stephen's immediate response to Bloom's expression of sympathy gives us a new view of his emotional state on his return to Ireland; clearly this had no connection with the vampirism of his morbid fantasies. We can see why he is able to respond to Bloom's kindness once again, on 16 June. At the end of 'Proteus' Joyce chooses to herald this imminent new development in Stephen's life with a cryptic epiphany:

He turned his face over a shoulder, rere regardant. Moving through the air high spars of a threemaster, her sails brailed up on the crosstrees, homing, upstream, silently moving, a silent ship.   (*U* 56)

In its combination of symbolic meaning, precision of language and verisimilitude this 'purple passage' might be compared to a Pre-Raphaelite painting. The threemaster is the *Rosevean* coming 'from Bridgewater with bricks' (*U* 249). Its appearance is ironically on cue, since Stephen needs reminding that he was to meet Mulligan and Haines at 'The Ship. Half twelve' (*U* 29). The ship is also an Odyssean symbol marking the next stage in Stephen's progress. 'Homing' or returning to port, it neatly cancels out the vision of the departing airman or 'hawklike man' (*P* 169) that Stephen imagined on Dollymount beach, and the 'black arms of tall ships' (*P* 252) that lured him away at the end of the *Portrait*. The vision of the ship, in fact, marks the passing of 'Stephen Hero'. His 'lovely mumming', with its virtuoso set of manic-depressive variations around the twin poles of artistic ambition and family conflict, turns out to be the prologue to another sort of drama with a quite different protagonist.

7   Bloom and Molly: the bourgeois utopians

Mr Leopold Bloom ate with relish the inner organs of beasts and fowls. He liked thick giblet soup, nutty gizzards, a stuffed roast heart, liver slices fried with crustcumbs, fried hencod's roes. Most of all he liked grilled mutton kidneys which gave to his palate a fine tang of faintly scented urine.

Kidneys were in his mind as he moved about the kitchen softly, righting her breakfast things on the humpy tray. Gelid light and air were in the kitchen but out of doors gentle summer morning everywhere. Made him feel a bit peckish.

(U 57)

Why 'Mr' Leopold Bloom? It is a title he shares with some other characters in *Ulysses* – Mr Best, Mr Dedalus, Mr Power – and it has both social and literary resonances. Socially, it conveys seniority, respectability (however attenuated in Mr Dedalus's case) and a certain distance. In literature, too, there is a distinction to be drawn between people described as 'Mr', people identified by surname only and people known familiarly by a Christian name or nickname. From the *Pilgrim's Progress* onwards the 'Mr' had denoted middle-class status, but it had taken a distinctly downward turn in the course of the nineteenth century. By the time Joyce was writing the usual 'Mr' in fiction was a comic petty bourgeois: Mr Pickwick, Mr Pooter, Mr Polly.

Mr Polly, in Wells's novel, begins with indigestion. Mr Bloom's dignity is undermined by his taste for the 'inner organs of beasts and fowls'. The careful diction of the opening sentence implies a gulf between comic character and fastidious narrator. As the paragraph goes on, however, Bloom's culinary tastes are recounted with mounting involvement and an almost salivary excitement, leading up to the tang of 'faintly scented urine' on his palate. There is then a smooth transition from external description to inside view ('Kidneys were in his mind'), and the style adjusts itself to Bloom's horizons until we meet a colloquialism that is unmistakably his, not the narrator's:

Made him feel a bit peckish.

Bloom is established from the start as comparatively gross but wholly engaging. Soon we are immersed in his mind, overwhelmed by his minute-to-minute sensations as we see what he sees and hear what he thinks. Bloom himself is a meticulous observer of life, so that we are aware both of the quality of his mind and of the extraordinary immediacy of Joyce's representation of it.

Leopold Bloom is the literal embodiment of 'middleness' or bourgeoisdom. He belongs to the middle of the Dublin lower middle class (lower than Menton, say, but higher than Paddy Dignam or Bob Doran). He occupies the middle of *Ulysses*, between 'Telemachus' and 'Penelope', and is a vaguely androgynous character described by the 'Cyclops' narrator as 'one of those mixed middlings' (*U* 336). In Lenehan's more charitable eyes he is a 'cultured allroundman', 'not one of your common or garden' (*U* 234). Thus he is midway between the artist (Stephen) and the common or garden (the cast of characters inherited from *Dubliners*?). Other extremes that he avoids are those of Unionist and Nationalist, Protestant and Catholic, and Christian and Jew. His job of advertising canvasser makes him a professional middleman. More poignantly, he represents the middle generation of the male line in a family in which both his father, Rudolph Virag, and his son, Rudy Bloom, have reached untimely deaths.

But if Bloom is the epitome of middle-class man, his portrayal goes far beyond the mixture of humour and sentimentality with which previous novelists had approached such a figure. Nor is he seen with Flaubertian aloofness. For all his cant phrases and secondhand notions, Bloom is far more than a collection of platitudes or walking *Dictionary of Received Ideas*. He is much more intimately and affectionately drawn than, say, Homais the chemist in *Madame Bovary*. Though his mind is cluttered with the small change of advertising, journalism, and modern print culture, he has the resourcefulness to put his own imprint on this debris of consciousness. Bloom gains in stature the moment he is compared with other characters in *Ulysses*. Among those few who are permitted interior monologues, the most startling contrast is with Father Conmee in 'Wandering Rocks' – a character who truly walks around in blinkers. Bloom is open to impersonal ideas and objective enthusiasms, where Molly on the whole is far more self-absorbed. Bloom's solitude is a little pathetic, and his prudence may be mocked at; yet it is the privacy and depth of his character which continues to fascinate the reader. No artist has paid a greater tribute to bourgeois man than did Joyce in the creation of Bloom.

If we seek a more precise definition of his social status we may be in

difficulties. By collating the mass of references to his past it is possible
to reconstruct a Bloomian biography, as John Henry Raleigh has
done.[1] From this it is clear he has held a number of jobs, working
mostly as a salesman. He has probably only worked for the *Freeman*
for a year or two. Once, in 1895, he was on the verge of bankruptcy.
His father, who put everything into the Queen's Hotel at Ennis, had
also ruined himself. The Blooms seem quite comfortably off in June
1904 and have money to spare on small luxuries. Bloom has a portfolio
of investments including £900 in Canadian government stocks. Just
what his prospects are it is impossible to say. His previous employment
record does not point to a long stay at the *Freeman*, and there is some
doubt about his earning ability. Nosey Flynn's opinion that 'He doesn't
buy cream on the ads he picks up' (*U* 177) seems representative, and
it is certainly borne out by Molly's account:

he ought to chuck that Freeman with the paltry few shillings he knocks out of
it and go into an office or something where hed get regular pay or a bank where
they could put him up on a throne to count the money all the day of course he
prefers plottering about the house so you cant stir with him any side whats your
programme today . . . pretending to be mooching about for advertisements
when he could have been in Mr Cuffes   (*U* 673)

Bloom works on commission and, during the morning, draws £1-7-6
that is due to him. He thinks he may make five guineas (not a bad sum
for 1904) out of Alexander Keyes's ad (*U* 259). The frequency of such
earnings depends on the weight we attach to Molly's 'paltry few
shillings'. Nor can her work as a professional soprano contribute more
than the occasional windfall to the household. Her last concert was in
May 1903 and her forthcoming tour with Blazes Boylan may or may
not turn out well.

Very occasionally we see Bloom thinking businesslike thoughts,
doing sums, working out costs, calculating potential profit and loss.
But Joyce's archetypal petty bourgeois is neither a moneygrubber nor
a frightened little clerk. Rather, like Wells's Mr Polly and Dickens's
Mr Wemmick, he is a dreamer. He enjoys the 'art of advertisement',
and is aware of its 'infinite possibilities hitherto unexploited' (*U* 604).
His plans for Stephen include, as a matter of course, the possibility of
marketing his work. Molly once thought her husband was a 'poet like
Byron', but now considers there is 'not an ounce of it in his
composition' (*U* 696). The truth is between these two extremes. Bloom
fantasizes about being a gentleman pursuing literary work and strongly
envies Mr Philip Beaufoy, the clubman and author of prize stories.

Without being a gentleman, however, he seems to have discovered the secret of leisure. His canvassing for ads permits him a good deal of idling. He has a number of visionary schemes for making money, and a very much more detailed idea (as we shall see) of the comforts and satisfactions he could buy with it. But he is also deeply aware of his present comforts and satisfactions, such as they are. His character and whole mode of consciousness exemplify the capacity for detachment and wonder celebrated in W. H. Davies's well-known verses:

> What is this life, if full of care,
> We have no time to stand and stare? –

('Leisure')

His programme for 16 June 1904 is a particularly leisurely one. He goes out to buy his kidney long after Stephen and Mulligan have breakfasted and after the school day (he passes a school on the way to the pork-butcher's) has begun. He visits the public baths and attends a funeral before going to business. During the afternoon he pauses at a secondhand bookstall to choose an erotic novel for Molly. His working day is over at 4 p.m., when he dines at the Ormond Restaurant. Though the day of a funeral is bound to be special there is no evidence that Wednesday 15th or Friday 17th would have seen him working much harder. (If indeed he has ordered breakfast in bed on the Friday, he will probably end up, after his late night, 'plottering about the house'.) The great attraction of advertisement canvassing for him is the freedom to move around and to arrange his own timetable. Despite Molly's wishes he will go a long way to avoid an office job with fixed wages and regular hours. His attendance at Dignam's funeral is part and parcel of his freedom. He and Dignam were, at most, very occasional companions, like Dignam and Charlie M'Coy (whose job at the morgue keeps him too busy to go to the funeral). A few months previously, Bloom has attended Mrs Sinico's funeral. Unlike some of his busier colleagues he always has the time, as well as the inclination, to pay his last respects to an acquaintance. His daytime obligations are as much social (going out to Sandymount to meet Mrs Dignam and discuss her life insurance; doing errands for Molly) as they are commercial. And many of his contacts have come about not through his own profession, but through his wife's.

Bloom is a literary character not a historical person, and Joyce's vagueness about his exact social position has the effect of broadening his appeal and perhaps even of making him more plausible. The range of his curiosity and the leisurely pace of his day give the impression of someone who is simultaneously at work and enjoying an unearned 'surplus value'. In part this is the consequence of his time of life. He has reached maturity, his health is good, his daughter has left home for the first time and alcoholism, which has claimed so many of his contemporaries including Paddy Dignam, has passed him by. Without any pressing financial worries, and with a job that makes no exorbitant demands upon him, Bloom is mentally free. He is free to indulge his irrepressible curiosity and to take a long view of his life, including its more sombre aspects.

'Calypso' begins with Bloom's culinary tastes and the grosser side of his nature. But we soon see him in a more intellectual light: explaining Greek philosophy to his wife whilst, downstairs, his kidney is burning. The word 'metempsychosis' (*U* 66) belongs to mythology and comparative religion and it is typical of Bloom that he knows that it means the transmigration of souls. 'Metempsychosis' is one of the innumerable reminders of death which beset Bloom − like Stephen − throughout the morning. Dignam's funeral is, no doubt, weighing on his thoughts, but then he is a man who makes a point of attending funerals. On the way to the cemetery he scans the newspaper obituary columns as if he thought of planning his next visit (*U* 93). Bloom's interest in exploring every aspect of the topic of death should not obscure the basic materialism of his outlook. Virginia Woolf once claimed that the episode in the cemetery failed 'because of the comparative poverty of the writer's mind'[2]. On the contrary, the poetry of materialism is present in these opening chapters of Bloomsday with a richness not seen in literature before or since.

Bloom has heard of the doctrines of spiritualism but feels no temperamental affinity for them. Stephen, we know, has seen his mother's ghost in a dream. He is prone to speculations like that about the mystic telephone line made up of umbilical cords:

The cords of all link back, strandentwining cable of all flesh. That is why mystic monks. Will you be as gods? Gaze in your omphalos. Hell. Kinch here. Put me on to Edenville. Aleph, alpha: nought, nought, one.   (*U* 43)

In one of its aspects *Ulysses*, like Beddoes's play, could have been called *Death's Jest-Book*. As an almanac of curious speculations about death and birth it was unrivalled, in 'mainstream' literature, since the seventeenth century. But where Stephen is still hag-ridden by the doctrine of the immortal soul, Bloom returns again and again to death's picturesque physical manifestations. Reverence for the dead is something that he plainly feels, but his reaction to the Christian commonplaces of the funeral is startling in its vehemence:

Mr Kernan said with solemnity:
   – *I am the resurrection and the life.* That touches a man's inmost heart.
   – It does, Mr Bloom said.
Your heart perhaps but what price the fellow in the six feet by two with his toes to the daisies? No touching that. Seat of the affections. Broken heart. A pump after all, pumping thousands of gallons of blood every day. One fine day it gets bunged up and there you are. Lots of them lying around here: lungs, hearts, livers. Old rusty pumps: damn the thing else. The resurrection and the life. Once you are dead you are dead. That last day idea. Knocking them all up out of their graves. Come forth, Lazarus! And he came fifth and lost the job.   (*U* 107)

'Old rusty pumps': Bloom's attitude to death is Buck Mulligan's, without the medical student's cynicism. Naturally, his favourite Shakespearian scene is the gravediggers' in *Hamlet*: that 'shows the profound knowledge of the human heart' (*U* 111). (We might remember that he was partial not only to kidneys but to 'stuffed roast heart', *U* 57.) Bloom's is a biological view of life, beginning with conception and midwifery ('Glad to see us go we give them such trouble coming', *U* 89) and ending with corpsegas, manure, and the breeding of maggots. Though his materialism is stiffened by an awareness of post-Darwinian science, in essence it is as old as the occupations of butcher and undertaker. He displays a certain affinity with the members of both professions: Dlugacz, the pork-butcher and a fellow Jew, Corny Kelleher who helps bail out Stephen in Nighttown, and John O'Connell, the 'decent fellow' (*U* 109) who is in charge of the cemetery.

It is on his trip to the pork-butcher's that we become aware of Bloom's tendency to see all flesh as meat. His vaguely lustful thoughts about the next-door girl who is buying sausages are mixed in with thoughts of the cattle-market. He admires her 'moving hams' and imagines her being cuddled by an offduty policeman – 'Prime sausage' (*U* 62). In 'Hades' he reflects that a corpse is 'meat gone bad' (*U* 116) and that butchers 'get like raw beefsteaks' as a result of their exposure to the bad gas of carcasses (*U* 105). In 'Lestrygonians' he imagines watching the journey of a pin, swallowed by mistake, through the human intestines. 'But the poor buffer would have to stand all the time with his inside entrails on show. Science' (*U* 179). For Bloom, part child of the scientific age and part traditional connoisseur of the grotesque, life seems to be a perpetual exhibition of the entrails.

His biological vision of life is the key to several facets of his character. First, there is his no-nonsense anticlericalism. 'The resurrection and the life. Once you are dead you are dead'. In 'Lotos-Eaters' he wanders idly into a church where holy communion is being celebrated. 'Rum idea: eating bits of a corpse why cannibals cotton to it' (*U* 82), he reflects. The same disinterested tone is apparent when he catches sight of a rat in the cemetery. 'One of those chaps would make short work of a fellow' (*U* 116). Nevertheless he is well aware of a connection between death and sex – 'Love among the tombstones. . . Spice of pleasure' (*U* 110) – and there is a certain necrophiliac interest in his repeated speculations. His triumph in 'Hades', however, is to combine scientific curiosity and sexual prurience with a firmly-expressed humanist attitude. He ends with a famous passage rejecting the morbidity and spiritualism we have earlier identified with Stephen:

I do not like that other world she wrote. No more do I. Plenty to see and hear and feel yet. Feel live warm beings near you. Let them sleep in their maggoty beds. They are not going to get me this innings. Warm beds: warm fullblooded life.   (*U* 116–17)

This takes its strength not only from the earlier presence of Molly in bed but from Bloom's remarkable ability, as he walks round the cemetery, to see through the monuments to the people they commemorate. The pious messages carved on gravestones should, he thinks, be replaced by something more lively:

Who passed away. Who departed this life. As if they did it of their own accord. Got the shove, all of them. Who kicked the bucket. More interesting if they told you what they were. So and so, wheelwright. I travelled for cork lino. I paid five shillings in the pound. Or a woman's with her saucepan. I cooked good Irish stew.   (*U* 115)

He thinks confusedly of Gray's *Elegy*, 'that poem of whose is it Wordsworth or Thomas Campbell', but this is a superb anticlerical riposte to the Christian argument of Wordsworth's 'Essay on Epitaphs'. Unpretentious and godless as it is, Bloom's way of honouring the dead points not to the nullity of the flesh but to the richness and diversity of human occupations.

His commitment to 'warm fullblooded life' is reached in defiance of the failures in his own life and, in particular, it is a rejection of suicide. He has come to terms with his father's suicide with the help of his generalized view of the human condition. The fantasy of repeating his father's act is briefly present in 'Sirens' (*U* 468), and in 'Ithaca' it is alleged that he fears 'The committal of homicide or suicide during sleep by an aberration of the light of reason' (*U* 641). But Bloom is content with his annual pilgrimage to his father's grave and his daytime thoughts, unlike Stephen's, are not dominated by his bereavement. His materialism is a robust and resilient doctrine.

Stephen has said that 'History is a nightmare from which I am trying to awake'. Bloom also connects his personal misfortunes with a historical tragedy, which is that of Israel rather than Ireland. Palestine, he thinks in a moment of sudden and shocking depression as he walks back from the pork-butcher's, is 'the grey sunken cunt of the world' (*U* 63). Immediately he tries to imagine a series of simple bodily expedients to help banish nightmarish thoughts like this: breakfast, Sandow's exercises and physical contact ('Be near her ample bedwarmed flesh', *U* 63). This moment reveals one of the underlying motivations for Bloom's constant recourse to biological thinking. It is because, like Stephen, he is afraid of history. He cannot 'face' history in the way that, for example, Marxists demand because for him it means personal failure (he bears the shame of his father's suicide, he has no son) and racial impotence. His biological vision of life, robust as it is, is something of a half-truth permitting him to continue to enjoy the sensation of freedom.

Bloom's Jewishness has been the subject of some agonized critical debate. However satisfying at the symbolic level, does Joyce, in this extraordinarily detailed characterization, show a convincing grasp of the nature of Jewish identity? Robert M. Adams has argued that he does not.[3] But Bloom is not circumcized, he has had only distant contacts with Judaism, and, like many others of his race in the late nineteenth century, he has adopted a secular materialism which leads him to identify with mankind in general rather than with any historical or ethnic grouping. Jewishness is something of which he is only intermittently conscious. His passing interest in the Palestinian planter's company, Agendath Netaim (for example), is more a matter of colonial investment than of incipient Zionism. Bloom is what H. G. Wells would have called a world citizen, a rationalistic believer in common humanity who – living in insurrectionary Ireland – calls for a non-violent settlement of world problems and denies that a nation is more than 'the same people living in the same place' (*U* 329). The future he looks forward to is a peaceful and prosperous one in which Western bourgeois civilization has been tempered with a mild dose of international socialism.

Bloom shares to the full the modern, materialistic understanding of history which grew up in opposition to Judaeo-Christian sacred history. It is a comparative history of human thought and also of the ways men have satisfied their basic physical needs such as food and shelter. This history is present in his mind not as a universal vision but as a bewildering array of fragments of that vision – pieces of 'general knowledge', half-digested details about the world's mass of cultures and civilizations, isolated facts. His share of universal knowledge is centred on the Mediterranean, though it makes valiant attempts to encompass the rest of the world. (His bookshelves contain volumes on the Russo-Turkish war, China, and Madagascar.) Its principal theme is the building, population, and destruction of cities.

Bloom's general knowledge is perpetually exhibited in his interior monologues. He has learnt what he knows in the 'university of life' (*U* 585) supplemented by a haphazard collection of reference-works and – much more importantly – by the daily newspaper. The newspaper indeed functions in *Ulysses* like a new form of scripture – 'give us this day our daily press' (*U* 567). Journalism is as comprehensive and varied as scripture, and it is followed as closely by its adherents. Each makes his own selection from its contents – whether it be the obituaries or the racing page – and in the 'Aeolus' episode newspaper style infects the writing of *Ulysses* itself. Newspaper culture, in the nineteenth century, had been deplored by educationalists such as Newman and Mill, who saw it as an agent of spiritual disintegration. Bloom if the charge holds good, is unquestionably a disintegrated spirit. He is a print addict who cannot perform such routine actions as going to the lavatory or walking home from the butcher's without the stimulus of something to read. The newspapers he buys, as he tells Bantam Lyons, are newspapers he was 'just going to throw . . . away' (*U* 87). His world-picture is thus the haphazard accumulation of what he saves from his throwaways.

One of the passages in which Bloom displays his sense of history most effectively is the following, from 'Lestrygonians':

His smile faded as he walked, a heavy cloud hiding the sun slowly, shadowing Trinity's surly front. Trams passed one another, ingoing, outgoing, clanging. Useless words. Things go on same; day after day: squads of police marching out, back: trams in, out. Those two loonies mooching about. Dignam carted off. Mina Purefoy swollen belly on a bed groaning to have a child tugged out of her. One born every second somewhere. Other dying every second. Since I fed the birds five minutes. Three hundred kicked the bucket. Other three hundred born, washing the blood off, all are washed in the blood of the lamb, bawling maaaaaa.

Cityful passing away, other cityful coming, passing away too: other coming on, passing on. Houses, lines of houses, streets, miles of pavements, piledup bricks, stones. Changing hands. This owner, that. Landlord never dies they say. Other steps into his shoes when he gets his notice to quit. They buy the place up with gold and still they have all the gold. Swindle in it somewhere. Piled up in cities, worn away age after age. Pyramids in sand. Built on bread and onions. Slaves. Chinese wall. Babylon. Big stones left. Round towers. Rest rubble, sprawling suburbs, jerrybuilt, Kerwan's mushroom houses, built of breeze. Shelter for the night.   (*U* 164)

He has the urge to generalize, persistently if somewhat feebly, but his generalizations invariably sink back into the morass of particular scraps and snatches of fact out of which they came. It is the sheer fluency and unpredictability of the facts at his command which makes a passage like this memorable. The 'Useless words' at the beginning of the paragraph represent a dismissal of politics; he has just been recalling the phraseology of Home Rule debates. A gesture of impotent resignation ('Things go on same; day after day') leads him to the consolations of universal biology and universal history. As so often he interprets society not as a theatre of historical decisions but of natural processes: birth and death; trams and 'squads of police'. The reality of the city lies in its houses, while its people are statistics condemned to the sterile opposition of landlord and tenant. Bloom is resolutely on the side of the tenant and he comes as close as he will ever do to a Marxist vision when he finds that there is a 'Swindle in it somewhere' – though he cannot say where. Like some of Dickens's characters, he is capable of social resentments, but not of social analysis. Far from identifying class as an abstract relationship, he goes straight on with his litany of half-remembered facts: 'Slaves. Chinese wall. Babylon'. History is a series of disconnected snapshots rather than thoughts.

Bloom has certain literary aspirations, but – like Mr Deasy, who composes a letter to the editor, and like Gerty MacDowell who has copied a poem out of 'the newspaper she found one evening round the potherbs' (*U* 361) – his literary horizons are circumscribed by journalism. During the day he is looking for a subject for a 'prize titbit' story like 'Matcham's Masterstroke'. He plays with the idea of '*The Mystery Man on the Beach*' (*U* 373) and, later, with '*My Experiences, let us say, in a Cabman's Shelter*' (*U* 567). He once published a letter in the *Irish Cyclist*. Another project, that of writing down Molly's remarks as she was dressing, involved the reporter's device of making notes on his shirt-cuff (*U* 71). (Molly returns the compliment here: 'if I only could remember the one half of the things and write a book out of it the works of Master Poldy' (*U* 675). Each of the Blooms regards the other as a literary 'character'.) Bloom's business day is partly spent in designing an advertisement. He engages in another literary activity, however, which has nothing to do with journalism. This is his clandestine correspondence with Martha Clifford, for which he has adopted the expressive pen-name of Henry Flower. The flirtatious letters to Martha represent a profound evasion of Bloom's actual problems. But then his whole mode of consciousness may be regarded from one point of view as a form of escapism.[4]

His biological vision helps to avert his eyes from historical and personal failure. Similarly, his incessant curiosity serves as a distraction, a way of banishing morbid and suicidal thoughts. General knowledge and universal history are a satisfying replacement for certain items of particular knowledge, such as his son's death and his father's suicide. During the day we see Bloom trying to soften the impact of a new development which might have been equally upsetting to his emotional balance: the knowledge of his wife's adultery.

From the moment he takes the post up to Molly ('Bold hand. Mrs Marion.' *U* 63), his day is comically full of occasions when it is necessary to avoid Blazes Boylan. Joyce rather cruelly makes their paths cross several times before the hour of Molly's assignation. There is no course of direct action, it seems, which can get rid of the threat of Boylan. It is, in part, his own behaviour that has driven Molly to take a lover. His habits of passive acceptance and mental escapism are, in many ways, limitations in Bloom's character. Yet when applied to his marital difficulties (given the stage these have now reached) they allow him to take the most sensible course, and to find comfort even in humiliation. For the reader it is a sad and amusing spectacle:

If he . . .
O!
Eh?
No . . . No.
No, no. I don't believe it. He wouldn't surely?
No, no.
Mr Bloom moved forward raising his troubled eyes. Think no more about that. After one. Timeball on the ballast office is down. Dunsink time. Fascinating little book that is of sir Robert Ball's. Parallax. I never exactly understood. There's a priest. Could ask him. Par it's Greek: parallel, parallax. Met him pikehoses she called it till I told her about the transmigration. O rocks!
Mr Bloom smiled O rocks at two windows of the ballast office. She's right after all. Only big words for ordinary things on account of the sound. She's

not exactly witty. Can be rude too. Blurt out what I was thinking. Still I don't know. She used to say Ben Dollard had a base barreltone voice. He has legs like barrels and you'd think he was singing into a barrel. Now, isn't that wit?

(*U* 153–4)

'If he' refers to the possibility that Boylan might give Molly a dose of venereal disease. The usually garrulous Bloom hints at this thought but, as Joyce indicates, he is successful in stifling it at birth. 'Think no more about that' he tells himself, and clutches zealously at the first general-knowledge item that comes his way. The theme of parallax has recently been described by Marilyn French and Hugh Kenner as one of the symbolic keys to *Ulysses*. French goes so far as to say that 'the term could have served as a title for this novel'.[5] This is its first appearance. Yet what is the thought of Sir Robert Ball's 'fascinating little book' but a desperate expedient to avert Bloom's mind from a subject which it would be torture to dwell upon? 'Parallax' leads to 'metempsychosis' and the bedroom conversation in which Molly showed a degree of respect for Bloom and his knowledge. In the remaining paragraph he labours to construct a very different Molly from the one who may be sullied by contact with Boylan. Now it is her wit, not her infidelity that he manages to focus upon.

Bloom's whole 'stream of consciousness', not merely his interest in parallax, is a demonstration of the inner resources he has built up to deal with life's disappointments. Even at his most weary and depressed he continues to make a positive adaptation to new circumstances:

I too, last my race. Milly young student. Well, my fault perhaps. No son. Rudy. Too late now. Or if not? If not? If still?
He bore no hate.
Hate. Love. Those are names. Rudy. Soon I am old.   (*U* 283–4)

'He bore no hate'; this at the moment when Molly and Boylan are probably meeting. Bloom indeed takes on new energy once the moment of assignation has come. His argument with the Citizen in Barney Kiernan's, his kindness towards Stephen and the attraction he exerts over Gerty MacDowell may not be heroic deeds, but they show something less than total passivity. The first two acts, especially, belie his normal reputation for caution and prudence. We cannot believe that he often gets involved in pub arguments,[6] and his late arrival at 7 Eccles Street with Stephen in tow is clearly unprecedented. In 'Cyclops' Bloom is the victim not of a lack of courage but of a lack of eloquence. Steeped in print culture, he has failed to acquire the gift of the gab so prized by his fellow-Dubliners. He has bored the Citizen and his cronies with information on various topics long before he invites their ridicule by advocating pacifism. Earlier he admired Simon Dedalus's 'amusing expressions' (*U* 105); he himself possesses arguments in plenty, but not the rhetoric – the voice – which would command the others' attention. His definition of a nation (quoted above) carries rational demystification to the point of absurdity. And it is hardly wise to speak of 'love' to this chauvinistic company:

> – But it's no use, says he. Force, hatred, history, all that. That's not life for men and women, insult and hatred. And everybody knows that it's the very opposite of that that is really life.
> – What? says Alf.
> – Love, says Bloom. I mean the opposite of hatred.   (*U* 331)

Naturally, as soon as he has gone, his manhood is impugned in the crudest way:

> – Do you call that a man? says the citizen.
> – I wonder did he ever put it out of sight, says Joe.
> – Well, there were two children born anyhow, says Jack Power.
> – And who does he suspect? says the citizen.   (*U* 336)

Bloom's defeat, in the world of the pub, is complete; yet strangely his floundering performance turns to eloquence on the printed page. Few remarks of his have been more quoted than his stubborn rejection of 'Force, hatred, history, all that', and none seems better calculated to confer on him a posthumous (if narrowly literary) heroism.

In Barney Kiernan's Bloom confronts the rhetoricians of Irish nationalism with a bald assertion of the virtues of charity and reason. He has already displayed these virtues in his attitude to Boylan and in a number of small acts of kindness (the beneficiaries include a blind man, a lunatic, a widow, and a woman in childbirth). Later on he will take Stephen home in 'orthodox Samaritan fashion' (*U* 533). But unlike the Samaritan he has actively pursued Stephen into Nighttown, so that his interest in him expresses much more than simple good nature. He feels an onrush of paternal affection and also the dawning of a plan of campaign. Just as Rudy's death began the dissolution of the Blooms' marital ties, so Stephen's presence in the household would somehow help restore those ties. The vision of Rudy in his Eton suit which is given to Bloom at the end of 'Circe' is, however, a romantic absurdity; and many of his other dreams and aspirations are mocked in the same episode. The whole basis of his efforts to come to terms with his cuckoldry is undermined by the masochistic scenes which suggest that he actively enjoys sexual humiliation. On the other hand, these Circean transformations are played off against the extended Saturnalian fantasy in which he wins civic recognition and becomes an absolute ruler. In his capacity as carnival king Bloom unfolds a utopian romance or vision of the 'new Bloomusalem' (*U* 459). Now at last he is a crowd-pulling orator whose speeches are peppered with the socialist and freethinking rhetoric of his day: 'New worlds for old' (the title of a 1908 book of Wells's advocating Fabian socialism), 'Free money, free love and a free lay church in a free lay state' (*U* 462). The new Bloomusalem is a burlesque of the classical utopian city: '*a colossal edifice, with crystal roof, built in the shape of a huge pork kidney*' (*U* 459). In case we should simply dismiss this vision of a Kidney Palace we read in the soberer mood of the 'Ithaca' episode of his 'desire to amend many social conditions, the product of inequality and avarice and international animosity' (*U* 617). A revolution, he believes, 'must come on the due instalments plan' (*U* 564) – another endorsement of Fabian socialism. He makes 'Utopian' plans for Stephen Dedalus's future (*U* 579).

'Utopian', in Joyce's time, was often used as a synonym for unattainable. Bloom's study of astronomy leads him to view the cosmos as a utopia (*U* 622). He is himself in more than one sense a utopian character. His political utopianism is no doubt suspect, since it is revealed at the height of a Carnival of Misrule. But he has a genuine yearning for social regeneration and, together with that, a more substantial and selfish vision of a personal utopia, to which Joyce gives the name of Flowerville. Perhaps the chief significance of both these utopian projects is that they help to stave off thoughts of despair.

Flowerville is a 'thatched bungalowshaped 2 storey dwellinghouse of southerly aspect', standing in '5 or 6 acres of its own ground' (*U* 633). Described as Bloom's 'ultimate ambition', the house and its contents are exhaustively inventoried in the 'Ithaca' episode. If the new Bloomusalem was ultra-socialist, Flowerville is a thoroughly bourgeois paradise. It is a self-contained heaven, stocked by Bloom in such a way as to provide a complete range of satisfactions from gentleman-farming to the 'lecture of unexpurgated exotic erotic masterpieces' (*U* 636). Here, Robinson Crusoe-like, Bloom would be surrounded by the appurtenances of the country gentleman, including a crest and coat of arms. He would have attained the magistracy at last, and his name would appear from time to time in the court circular ('Mr and Mrs

Leopold Bloom have left Kingstown for England', *U* 637).

The architecture of Flowerville is a weird confusion of styles. The actual English houses of the period from 1870 to 1910 − the great period of middle-class domestic architecture − have been described as aspiring to the condition of 'dream houses', 'dreams of a world of lost perfection, which even as they are dreamt the dreamer knows is of a future that is not to be'.[7] Flowerville, however, is a dream house in the double sense that Bloom will never be able to afford it and that, even if he were, no architect would consent to build it. A mixture of bungalow, thatched cottage, town house and country mansion, with ivy-covered porch, 'stucco front with gilt tracery at eaves and gable' and 'balcony with stone pillar parapet', it represents yet another instance in *Ulysses* of the aesthetics of the grotesque.

The fact that Bloom of Flowerville is pictured as an Anglo-Irishman is particularly ironic. Joyce was writing the 'Ithaca' chapter shortly after Yeats, in 'Nineteen Hundred and Nineteen', had lamented the passing of the constitutional ideals which sustained British rule in Ireland:

We too had many pretty toys when young:
A law indifferent to blame or praise,
To bribe or threat; . . .
O what fine thought we had because we thought
That the worst rogues and rascals had died out.

Bloom, like an eighteenth-century country gentleman, dreams of 'ameliorating the soil, multiplying wisdom, achieving longevity' (*U* 636) and administering British justice to the local malefactors. Such a dream may have persisted in 1904; when *Ulysses* appeared in 1922 Ireland was partitioned and ravaged by the Troubles, with the country retreat no more than a nostalgic memory.

It would be wrong, however, to judge Flowerville simply as a private fantasy. It is no accident that Bloom, its designer, is an advertisement canvasser and that the inventory of the house and its grounds resembles an estate agent's brochure. Wondering how he could raise the mortgage on such a house, Bloom meditates a dazzling variety of capitalist schemes, all of them far beyond his slender entrepreneurial talents. It is a safe bet that were he actually to possess Flowerville he would be unhappy, out of place, and bewildered in it. The dream house is a deeply satisfying utopian fantasy in the genre of the 'lifestyles' sold by the modern advertising industry. Here is a prophetic example of advertising's 'infinite possibilities hitherto unexploited' (*U* 604).

Flowerville anticipates the era of the glossy magazine and makes an incomparably greater appeal to narcissism and 'self-image' than do the purely functional advertisements with which Bloom is concerned in his professional life. One index of this narcissism is that the family, which normally means so much to Bloom, has disappeared from sight. 'Mrs Leopold Bloom' is now merely a name in the court circular and (presumably) an occupant of the lady's hammock. The only other living member of the household he envisages is the 'fingertame parrot (expurgated language)' (*U* 634).

Yet Bloom as magistrate plans to uphold the law not only against 'all perpetrators of international animosities' but against 'all menial molestors of domestic conviviality, all recalcitrant violators of domestic connubiality' (*U* 637). This is a clear signal that Flowerville, the fantasy retreat, represents a utopian opposite to the actual conditions of his life. His whole day has been spent coming to terms with a violation of his own connubiality. His response, as we have seen, is to seek refuge in the consolations of privacy. Such consolations include his masturbation, his clandestine correspondence with Martha Clifford, and even the bath that he anticipates so vividly at the end of 'Lotos-Eaters'. His constant, free-ranging mental activity is another form of consoling self-therapy. And yet it is this mental activity, with its serendipity and freedom from obsession, which makes the presentation of Bloom as Everyman possible.

Bloom is not only a highly individualized creation but the first embodiment of Joyce's encyclopaedic ambitions. There is a clear continuity between the fragments of world history and universal knowledge embedded in Bloom's mind, and the encyclopaedism of *Finnegans Wake*. The difference is that Bloom is, by and large, a fictional character in the conventional sense; HCE, the Everyman figure in *Finnegans Wake*, is not. Joyce's particular triumph in *Ulysses* rests to a very considerable extent on the profound fit between Bloom's personality and his literary role as the vehicle of Joycean universalism. Joyce would not attempt this again; HCE has no personality in the accepted sense. In this he is closer to the conception of universal man than Bloom could ever be.

That Bloom is Everyman is, in the end, a magnificent paradox. He began as 'Mr' Bloom, the gross petty bourgeois, but we soon come to know him as a dreamer, an evader, a utopian. Again (with Flowerville still in mind) some lines of Yeats provide an ironic counterpoint:

O what if levelled lawns and gravelled ways
Where slippered Contemplation finds his ease . . .
But take our greatness with our violence?

('Ancestral Houses')

Bloom's ideal is one of slippered contemplation and (unlike HCE) he
lacks both greatness and violence. He is the expression, on Joyce's part,
of a deep and courageous rejection of the tarnished heroic ideals of
Irish life (and of politico-military heroism everywhere). But however
attractive we find his humility, open-mindedness, and pacifism, it is
clear that the whole of life is too much to be represented by any such
personality or set of attitudes. Most writers, faced by this dilemma,
would abandon the aim of creating an Everyman figure to represent
the whole of life. Joyce, on the contrary, chose after *Ulysses* to
abandon the notion of individual personality in literature. He had in
mind the first, tentative steps towards such an abandonment when he
showed Bloom falling asleep and Molly beginning her monologue.

Joyce's portrayal of Bloom is firmly grounded in the modes of
realism. Our sense of his mythic and universal functions remains
subordinate to his realistic presence. In Molly Joyce spoke of producing
a more overtly mythical figure. She was to represent the earth-goddess
Gea-Tellus, 'perfectly sane full amoral fertilisable untrustworthy
engaging shrewd limited prudent indifferent *Weib*' (*SL* 285). The
notion that Molly represents the essence of femaleness has been a
popular one. C. G. Jung praised the 'Penelope' chapter, in a letter to
Joyce, as 'a string of veritable psychological peaches. I suppose the
devil's grandmother knows so much about the real psychology of a
woman, I didn't'.[8] Jung is speaking as a psychoanalyst but his words
are nevertheless symptomatic of an attitude towards Molly which today
arouses considerable unease. Putting Auerbach and Jung together it
would seem that, whereas the Everyman theme demands a synthesis of
universal cultural history, Everywoman is simply a problem in
psychology! (Nora, Joyce's wife, said of her husband that 'He knows
nothing at all about women',[9] but she never read his books and so this
is not a comment on the literary evidence.) What may be said is that
Molly is more obviously a utopian conception, or ideal type, than
Bloom is; that the ideal was conceived as a deliberate contrast to Bloom
– her monologue, Joyce said, was the 'indispensable countersign to
Bloom's passport to eternity' (*SL* 278); and that the contrast is loaded
with preconceptions about gender. Molly is a splendidly vital
embodiment of some easily recognizable superstitions about women.

To Bloom, who is sexually as well as morally passive, the woman is pre-eminently the initiator of life. He remembers the morning of Rudy's conception when Molly was aroused by the sight of a pair of dogs copulating in the street. 'Give us a touch, Poldy. God, I'm dying for it. How life begins' (*U* 90), he reflects. It is how Life begins, not how a particular life began. Bloom's whimsical detachment as he recalls such moments is not the sort of thing we would expect from Molly. Unlike Bloom, with his sense of the impersonal past and the possible future, Molly's monologue is uninterruptedly personal and her ideas of the future hardly extend beyond the middle of next week.

Her monologue, though divided into eight long paragraphs, is otherwise unpunctuated. This comic device has the advantage of sharply distinguishing her style of thought from those of Bloom and Stephen. Moreover, it is the culmination of a loosening and lengthening of the sentence which may be seen throughout the later episodes. The lack of punctuation conveys a breathless effect but rarely impedes understanding. Its most drastic consequences are felt on the third-person pronoun. Molly's ubiquitous 'he' is frequently ambiguous at first reading; the individual men to whom it refers thus tend to merge into a single Other who is at once antagonist and sexual partner. Her 'I', on the other hand, is conspicuously capitalized (in a text without sentence-breaks). The capitalized 'I' surveying her anonymous 'hes' is indeed like a goddess on a pedestal.

Molly, beside Bloom and Stephen, is an unselfconscious egotist. She has a vigorous but very restricted imagination which hardly ever strays outside her own immediate concerns. She is capable of picturing events on the other side of the world ('I suppose theyre just getting up in China now combing out their pigtails for the day', *U* 702), and of identification with another's point of view ('imagine Im him', *U* 661). But in both cases the projection is momentary and leads straight back to herself. Molly is content with these mental limitations, as her attitude towards politics shows. She was once captivated by Bloom's 'blather about home rule and the Land League' (*U* 692), but now 'I hate the mention of politics' (*U* 670). It is true that, in one or two remarks, she displays an instinctively feminist attitude. She complains of women being 'always chained up' (*U* 698), and thinks 'itd be much better for the world to be governed by the women in it you wouldnt see women going and killing one another and slaughtering' (*U* 699). But these are just received opinions. Molly is unlikely to follow her political instinct and she relies on the men in her life to broaden her mental horizons.

Molly, then, is ungrammatical, egotistical, shrewd, and ignorant. If she is in revolt against the 'chains' imposed on women, that revolt (which is compromised anyway) is largely confined to the fields of language and sex. She is uninhibited in both and, even as a girl, was not made to blush by a smutty story: 'why should it either its only nature' (*U* 698). She is understandably pleased about her afternoon with Boylan and looks forward to further bouts of anarchic sexuality in the immediate future. Yet she knows that their affair is purely a matter of physical release, 'do it and think no more about it' (*U* 661), and she views her lover with friendly contempt: 'of course hes right enough in his way to pass the time as a joke', but 'you might as well be in bed with what with a lion' (*U* 698). (There is a submerged implication here of 'Leo the Lion'; but her once sexually potent husband has become the emasculated Poldy.)

What Boylan lacks, and Bloom once offered, is the spice and sustenance of erotic romance. For Molly, in addition to her other 'female' qualities, is a dyed-in-the-wool romantic. Her romanticization of past experience is as powerful a technique as any that Bloom or Stephen possess for escaping from the disappointments of real life. Molly, indeed, is the creator of her own myth, and comic detachment passes over into lyrical identification as Joyce makes her retell the story of her own life with ever-increasing fluency, rising to a crescendo modelled upon (yet immeasurably surpassing) the pornographic fiction she reads. Molly as the archetypal woman combines total candour and lack of refinement with the gush usually associated with a certain sort of female novelist. In this respect she is an older, coarser and more worldly-wise counterpart of the other main female character of *Ulysses*, Gerty MacDowell. Molly looks back to her adolescence in Gibraltar, her virginal dreams, her earliest love-letters. The life-story she tells herself (the mature equivalent of Gerty's dream of dark strangers) consists of an apostolic succession of lovers: Mulvey, Bloom, Gardner, Boylan, and (should the opportunity arise) Stephen Dedalus. Her ideal list of lovers is, in a sense, to Molly what Flowerville is to Bloom: a monument to romantic narcissism, carefully edited in accordance with her emotional needs, at once belonging to and quite separate from the actualities of existence. Bloom's myth is set in an ever-receding future; Molly's in a constantly updated past. Of the two myths hers is therefore the most substantial, though we may be surprised by its meagre realistic basis – especially when contrasted with Bloom's suspicions. When the catechist in 'Ithaca' listed Molly's admirers he came up with a series of no less than twenty-five names; twenty-seven, if Bloom himself and Gardner — of whose passion her husband is either ignorant or oblivious — had been included. Bloom is incomparably the most significant member of Molly's list. His entry into her life was foreshadowed at Gibraltar, when she pretended to be engaged to one 'Don Miguel de la Flora' (*U* 680). Now he is blamed for her adultery: 'its all his own fault if I am an adulteress as the thing in the gallery said' (*U* 702). She is alternately tolerant and impatient towards his sexual peculiarities, which scarcely involve her and leave her frustrated and bored. Nevertheless, Bloom remains a figure of wonderment to her: 'I suppose there isnt in all creation another man with the habits he has' (*U* 693). In contrast to the transparent Boylan — 'Hugh the ignoramus that doesnt know poetry from a cabbage' (*U* 697) — she would no doubt agree with Lenehan that Bloom is 'not one of your common or garden' (*U* 234). It is through contact with Bloom, above all, that her mental horizons have been broadened.

Molly is, as Marilyn French points out, in one of her aspects a 'middle-class woman with an eye to respectability'[10]. The climax of her romantic autobiography is the day of betrothal on Howth Head when she was able to combine the satisfactions of anarchic sexuality with those of entering a marriage contract. Molly remains deeply aware of her married state, and has no thought of giving up its responsibilities. Even her adultery has taken place under the marital roof and in the connubial bed. Though she has a moderately successful singing career she takes her professional duties lightly and certainly does not fit the idea of a career woman. Her reputation in the Dublin musical world is based as much on her physical as her vocal charms. Her thoughts, when not directly concerned with erotic romance, belong largely to the categories of 'business for women', 'clothes and cooking and children' (*U* 691). Her outlook is thoroughly domestic, with Bloom himself preoccupying her far more than anyone else does, and it is apparently a domestic event which has provoked the present crisis. Tension has been rising in the Bloom household since the arrival at puberty of Milly, their daughter, in September 1903. Molly 'couldnt turn round with her in the place lately unless I bolted the door first gave me the fidgets coming in without knocking first' (*U* 687). Bloom in turn has felt restricted by 'reiterated feminine interrogation' as to his comings and goings, with the result that 'complete corporal liberty of action had been circumscribed' (*U* 657). Milly's absence, engineered by Bloom, is Molly's opportunity. Her occasions and (perhaps) her inclination for casual adultery are likely to fade once Milly is back home and pursuing her own newly discovered interest in the opposite sex.

Molly's unconventionality is the result of her frank and highly-sexed nature. Apart from that, she does rather little to challenge the conception of women's role enjoined by bourgeois society. To the extent that she was intended as a universal symbol, she is less extensively and subtly developed and has not stood the test of time as well as Bloom. At the same time, she is an ebullient creation who embodies a mode of life utterly different from that of either Bloom or Stephen. Her conflicting qualities of complacent earthiness and narcissistic romanticism come together at the climax of her monologue. Her final 'yes' is at once an erotic culmination and a profound endorsement of the marriage ideal (and hence of Bloom's own patient and stoical commitment to their marriage). The 'yes' is a utopian affirmation, conveying the possibility of renewed marital harmony much as Odysseus's return promises the restoration of harmony to Ithaca. Tradition tells us that Odysseus eventually grew restless on his island, nor need we suppose that the Blooms lived happily ever after; it is enough that the romantic notion is present and the possibility is glimpsed. Joyce described Molly as 'human, all too human' (*SL* 278), and to her stereotype qualities of earthiness, egotism, ignorance and romanticism we should add her underlying loyalty. It is loyalty on her own terms, not Bloom's. But he has had the good sense not to force her to come to terms, and the fact that she apparently does so at last is the ratification of his homecoming.

8   The styles of *Ulysses*

Ulysses has been well described by Arnold Goldman as an 'encyclopaedia of styles'.[1] Joyce deliberately set out to devise 'a new style per chapter',[2] and – through Gilbert and others – offered a series of justifications for these styles, usually relying on the Homeric parallels. Thus the 'Aeolus' episode uses newspaper headlines and overblown rhetoric because journalism and oratory are the modern equivalents of Ulysses's bag of winds. The parodic history of English prose styles in the 'Oxen of the Sun', on the other hand, was justified by its setting in a maternity hospital; the development of English prose was the literary equivalent of the growth of an embryo. These explanations have their place in commentaries on Joyce but we need not perhaps take them very seriously. They belong, rather, to the time-honoured category of Irish bulls.[3]

Some, though not all, of the later chapters of *Ulysses* are stylistic encyclopaedias in themselves. 'Aeolus' runs through a vast repertoire of rhetorical figures, 'Sirens' reproduces hundreds of musical forms, and the 'linguistic gigantism' of 'Cyclops' parodies a series of texts ranging from the Bible and Celtic epic to a child's reading-book. Yet the concept of an encyclopaedia will not in itself explain the styles of *Ulysses*. It is only very recently that critics have felt able to state their rationale.

Joyce contradicted his prescription of 'one style per episode' when he spoke of an 'initial style', composed of third-person narrative interspersed with passages of interior monologue, which runs right through the early episodes.[4] The initial style holds good until the end of 'Hades', after which it is modified and then – in various episodes – wholly abandoned. With this in mind, we can read *Ulysses*, along the lines suggested by Walton Litz, as a 'two-part performance in which the modern novel is built up and then disintegrated into its original components'.[5] Litz's formulation is a reminder that the initial style was itself highly experimental and innovative when *Ulysses* was published. In the 1920s this was the most influential aspect of Joyce's

writing, stimulating the 'stream-of-consciousness' experiments of
Faulkner, Woolf and others. His influence began, not with the book
publication of *Ulysses*, but with the instalments printed in the *Egoist*
and *Little Review*. Much recent scholarly work has explored the
differences between manuscript, serial, and book versions. From this
it is evident that the earlier chapters of *Ulysses* were greatly affected and
sometimes transformed by Joyce's revisions. The 1918 serial version
of 'Aeolus', for example, is written in the initial style. It was in
mid-1921, when most of the later episodes had been drafted, that Joyce
broke up the text with newspaper headlines and systematically extended
his catalogue of rhetorical tropes.[6] By the 'later' developments of style
in *Ulysses* we thus mean both those which come further on in the book
and those which were chronologically late in the process of
composition. These developments betray Joyce's recognition of the
inherent limitations of his initial style. And it is that style we must seek
to define first.

The early interior monologues − unlike that of Molly which
concludes the book − are set in context by the use of a third-person
narrator. The narrator is Flaubertian in that he subscribes to the
doctrine of artistic impersonality (which was reaffirmed by Stephen in
the *Portrait*) and strives fastidiously after *le mot juste*:

Stately, plump Buck Mulligan came from the stairhead, . . .   (*U* 9)

Mr Leopold Bloom ate with relish the inner organs of beasts and fowls.(*U* 57)

Perfume of embraces all him assailed. With hungered flesh obscurely, he
mutely craved to adore.   (*U* 168)

The last of these three extracts is the subject of a famous anecdote
recounted by Frank Budgen.[7] Budgen went to see his friend one day
and asked how the great work was progressing. Joyce replied that he
had spent the whole morning toiling over two sentences. In the
'Lestrygonians' episode in Homer there was a seduction motif (the
cannibal king's daughter). Joyce's way of alluding to this was to show
Bloom being momentarily aroused by women's underwear in a shop
window. The problem was not one of finding the right words for his
two sentences, he explained − he already had them − but of putting
them in the best order. Hugh Kenner has cast some doubt on this
anecdote,[8] but assuming it is not wholly false we should note that the
sentences belong to the narrator and are not a fragment of interior
monologue. They should be reinserted into the context from which they
came:

*Paragraph
no.*

1   High voices. Sunwarm silk. Jingling harnesses. All for a woman, home and houses, silk webs, silver, rich fruits, spicy from Jaffa. Agendath Netaim. Wealth of the world.

2   A warm human plumpness settled down on his brain. His brain yielded. Perfume of embraces all him assailed. With hungered flesh obscurely, he mutely craved to adore.

3   Duke street. Here we are. Must eat. The Burton. Feel better then.

4   He turned Combridge's corner, still pursued. Jingling hoofthuds. Perfumed bodies, warm, full. All kissed, yielded: in deep summer fields, tangled pressed grass, in trickling hallways of tenements, along sofas, creaking beds.

5   – Jack, love!
    – Darling!
    – Kiss me, Reggy!
    – My boy!
    – Love!   (*U* 168)

What strikes us first here is the fluid, spontaneous impressionism of Joyce's writing. The toil of which he spoke to Budgen is as hidden as it could well be. The more daring the modulations of style and mode, the more immediate is the illusion of being exposed to the minute-by-minute phantasma of another mind.

As soon as we start to analyse the passage we are likely to score it, so to speak, for dramatic production. Paragraphs 1 and 3 are in Bloom-voice, rapt and sensuous in 1, hoarse and breathless in 3. Paragraph 2 and the first sentence of 4 are in the voice-over of a precisely toned narrator. The prostitutes' voices are 'staged' in the text by being set out as direct speech; echoing apparently in Bloom's mind, they appeal to a stereotyped notion of vulgar seduction. We have here an orchestration of different voices, as in radio drama. Yet what is also noticeable is the unified effect of the passage on the printed page. The whole is a single dramatized scene, taking place in Bloom's mind and to be read, we feel, at the same pace as the mental events it portrays. The paragraphs blend into one another and, with the exception of the prostitutes' voices, it is by subtle syntactic and verbal shifts that the text invites a polyphonic reading.

Though all the voices 'describe' Bloom, what I have called a Bloom-voice is close to the level of speech and bears the stamp of his individual personality. We may contrast the Bloom-voice with a comparable passage of Stephen's monologue:

Come. I thirst. Clouding over. No black clouds anywhere, are there?
                                                                (*U* 56)

Already (for the paragraph goes on for another three lines, and includes
a Latin quotation) we are aware of Stephen's slightly facetious
literariness, as against Bloom's stolid materialism. 'Come. I thirst' is
deliberate Wardour Street English (the language of Victorian historical
romances and costume dramas). What it has in common with Bloom's
'Must eat. . . . Feel better then' is that they are both characteristic
phrases which we can easily imagine these particular individuals
speaking to themselves. The sequence beginning 'High voices.
Sunwarm silk' is not so easily classifiable. Subliterary clichés such as
'All for a woman' and 'Wealth of the world'[9] represent the sort of
cultural detritus that typically speaks through Bloom. The phrases
evoking silk and spices, however, are as close to the idiom of the
narrator (or of Stephen) as they are to that of Bloom.

   'Agendath Netaim' in paragraph 1 represents another stylistic trick
– the personal mnemonic. The words come from the newspaper
advertisement that Bloom read in 'Calypso'. On another occasion a
different mnemonic, such as 'Bleibtreustrasse', will be used to recall
the same advertisement. The mnemonic has the effect of permitting a
moment of flashback without interrupting the narrative flow. At the
same time, it emphasizes the artificiality of a verbal representation of
the 'stream of consciousness'. We begin to see how much this depends
on the adroit manipulation of counters and symbols.

   In the initial style sense-impressions, such as sight and sound, are
given verbal representation by traditional poetic means. For sounds,
an onomatopoeic choice of vocabulary ('jingling hoofthuds') will be
appropriate; for sights – whether seen in actuality or with the mind's
eye – a series of compressed images, verbal metonymies, such as
'creaking beds' and 'tangled pressed grass'. The result is a complex
blend of narrative elements. As a general rule, the levels of
consciousness closest to speech are represented by mimicking the
character's idiolect, while physical sensations and the visual
imagination are represented by means of the poetically precise language
we attribute to the narrator. Local repetition (such as that of the word
'silk' in the quoted extract and the paragraphs immediately preceding
it) is used for thematic intensification and may affect the reader
subliminally. Long-range, mnemonic repetition (the so-called
leitmotivs such as 'Agendath Netaim') is, however, less an imagistic
device than a memory-test to jolt the reader into attention. While at one

level it stresses continuity of character – the Bloom who remembers 'Agendath Netaim' being manifestly the same figure who earlier found it in a newspaper advertisement – at another and perhaps more significant level it operates, like the rest of the book's symbols and literary allusions, to deepen our sense of the incrustation of Joyce's text, its meticulously arranged and richly decorated surface.

These remarks are, at best, a merely preliminary account of the narrative features of the initial style. They are intended to point out the highly conventional and artificially constructed nature of that style's realistic facade. For a dramatic example of the extent to which Joyce's 'stream-of-consciousness' writing *is* a facade – rather than the method of ultimate realism it may at first resemble – we have only to recall Joyce's handling of the vampire poem in 'Proteus'. Far from incorporating the words of the finished poem into Stephen's monologue as would seem natural, Joyce simply uses the narrative voice to describe the action of writing it down (*U* 53). The poem itself crops up in the 'Aeolus' episode very much later. Clearly this is a compositional game, designed to intrigue and puzzle the reader and, perhaps, to warn him of the deceptiveness of narrative realism. Selection, perspective, foregrounding and other conventional devices play as great a part in the transparent narrative at which Joyce aimed (or pretended to aim) as they do in any other form of storytelling. Joyce could boast both of creating a new form of realism, and of ensuring his immortality by the mass of enigmas and puzzles he had put into *Ulysses*.[10]

The verisimilitude of the initial style is sharply at variance with its underlying reality. We may itemize the appearance of the style – the realistic illusion it creates – as follows. Joyce's interior monologues seem to be

(i)   spontaneous and free-flowing,
(ii)   transparent and directly expressive of mental events,
(iii)   objective and impartial in reporting these events,
(iv)   capable of expressing any form of experience,
(v)   faithful to the subjectivity of experience and its filtering through an individual personality or temperament, and
(vi)   they appear to proceed at exactly the same pace as the events they describe.

It is entirely appropriate that this style, which creates such a powerful realistic illusion, should have sustained its interest and technical ingenuity over a number of chapters. When Joyce abandons it, it is for a series of ostentatious, and inherently provisional, narrative structures. It has become a familiar point that Joyce thus exposes the relativity of all styles.[11] The later chapters may be read as the profound and unforgettable demonstration of a series of axioms which have played a fundamental part in modern stylistics. These axioms – stated as a sequence of counter-propositions to the six aspects of the realistic illusion cited above – may be put as follows:

(i)   All narrative is an artificial structure imposed on the 'free flow of events'.   ('Aeolus', 'Wandering Rocks')

(ii) Far from being transparent, narrative is like a musical score waiting to be interpreted and performed by the reader.   ('Sirens')

(iii) There is no objective or neutral style. There are only degrees of explicitness in the narrative bias.   ('Cyclops', 'Nausicaa')

(iv) Stylistic resources vary from age to age and with the accumulation of past styles. All styles have their limits; but beyond the euphony of styles lies the cacophony of language.   ('Oxen of the Sun')

(v)   'Subjectivity' and 'personality' are constructs arising within the literary text and varying from one genre to another.   ('Circe', 'Eumaeus')

(vi) There is no 'unity of time' in narrative fiction. The narrator is both hare and tortoise and all narrative is alternately summary and digressive.
                                                                        ('Ithaca')

The rationale of Joyce's styles in the later parts of *Ulysses* will appear if we apply these axioms one by one.

(i)   *Narrative is an artificial structure*

At the level of overall narrative structure this is a truism. The discontinuities between 'Telemachus' and 'Nestor' (omitting Stephen's journey from Sandycove to Mr Deasy's school), or between 'Proteus' and 'Calypso' (switching from Stephen at midday to Bloom four hours earlier), are examples of a perfectly conventional sort of narrative surprise. Within a given scene the effect may be more disconcerting, as was shown by the example of the vampire poem. It is no accident that the poem reappears in 'Aeolus', the first of Joyce's episodes to be cut into by blatant discontinuities in the narrative. If the textual breaks in 'Aeolus' reflect the style of headline journalism, those in 'Wandering Rocks' suggest rather the language of the cinema. The scene-switching here (we could use such words as montage, jump-cuts, visible or invisible editing) became conventional in modernist fiction as a result of its widespread adoption by Joyce's contemporaries, such as Dos Passos, Aldous Huxley and Virginia Woolf. In any case, it had been pioneered sixty years earlier by Flaubert in the *comices agricoles* scene of *Madame Bovary*. This example suggests that readers soon become accustomed to the artificiality of any particular form of narrative. It becomes 'naturalized' and they do not notice it. It is the extraordinary variety of the styles in *Ulysses* which highlights their artificiality. Joyce differs from other novelists in his refusal to allow his readers to settle in to any single storytelling convention.

(ii)   *Narrative is like a musical score*

The opening of 'Sirens' could have a totally baffling effect on the first-time reader. Yet once he has grasped the idea of a summary statement of 'musical' themes, following the same sequence as that in which they appear in the narrative proper, he will have no difficulty in reading on (though it is a slightly unusual kind of reading). Another problem is posed by the deliberate deformation of language at points in this episode. If language were really the transparent medium it seemed to be earlier in *Ulysses*, then the deformations of the 'Sirens' would be merely infantile:

Bald Pat who is bothered mitred the napkins. Pat is a waiter hard of his hearing. Pat is a waiter who waits while you wait. Hee hee hee hee. He waits while you wait. Hee hee. A waiter is he. Hee hee hee hee. He waits while you wait. While you wait if you wait he will wait while you wait. Hee hee hee hee. Hoh. Wait while you wait. (*U* 279)

Read flatly as 'words on the page', this is nonsense. Set to music and chanted, however, it has a catchy and cheerful tune − the sort of beguiling triviality against which Ulysses stopped up the ears of his crew. But the tune is a literary cadenza − a passage the reader must improvise himself, with only limited help from the author. It takes a very considerable departure, such as this one, from conventionally acceptable narrative to force us to recognize the element of interpretation, not to say improvisation, involved in all reading. For this reason it is not enough to describe 'Sirens' as the musical chapter of *Ulysses*. Music is the stalking-horse to bring language into our sights. Or, to change the metaphor, just as one of Ben Dollard's love-songs would 'burst the tympanum of her ear . . . Not to mention another membrane' (*U* 269), so Joyce breaks the membranes of language by way of expressing his feeling for it. In retrospect, the Teutonic abhorrence of the hyphen (as in 'scrotumtightening', etc.) throughout his work might be seen as the breaking of a membrane. But it is in 'Sirens' that he first uses compressed compounds or portmanteau-words, in anticipation of the process of linguistic deconstruction and reconstruction in *Finnegans Wake*. Thus 'Yes' and 'Essex bridge' give us 'Yes, Mr Bloom crossed bridge of Yessex' (*U* 260). One difference between 'Sirens' and the *Wake*, however, is that most of these transformations in the earlier text are specifically justified by their musical resonance.

> — O Greasy eyes! Imagine being married to a man like that, she cried. With his bit of beard!
> Douce gave full vent to a splendid yell, a full yell of full woman, delight, joy, indignation.
> — Married to the greasy nose! she yelled.
> Shrill, with deep laughter, after bronze in gold, they urged each each to peal after peal, ringing in changes, bronzegold goldbronze, shrilldeep, to laughter after laughter. And then laughed more. Greasy I knows. Exhausted, breathless their shaken heads they laid, braided and pinnacled by glossycombed, against the counterledge. All flushed (O!), panting, sweating (O!), all breathless.
> Married to Bloom, to greaseaseabloom.   (*U* 259)

Here the verbal playfulness, arising out of the dialogue, is 'set to music' by the metaphor of bells pealing. The progression greasy eyes — greasy nose — Greasy I knows — greaseaseabloom can be heard as the note of the bells. This set of transformations is not wholly gratuitous. Explicitly it helps to rub in the ignominy (at least as far as the barmaids are concerned) of being 'Married to Bloom'. Implicitly, it makes a major thematic reference, with the compound 'seabloom' which contains the idea of Bloom as archetypal sailor. 'Seabloom' makes his reappearance at the end of the chapter:

> Seabloom, greaseabloom viewed last words. Softly. *When my country takes her place among.*
> Prrprr.
> Must be the bur.
> Fff. Oo. Rrpr.
> *Nations of the earth.* No-one behind. She's passed. *Then and not till then.* Tram. Kran, kran, kran. Good oppor. Coming. Krandlkrankran. I'm sure it's the burgund. Yes. One, two. *Let my epitaph be.* Karaaaaaaa. *Written. I have.*
> Pprrpffrrppfff.
> *Done.*   (*U* 289–90)

It will be seen how this ending builds on the narrative conventions already established in the 'Sirens' and earlier. 'Bur' stands for burgundy and 'oppor' for opportunity — this is recognizable Bloom-speak. Nonsense-words like 'Prrprr' and 'kran' are easily decipherable cases of onomatopoeia. Robert Emmet's last words, though cut up into seven sections, are set in italics and have already been named in the text (*U* 289). This passage presents no difficulties of interpretation, though it clearly invites and depends upon a vigorous performance. And when performed it is both transparent and self-reflexive (not to say laxative). It is both an account of a man farting in front of Emmet's picture, and a piece of writing uproariously and finally '*Done*'.

(iii)   *There is no objective or neutral style*

It may be said that the real point of the passage we have just quoted is its scatological debunking of Irish pieties. There is a sniggering, schoolboy delight in the treatment of Emmet's last words which it would be dishonest to describe as either impersonal or accidental. The passage betrays no 'death of the author' but, on the contrary, Joyce amusing himself. Yet his amusement is conveyed through what is, formally, still an interior monologue. As in all deliberate comedy, there is bias implied here − though the bias might be read differently by different readers. There are, in all probability, many nations of the earth in which a novel whose protagonist farted to the accompaniment of the words of a patriotic hero could not be published.

There is bias simply in the claim that Bloom is a character whose minute-by-minute thoughts merit the space Joyce gives to them. (Imagine the same space being devoted to smug Father Conmee, whose brief monologue is found in 'Wandering Rocks'!) Yet the interior monologue is a style which hides its bias, more or less, until Bloom's final outburst of flatulence. With his discharge in front of Emmet's picture *Ulysses* enters the anarchic realm of the carnival, the satyr-play and the pillory. From now on bias, disrespect, lewdness and mockery will take over the text and destroy all pretensions to neutrality of style.

We begin with 'Cyclops', an episode partially narrated by a bilious and nameless Dublin debt-collector which shows Joyce's rehandling of the Homeric material at its most impressive. The narrator and the Citizen − Bloom's antagonist in Barney Kiernan's pub − are both biassed and 'one-eyed' men like Homer's Cyclops. Joyce described the style as 'linguistic gigantism', and one (perhaps unintended) aspect of this is that 'Cyclops' is one of the longest episodes in the book, being only exceeded by 'Ithaca' and the gargantuan 'Circe'. The length of 'Cyclops' is partly due to its being a richly dramatized episode, and partly to the expansiveness of bombastic language (and the even greater expansiveness of parodies of bombast). The set-pieces, such as the astonishing lists of names, are filled to the utmost by Joyce's powers of inventiveness. Had he been able to, he would probably have gone on adding to these passages. He wished to add the name 'Boris

Hupinkoff' to the Friends of the Emerald Isle (*U* 305), but the French printer marked the correction *trop tard*.[12]

Though 'Cyclops' is a masterpiece of parodic style it is (like 'Circe' but not, perhaps, like 'Oxen of the Sun') far more than merely a matter of style. It is the most politically committed piece of fiction that Joyce ever produced. Its message is a rejection of the violence and hatred engendered by two opposing political systems, British imperialism and Irish nationalism. The ugly face of British imperialism is present only by implication, though we shall see it later, in the persons of Private Carr and Private Compton. The ugly face of Irish nationalism is that of the Citizen, a caricature of Michael Cusack, the founder of the Gaelic Athletic Association. (One wonders which Joyce detested more – its Gaelicism or its athleticism?) The narrative, however, is a complex satire working by means of a double displacement. The nameless debt-collector who tells the story is violently anti-British and also contemptuous of Bloom. His view of the Citizen, too, is fairly jaundiced. Yet he is himself apparently a victim of venereal disease[13], and in this and other ways is a plain embodiment of the spiritual paralysis Joyce had attacked in *Dubliners*. Our appreciation of Bloom's rational and pacifistic attitude depends on our perceiving the unreliability of the debt-collector's narration. Joyce has made this easy for us by the series of parodies, from the Biblical style to that of the Nationalist press, which suggest that no form of public language is to be trusted. Thus three different stylistic levels in descending order of dignity are included in the final sentence of the episode:

And they beheld Him even Him, ben Bloom Elijah, amid clouds of angels ascend to the glory of the brightness at an angle of fortyfive degrees over Donohoe's in Little Green Street like a shot off a shovel.   (*U* 343)

The progression is from Holy Scripture by way of newspaper reporting ('over Donohoe's in Little Green Street') to the vernacular narrator telling his colourful tale to a group of fellow-drinkers in a pub. Though an eye-witness, he is deeply suspect (and indeed he admitted in his opening sentence to having his eye nearly put out by a sweep, *U* 290). The other styles are no more truthful. What we are left with in 'Cyclops' is not the illusion of an objective or neutral narrative, nor, exactly, the traditional sense of a hierarchy of styles, for the styles are all getting jumbled together. The stilted sublime runs into the vividly bathetic.

From the shot off the shovel we move straight on to summer's mysterious embrace:

The summer evening had begun to fold the world in its mysterious embrace.
                                                              (*U* 344)

Lame Gerty MacDowell is a prisoner of language. The style of
'Nausicaa' at once expresses her feelings — in a different style she
would be a different character — and makes fun of them. We are to
think of her as a teenage girl from much the same background as the
other characters of *Ulysses*, lounging with her friends on a public
beach. But in this episode language itself constitutes a pastoral setting
which cuts her off from reality. Warmth, twilight, the domesticized
landscape (in Gerty's eyes the beach-girls are sitting in a 'favourite
nook' guarded by 'dear old Howth', *U* 344), and the Byronic presence-
yet-absence of Bloom, conspire with Gerty's language to make up the
'mysterious embrace' which envelops her. Joyce gives several hints as
to the possible sources of Gerty's narrative. '*The Lamplighter* by Miss
Cummins' (*U* 361), 'the Woman Beautiful page of the Princess
novelette' (*U* 347), the *Lady's Pictorial*, and the poem '*Art thou real,
my ideal?*' by Louis J. Walsh of Magherafelt (*U* 361) are cherished
items of Gerty's reading. Stanley Sultan has claimed Miss Cumming's
(sic) *The Lamplighter* as Joyce's source for the episode,[14] but an
examination of that deservedly forgotten novel shows that all that he
took from it were certain stylistic tricks. The style of 'Nausicaa' is a
complex and original parody. It blends the high-flown sentiments of
the lady's novelette with a series of lapses into the earthiness of Gerty's
vernacular. Characteristically these are caused by things she cannot
ignore or gloss over in the outside world, such as the unruliness and
incontinence of Cissy Caffrey's younger brothers. There is one lapse
that Gerty will not permit herself, and that is to let the reader in on the
secret of her lameness. Joyce enjoys coming close to it, with references
to her accident, her health ('those iron jelloids she had been taking of
late', *U* 346), and to legs and feet ('the scatty heel of the loaf of brown
bread', *U* 344). The exhibitionist act she performs before Bloom is
designed at once to reveal her legs and to hide their most significant
feature. Even at the end of her narrative, the imprisoning style refuses
to admit the word 'lame' (*U* 365), preferring instead to trail off in mid-
sentence. It is left to Bloom, once his monologue resumes, to utter the
word. And though Bloom takes over from Gerty with a richly reflective
monologue in the initial style, he too is imprisoned by a word he cannot
utter. We see this from his unfinished message to Gerty — 'I. AM. A.'
(*U* 379) — scrawled in the sand. The unfinished message corresponds
to her unfinished sentence. And if her narrative cannot admit that

she is lame, Bloom in his turn cannot bring himself to write the word cuckold. This is the explanation of the ending of 'Nausicaa', in which Bloom, tired after his exertions, has dropped off to sleep. The cuckoo clock in the priest's house can say

> *Cuckoo.*
> *Cuckoo.*
> *Cuckoo.*   (*U* 380)

but so, as we see in the following paragraph, can Gerty MacDowell. And if this is Bloom's dream it raises the possibility that the whole episode, far from offering a free-standing characterization of Gerty, might simply be read as the expression of Bloom's masturbatory imagination. No wonder the style imprisons its subject.

(iv)   *Stylistic resources vary from age to age*

But all styles imprison their subjects − or so, at least, modern linguistics has tended to claim. The influential Sapir–Whorf hypothesis holds that 'a speaker's native language sets up a series of categories which act as a kind of grid through which he perceives the world, and which constrain the way in which he categorizes and conceptualizes different phenomena'.[15] Whatever can be said of whole languages is, of course, true *a fortiori* of the different styles and registers which shape an individual writer's or speaker's use of language. The familiar notions of literary convention and stylistic decorum entail that, within any particular style, there are things that cannot be said. In the earlier parts of *Ulysses* Joyce has created the individual styles of Stephen and Bloom, and also of such minor characters as Father Conmee, the 'Cyclops' narrator, and Gerty MacDowell. In 'Oxen of the Sun' he turns his attention from individual styles to the historical development of literary language. Literary prose is separated from oral narrative by a self-consciousness stemming from the preservation of its own past. The styles, however functional they may have been in their own time, acquire a lapidary and monumental quality once they take their places in the cultural museum. 'Oxen of the Sun' resembles a literary museum containing, not pickled foetuses, but specimens of writing. The exhibits are historically evocative even to readers who lack the expertise to date them precisely. The effect of the chronological sequence is to give styles which may have served very different purposes (the Biblical, the courtly, the journalistic, the Gothic, the novelistic and so on) the appearance of forming a continuous tradition. The theme of this tradition is the emergence of a 'mature' prose reflecting the individuality of the writer. The cult of personality in literature and the rise of the individual stylist takes place from the seventeenth to the nineteenth centuries. Hence, in 'Oxen of the Sun', Joyce moves from early parodies of anonymous and communal styles to the idiosyncrasies of particular authors such as Sterne, Goldsmith, Lamb, de Quincey, Dickens, and Carlyle. The episode ends not with a euphonious narrative voice such as these, but with the chaotic hubbub of conversation in Burke's pub. It is as if his tour of the stylistic museum had ended with a rejection of style – and hence of literature – altogether.

Joyce's view of the stylistic museum is (as some pedantic critics have rather mercilessly insisted) a highly idiosyncratic one. It is now clear that he rested heavily on two widely available cribs, Saintsbury's *History of English Prose Rhythm* and Peacock's World's Classics anthology of *English Prose: Mandeville to Ruskin*, when writing the chapter.[16] The result is brilliant literary pastiche, though the learning behind it is much more apparent than real. The implicit tone of the chapter is balanced between antiquarian glee and a reductive, even dismissive, view of the past. The limitations of each style are fully (if affectionately) exposed. No previous episode of *Ulysses* has opened as dully as 'Oxen of the Sun', with its medieval Latin sentence ('Deshil Holles Eamus', *U* 380) repeated three times. The medical students carousing in the maternity hospital are initially stock figures, 'young learning knights' (*U* 384) and 'right witty scholars' (*U* 386). Leopold Bloom makes his first appearance as 'Some man that wayfaring was' (*U* 382), 'The man that was come into the house' (*U* 383); later he graduates to the status of 'childe Leopold' (*U* 385), 'sir Leopold' (*U* 387), 'Mr Cautious Calmer' (*U* 387), 'Mr Canvasser Bloom' (*U* 407) and so on. There is further amusement to be gained from describing such industrial products as a contraceptive sheath and a sardine-can within the decorum of the traditional styles.[17] We may detect an iconoclastic purpose beneath the comedy. Joyce in the later chapters of *Ulysses* (as we have seen) was undermining his *own* initial style. He certainly did not wish to suggest that the answer could be a reversion to previous styles.

Thanks to the self-consciousness of this episode its narrative is difficult to follow. For this reason, not all readers may appreciate that 'Oxen of the Sun' is a piece of sustained satire, in which the limitations of the styles themselves are reinforced by the traditional and platitudinous nature of what they have to say. We are faced with long diatribes against the slaughter of the 'sacred oxen' (ie. the male sperms) of human fertility by such practices as masturbation ('those Godpossibled souls we nightly impossibilise', *U* 387) and contraception. Bloom, as we know, resorts to both habits, and eventually we reach an imprecation in Carlylean English ('let scholarment and all Malthusiasts go hang', *U* 420) directed at both him and Stephen. The pretended narrative stance is more or less that of Roman Catholic theology. In 'Nausicaa' Joyce portrayed Bloom's masturbation side by side with the celebration of Mass by Canon O'Hanlon and Father Conroy — an act of near-desecration. Here orthodoxy is allowed its revenge, culminating in a thunderstorm, a fire-engine in the streets, and divine vengeance being preached in the voice of the evangelist Alexander J. Dowie. At issue is the proper degree of reverence due to the mysteries of human reproduction and fertility, and the sanctity of the nursing profession. If Bloom's pagan curiosity and natural kindness are to be admired, he must also face charges of sexual hypocrisy, and above all the existence of a 'consort neglected and debauched' (*U* 407), as the price of his 'Malthusiasm'. But against Bloom are set the raucous medical students, led by Buck Mulligan whose crude application of the injunction to 'Increase and multiply' — 'the noblest task for which our bodily organism has been framed' (*U* 399) — can claim the sanction of orthodoxy. Mulligan's plan for a 'national fertilising farm' is, however, in defiance both of common decency and of the rational principles of population control in which Bloom (and, one would assume, Joyce too) believes. 'Increase and multiply. Did you ever hear such an idea? Eat you out of house and home', Bloom has earlier reflected, adding that priests have 'No families themselves to feed' (*U* 151). In 'Oxen of the Sun' there is an unhealthy alliance between the views of 'Trinity medicals.... All prick and no pence' (*U* 427) and those of the priests.

There is no single point at which 'Oxen of the Sun' passes from a succession of euphonious styles to a medley of voices. The last individual writer to be parodied — Carlyle — is so full of quotations, allusions, and archaisms, and so indiscriminate in his choice of rhetorical weapons, that already we are prepared for the cacophony of the final pages, which are like a tape-recording of innumerable conversational fragments overheard in the street and in the pub. It is as if the decadence of literary narrative style were to lead inevitably to a return to oral language, prodigious in its variety and utterly promiscuous in the registers, idioms, and tones of voice on which it draws. The final pages of 'Oxen' invite performance, just as the musical prose in 'Sirens' did; and the possibilities of performance – the number of voices involved and the distribution of tones – are almost infinite.

The ordinary reader's business is not to give a dramatic rendering of the end of 'Oxen', but to read it. In some ways this is a decoding exercise akin to the reading of *Finnegans Wake*, in which certain well-defined utterances emerge very clearly from the surrounding noise. Notably, there is the sound of Buck Mulligan unscrambling the telegram that Stephen had earlier sent him at the Ship:

Mummer's wire. Cribbed out of Meredith. Jesified orchidised polycimical jesuit! Aunty mine's writing Pa Kinch. Baddybad Stephen lead astray goodygood Malachi.   (*U* 422)

Most of the rest of the passage can be deciphered easily if we are attuned to the various types of jargon Joyce evokes, from student jocularity to the argot of thieves. The difference between the cacophony of the *Wake* and of 'Oxen' is, finally, that here Joyce stops short of the replacement of traditional literary style by a new form of language. Everything that is outside the museum of styles in this chapter can be placed under the heading of slang, or language which is not only oral but also in its nature ephemeral. It is as if we had been taken into a different museum. Already its contents seem quaint – much as the parodied styles seem quaint – and perhaps no other passage in *Ulysses*, apart from the torrent of literary quotations in 'Proteus', will demand so much annotation in the future.

(v)   *'Subjectivity' and 'personality' are constructs arising within the literary text and varying from one genre to another*

If 'Oxen of the Sun' is a museum of literary styles, 'Circe' is a vast freak show, an encyclopaedia of monstrosities lurking in the underworld of the life defined by Bloom and Stephen. Its relationship to the rest of *Ulysses* is one of phantasmagoria and carnival. Here in the Nighttown chapter restraints are overturned, values are inverted and primitive hungers and drives are unleashed. Themes, incidents and memories from earlier in the day come back, in grossly exaggerated and distorted forms. At the centre of 'Circe' is a Feast of Misrule in the course of which Bloom is made Lord of Misrule and then pelted with 'soft pantomime stones' (*U* 467). This and the other dramatic set-pieces follow one another like scenes in a pageant or floats in a carnival procession. Specifically appropriate to the carnival theme are the transvestite fantasies (a combination of traditional festivity and Victorian pornography).[18] The episode is full of distorted bodies and physical grotesques, as is appropriate in an episode based on Homer's Circe who turned men into swine. We enter Nighttown through a tableau of 'stunted men and women' (*U* 425), we see such sights as a navvy ejecting a jet of snot (*U* 428) and a woman pissing 'cowily' in an archway (*U* 437), and we hear depositions such as that of Mr Philip Beaufoy, author of *Matcham's Masterstroke*, concerning Bloom's earlier behaviour: 'a specimen of my maturer work disfigured by the hallmark of the beast' (*U* 443). Back in the National Library Stephen remembered the Parisian whore who solicited him with the suggestion that '*Nous ferons de petites cochonneries* ' (*U* 202). 'Circe' is full of *grandes et petites cochonneries*.

The existence of these horrors in forms that are personalized to Stephen and Bloom makes it inevitable that we should read 'Circe' as an exercise in depth psychology. Is Joyce not exploring the recesses of personality, portraying hallucinations and phantasmagoria akin to the dreams which are studied by psychoanalysts? The answer is not at all clear-cut. To fit the specifications for Freudian dream-interpretation, the hallucinations of 'Circe' would all have to emanate from a particular individual (Bloom or Stephen), they would all have to involve wish-fulfilment and they would have to draw on the events of the previous day. These conditions are sometimes fulfilled, but not invariably so; and for much of the time the characters' traumas and obsessions are openly dramatized, rather than being distorted and obscured by the 'dream-work'. Is it that Joyce, far from remaining at the dream-level where censorship has already taken place, is plunging the reader direct into the unconscious itself? This explanation is equally unsatisfactory. Critics have agreed that the hallucinations cannot all be assigned to individual characters, and that there are elements in 'Circe' which defy psychological rationalization.[19]

'Circe' is written with profound psychic knowledge, yet it cannot be reconciled with what psychologists tell us of the individual human personality-structure. Where Joyce draws on psychological research in this chapter, he does so less for the sake of individual characterization than to give a comprehensive view of the occult peculiarities of the mind. Thus, in one of its aspects, 'Circe' is an encyclopaedia of sexual perversions, competing in its account of sadism, masochism, transvestism, fetishism, voyeurism and coprophilia with the sexology of Krafft-Ebing and Havelock Ellis.

Even if all these deviations are potentially present in the average person's sexual make-up, it strains credulity to hold that such an array helps to establish the individuality of Bloom. Far more relevant is the fact that he is visiting a brothel, and that a brothel is a place of sexual theatre. He experiences the perversions because they provide such a key part of the sexual-theatrical repertoire. In 'Circe' we see not Bloom and Stephen as they 'really' are, but Bloom and Stephen transformed by the power of universal obsessions.

The literary vehicle of these transformations is Joyce's switch from narrative to drama. The dramatic mode varies from naturalist to expressionist, looking backwards to Strindberg and forward to surrealism and the experimental film. Perhaps the most startling expressionist innovation is the attribution of speech to inanimate objects. These fetishized objects are invested with, and deprived of, personality at will. Midway between human beings and fetishized objects are the ghosts and revenants which make so many appearances. The doctrines of spiritualism are as important to 'Circe' as are those of psychoanalysis. The episode is constantly becoming a dramatized séance. The spirits called up range from Shakespeare to Paddy Dignam via Stephen's mother and Bloom's parents, son, and grandfather. Another revenant is Mananaan Maclir, the Irish god of the sea who spouts the theosophical and occultist jargon which Joyce knew from the books of Madame Blavatsky.[20] The return of the shades is partly pure slapstick and partly a reassertion of guilty and fearful memories. Stephen is tortured by his mother's ghastly reappearance; Bloom has to confront his father and his son.

There are other kinds of drama at work in the episode. Bloom's fantasies tend to turn into nightmares of the courtroom and of 'petticoat government' (*U* 486); Stephen's into nightmares of the Inquisition. When Stephen finally smashes the lamp and runs out into the street the episode becomes a political drama on the theme of heretical rebellion. Stephen has the Black Mass behind him and is sustained by his drunken intention of killing 'the priest and the king' (*U* 521) in his own mind. But his mention of killing unleashes the forces of Irish patriotic unreason, such as Kevin Egan, the Croppy Boy, and Old Gummy Granny (Cathleen ni Houlihan) who thrusts a hallucinatory dagger towards his hand. 'Armed heroes spring up from furrows' (*U* 526), and the meaningless brawl with the British soldiers carries with it the menace both of Armageddon and of Easter 1916. This is the nightmare of history from which he cannot awake. After his beating recovery will come, thanks to the charity of Leopold Bloom who has successfully withstood his own ordeal by 'petticoat government'. 'Circe' marks an abandonment of characterization in narrative for a mode which is alternatively carnival, pageant, brothel-play and séance. But it also shows the protagonists of *Ulysses* placed on trial and, at length, lucky to escape with their lives.

'Eumaeus' is the ugly duckling of *Ulysses*. Bloom and Stephen, drained by Nighttown, are shown wending their way homeward through fifty pages of long-winded and cliché-ridden prose. During the episode Leopold Bloom reflects for the first time that the experiences he is undergoing have a certain literary potential:

To improve the shining hour he wondered whether he might meet with anything approaching the same luck as Mr Philip Beaufoy if taken down in writing. Suppose he were to pen something out of the common groove (as he fully intended doing) at the rate of one guinea per column, *My Experiences*, let us say, *in a Cabman's Shelter*.   (*U* 567)

Recent criticism has debated the possibility that the narrator of 'Eumaeus' is none other than Bloom himself. Hugh Kenner writes that in this episode we are 'entrapped inside a novel with Leopold Bloom in possession of the pen'.[21] Marilyn French, on the other hand, notes the stilted diction and extensive vocabulary of the 'Eumaeus' style and claims that it 'lacks Bloom's acuteness and honesty'.[22] These observations do not preclude the possibility that stiltedness and humbug might be precisely the pitfalls in which Bloom would be trapped if he tried to fulfil his literary ambitions. Bloom's personality as Joyce's fictional character is one thing; the 'personality' he might create for himself if he set out to 'pen something out of the common groove' (that is, to attempt literature) is quite another. Do we, then, have an episode in which Bloom − trying desperately hard to be his own advocate − has inadvertently squandered most of the good qualities Joyce has taught us to admire in him?

The theme of 'Eumaeus' is one of sincerity struggling to overcome disguise. The Homeric story shows Ulysses, literally disguised, enlisting the help of the faithful shepherd. In 'Eumaeus' there is a rogue sailor, W. B. Murphy, who is confused about the identity of Simon Dedalus. The shelter-keeper may or may not be Skin-the-Goat who was involved in the Phoenix Park murders. Deceptive documents abound: Murphy's discharge papers, his South American postcard, the evening paper with its bungled account of the funeral, and the still more fictitious morning paper which (it is said) will one day report the '*Return of Parnell*'

(*U* 569). We have seen that Bloom's account of these disguises and faked documents may form the (comparably misleading) narrative we are reading. Nevertheless, within the narrative he firmly produces the one sort of document – a photograph – which proverbially cannot lie. The photograph of Molly, 'showing a large sized lady, with her fleshy charms on evidence in an open fashion' (*U* 573), is the bait to lure Stephen to the Blooms' house at 7 Eccles Street.

Bloom believes that the photo 'simply wasn't art' (*U* 573). The style of 'Eumaeus', by contrast, tries to be all too artful. From the very beginning it is determined to create sympathy for Bloom, though its way of doing so is impossibly clumsy:

Preparatory to anything else Mr Bloom brushed off the greater bulk of the shavings and handed Stephen the hat and ashplant and bucked him up generally in orthodox Samaritan fashion, which he very badly needed.   (*U* 533)

Bloom's Samaritanism, his considerateness and sense of responsibility, are harped on throughout the episode. Characteristically he remembers picking up Parnell's hat in a crowd and giving it back to the great man. Others might have stolen it or claimed it as a souvenir – but not Bloom. The sad thing is that, for all his efforts, reading between the lines will suggest that Bloom's goodwill is of very little account. He is virtually ignored first by Corley, then by the supposed sailor and Skin-the-Goat. Stephen is his captive listener, but Stephen's openness to Bloom's persuasion is doubtful in the extreme. The episode ends with yet another figure who ignores him, the streetsweeper who 'never said a word, good, bad or indifferent' (*U* 586). In the final paragraph it is the sweeper's point of view, not Bloom's, that is represented. Bloom's special pleading is over. 'Eumaeus' shares the disadvantage of all other literary efforts at deliberately bad writing. But Joyce clearly intended the discrepancy between style and subject-matter, and between Bloom's personality as expressed in this narrative and the Bloom of earlier chapters. In order to recover the 'Bloom-voice', we must penetrate the disguise of an exceptionally florid – but very conceivably Bloomian – mode of writing.

(vi)   *There is no 'unity of time' in narrative fiction*

A crucial aspect of the realistic illusion created by Joyce's initial style is its rendering of time. In an interior monologue, portraying the minute-by-minute flow of the mind, the mental events appear to proceed at exactly the same rate as the words on the page. Clearly some sleight-of-hand is involved here – an hour of narrative time may pass in the course of an episode which takes half an hour to read – but in interior monologue, as in direct dialogue, we seem to follow the stream of events as they happen, with no interventions of summary or digression on the part of the narrator.

On the face of it, *Ulysses* observes the neoclassical 'unity of time' which dictated the scope of a dramatic performance. Had it been strictly applied, the unity of time would have limited a play lasting three hours to three hours' duration of plot. In fact the division of act and scene was held to allow a plot to extend over twenty-four hours. The time-span of Joyce's work is about eighteen hours and, as was shown by the Radio Telefis Eirann production on 16–17 June 1982, a dramatized reading of the complete text takes a few hours longer. Nor does Joyce indulge in the anticipations and flashbacks (prolepses and analepses) which are so marked a feature of modern narration. The movement of time, at least in the interior monologue chapters, is steadily and unremittingly forward. And far from measuring time by the calendar or the individual life-span, as novels usually do, *Ulysses* measures it by the clock.

Both Stephen and Bloom are more time-ridden than any previous fictional characters had been. Joyce here was faithfully reflecting the nature of modern urban society. Stephen's time is controlled by his teaching obligations and his appointment to meet Buck Mulligan at the Ship (which, however, he breaks off by telegram). Bloom's time is controlled by the funeral, by office hours and newspaper deadlines, and by an arrangement to meet Martin Cunningham. Molly has a 4 p.m. assignation with Boylan. The timing of the Gold Cup race at Ascot – the result being instantly available in Dublin – is also significant in the story. The attention it gives to clock-time is one of the most innovatory features of *Ulysses*. Not only are Bloom and Stephen constantly aware of the time; the very pace of their monologues seems to tick along like a metronome.

But this is necessarily an illusion. It equates chronology with narrative sequence and ignores the conventional nature of language. For example, in life two events can take place at the same moment. In a stream-of-consciousness narrative there is no simultaneity, only a linear relation. To describe two events as having happened at the same time would require precisely the sort of digressive commentary that Joyce's initial style forbids. The question of narrative time is further complicated by the fact that, while units of time are infinitely divisible, semantic units are not. Whether we take the unit of narrative to be the word, the clause, the sentence or the paragraph, any equation of narrative sequence with time-sequence is both approximate and arbitrary. It is true that thoughts expressed in long sentences may take longer to think than those expressed in short sentences (though even this proposition is highly disputable); but feelings, sensations, and events are a quite different matter. If clock-time is like the proverbial tortoise then all narratives, including stream-of-consciousness narratives, proceed like the hare by fits and starts. The regular progression of the interior monologue is only apparent.

Nevertheless, to achieve this apparent regularity is no easy task. It made very great (and in the long run intolerable) demands on Joyce's technique. It meant that his early chapters had to be all 'scene' without any 'setting' and that contextual information regarding the characters and events could only be supplied through dialogue or within the interior monologue − by inserting it into the consciousness, that is, of the characters themselves. What Bloom or Stephen could not be made to hear or think or remember, the reader could not be told. Towards the end of *Ulysses* it is as if Joyce has a vast backlog of information about Bloom in particular which he has still not managed to incorporate. In 'Ithaca' he at last chose a form within which to unloose the data-bank.

'Ithaca', however, is not the first episode to disturb the illusion of linear narrative time. In the 'Oxen of the Sun' Joyce introduced a different scale of time − that of literary history moving forward − which claimed the reader's primary attention. Narrative progress continued, but could now be seen as a secondary matter. In 'Circe' there is again a clash of time-streams. Often the naturalistic time-frame seems to be suspended while, at a more hallucinatory level, the action still moves forward. For example, when the 'massive whoremistress' Bella Cohen makes her entry she announces, plausibly enough, that she's 'all of a mucksweat' (*U* 486). Her attention lights upon Bloom and there follow nearly twenty pages of ritual humiliation of this slave to 'petticoat government'. When Bloom emerges from his ordeal Bella speaks 'realistically' again:

Here. This isn't a musical peepshow. And don't you smash that piano. Who's paying here? (*U* 502)

It is as if the clock, having been stopped for a number of pages, now starts up again. At the naturalistic level Bella is a businesslike brothel-keeper and is saying what she would have said very soon after entering the room.

It is in 'Ithaca' that Joyce abandons the pretence of observing the unity of time altogether. The method he chooses is one of catechism or impersonal interrogation. The purpose of interrogation is often to prompt the victim into an exhaustive analysis of events, pausing over them for as long as is needed to evince the details the interrogator seeks. The narrative unit, here, is the question-and-answer. The questions are arranged in chronological sequence, but the pace of the sequence can be varied at will. In 'Ithaca' the effect is as if time were no longer continuous, but had been chopped up into quanta for the convenience of narrative exposition. The tortoise has given place to the hare.

But who is the catechist, and what is the purpose of his analysis? The information given us in 'Ithaca' is so varied that we cannot assign to it any obvious human purpose. It is a gathering of heterogeneous logical and scientific data – the latter including the longitude and latitude of 7 Eccles Street, the description of the 'phenomenon of ebullition' (U 594), and the inventory of Bloom's bookshelf – for reasons wholly inscrutable. Here Joyce is exposing yet another narrative convention, that of relevance, for the arbitrary device it really is. Henry James wrote in the preface to *Roderick Hudson* that 'really, universally, relations stop nowhere, and the exquisite problem of the artist is eternally but to draw, by a geometry of his own, the circle within which they shall happily *appear* to do so'.[23] Leopold Bloom is an amateur of science, portrayed in 'Cyclops' as holding forth 'with his jawbreakers about phenomenon and science and this phenomenon and the other phenomenon' (U 303). The catechist of 'Ithaca' is also obsessed by phenomena. He is a 'phenomenologist', so to speak, far removed from the assertive and clamorous world of human desires. His impersonal curiosity might extend to anything and everything concerning Bloom and Stephen (but especially Bloom). All this has its aesthetic justification well outside any narrow or preconceived notion of narrative relevance. The episode not only tells us a great deal about Bloom, Stephen and their surroundings that we should never have thought to ask; it also has an austere and peculiar beauty.

Joyce's published statements about 'Ithaca' show that he was deeply aware of the contrast it would made with his final chapter, 'Penelope'. He wrote in May 1921 that he was 'struggling with the acidities of Ithaca – a mathematico-astronomico-physico-mechanico-geometrico-chemico sublimation of Bloom and Stephen (devil take 'em both) to prepare for the final amplitudinously curvilinear episode *Penelope*'.[24] In 'Ithaca', he told Frank Budgen, 'not only will the reader know everything and know it in the baldest coldest way but Bloom and

Stephen thereby become heavenly bodies, wanderers like the stars at which they gaze' – all this in contrast to the 'last word (human, all too human)' of 'Penelope'.[25]

It is not true that the human interest of Bloom and Stephen is diminished by 'Ithaca'. Without it we should have a considerably impoverished picture of Bloom, in particular. In her essay 'Modern Fiction' Virginia Woolf argued that the novelist seeking to capture 'life' should portray the 'semi-transparent envelope' of her characters' consciousness – not their material features and surroundings.[26] Joyce's interior monologues had heavily influenced this prescription for the contemporary novel. In 'Ithaca', however, he reverts to a materialist standpoint and tells us very little about the movement of the characters' minds, foregoing both dialogue and stream of consciousness. We do not know why Stephen eventually leaves, and his conversation with Bloom over mugs of cocoa is baldly summarized by the catechist:

Did Bloom discover common factors of similarity between their respective like and unlike reactions to experience?

Both were sensitive to artistic impressions musical in preference to plastic or pictorial. Both preferred a continental to an insular manner of life, a cisatlantic to a transatlantic place of residence. Both indurated by early domestic training and an inherited tenacity of heterodox resistance professed their disbelief in many orthodox religious, national, social and ethical doctrines. Both admitted the alternately stimulating and obtunding influence of heterosexual magnetism.

Were their views on some points divergent?

Stephen dissented openly from Bloom's views on the importance of dietary and civic self-help while Bloom dissented tacitly from Stephen's views on the eternal affirmation of the spirit of man in literature.   (*U* 586–7)

The actual words they used (it is implied) are so much hot air. The 'phenomenologist's' concern is with logical classifications of similarity and difference, with enumeration and epitomization. 'Ithaca' contains a remarkable series of inventories and lists: Bloom's itemized (and also bowdlerized[27]) budget for the day, the contents of his shelves and desk drawers, details of the living-room furniture and its rearrangement, and the provenance of his mains water. There is much to be learnt from these lists, as there was from the 'materialist' narratives against which Virginia Woolf protested. Towards the end of the episode the catechist's impersonal concerns are contrasted with Bloom's self-interrogation – including his exhaustive inventory and survey of Flowerville – which he practises to alleviate fatigue and ensure 'sound repose and renovated vitality' (*U* 641). Still more are they contrasted with the 'feminine interrogation' (*U* 657) he faces, once he has entered the bedroom, from a reawakened Molly. The impersonal catechism of 'Ithaca' poses a model of questions answered with total, machine-like efficiency. But Bloom's answers to Molly's enquiries are both glib and circumspect. There follows Molly's monologue which, however exhaustive and repetitive it may be, has nothing machine-like about it.

It may be asked why, after the six-point demonstration of the limitations of the initial style that we have traced, Joyce should have closed the book with yet another interior monologue. In part, it is precisely because the realistic illusion of this style is 'human, all too human'. After the rigours of 'Sirens', 'Cyclops', 'Oxen', 'Circe', 'Eumaeus', and 'Ithaca' Joyce was ready to end his odyssey with a homecoming even at the level of style. 'Penelope', however, is the initial style transformed. Without interruption, without punctuation, without a narratorial presence it is still closer to the transparent 'stream of consciousness' than are the monologues of Bloom and Stephen. At the same time its deliberately composed rhetorical, rhythmical and syntactic features are much more overt. The earlier monologues had a haphazard structure and came to an end arbitrarily, or so it seemed, simply because time had run out. Molly's, by contrast, has a spiralling intensity and builds throughout its forty pages to a famous climax. Joyce described it in a 1921 letter to Budgen in remarkably symbolic terms:

Penelope is the clou of the book. The first sentence contains 2500 words. There are eight sentences in the episode. It begins and ends with the female word *yes*. It turns like the huge earth ball slowly surely and evenly round and round spinning, its four cardinal points being the female breasts, arse, womb and cunt expressed by the words *because, bottom* (in all senses bottom button, bottom of the class, bottom of the sea, bottom of his heart), *woman, yes. . . . Ich bin der Fleisch der stets bejaht.*   (*SL* 285)

Whatever we make of this it cannot be discussed in terms of style. We need to enter more deeply into the poetics of *Ulysses*, which is, as Joyce insisted on several occasions, a poetics of the body. The German sentence in the above extract may be translated 'I am the flesh that always affirms'.

9   The ultimate symbol

The ultimate symbol of *Ulysses* is Molly's 'yes' and the memory to which it refers – a memory of shared sexual joy, of a marriage proposal, and above all of a kiss. Bloom has earlier recalled the same kiss. As he sips his lunchtime burgundy in Davy Byrne's pub he senses a 'secret touch telling me memory' (*U* 175). The scene which comes back, with the young lovers 'Hidden under wild ferns on Howth' and the sweep of bay underneath, is startlingly sensual and vivid. Both Molly and Bloom recall that he ate a piece of seedcake, 'sweet and sour with spittle' (*U* 176), from out of her mouth. Both recall a full bodily contact, the first time (presumably) that Bloom had felt Molly's breasts. And Bloom's memory includes a curious moment of goatish irrelevance:

Pebbles fell. She lay still. A goat. No-one. High on Ben Howth rhododendrons a nannygoat walking surefooted, dropping currants. Screened under ferns she laughed warmfolded. Wildly I lay on her, kissed her; eyes, her lips, her stretched neck, beating, woman's breasts full in her blouse of nun's veiling, fat nipples upright. Hot I tongued her. She kissed me. I was kissed. All yielding she tossed my hair. Kissed, she kissed me. (*U* 176)

This should remind us of the later occasion when the Blooms made love as a result of Molly's excitement at seeing a pair of dogs copulating in the street. Both scenes contrast with conventional lovemaking by their stress on the profane, the goatish, the indecent. There could be no better example of Joyce's use of fiction to explore hitherto unexpressed joys, secret desires and secret shames.

But if Joyce at such moments is an 'adult' writer – a phenomenologist of the emotions – he is also an artist with a meticulous sense of design. It is entirely appropriate that the two passages describing the kiss on Howth Head come roughly at midday and midnight, and that Bloom's association of the wine with the seedcake carries a strong suggestion of Holy Communion. The kiss is a sacramental act on the part of Joyce's characters who (as Richard Brown has put it) disbelieve in religion but believe in sex.[1] Here is the

187

fulfilment of an ambition Joyce had expressed as a young man, when he wrote of 'converting the bread of everyday life into something that has a permanent artistic life of its own'.[2] Neither 'style' nor 'character' – essential as these approaches are to a reading of *Ulysses* – can sufficiently determine the place of the kiss in the artistic economy of the book as a whole.

As an epic work based on Homer's *Odyssey*, we should expect *Ulysses* to tell the story of a homecoming. As a symbolic work, we should expect some moral or spiritual revelation to emerge. Most critics would agree that *Ulysses* contains a homecoming and a revelation, but there has been endless controversy as to how these should be understood. In large part this is because Joyce refuses some of the opportunities he himself creates to bring *Ulysses* to a traditional sentimental climax. At the end of 'Circe', for example, Bloom envisions his dead son Rudy as he stoops over the prostrate body of Stephen. The saccharine, Little Lord Fauntleroy aspect of this '*fairy boy of eleven*' (*U* 532) has offended readers of the 'Is nothing sacred?' school, who object to Joyce's irreverent parody of the classic melodramatic recognition-scene. Yet Rudy is simply the last in the line of deceased relatives called back to Earth, and Joyce's handling of his reappearance is consistent with the debunking of spiritualism and séances which has gone on throughout the episode. Later Joyce further disappoints whatever sentimental hopes we might have attached to the spiritual-father-and-son theme. Despite Bloom's proposals that he should join the household, take music lessons and 'practise literature in his spare moments' (*U* 585), Stephen simply vanishes without explanation into the night. Frank Budgen speaks for our intuitive conviction when he suggests that the two are unlikely to meet again.[3]

When we turn to the resolution of Bloom's and Molly's relationship, we are bound to remember that the *Odyssey* concludes with the bloody and triumphant spectacle of Odysseus slaughtering the suitors. Many readers have been anxious to show that Bloom, returning home to a bed which a few hours earlier felt the conquering impress of Blazes Boylan, can lay claim to a similarly Homeric triumph. And yet his homecoming seems a routine, complaisant, slightly furtive act. One theory which has attracted disproportionate notice is that his apparent request for breakfast in bed with two eggs in the morning constitutes the missing act of aggression . . . or is this, as Hugh Kenner claims, the result of Molly's mishearing of his sleepy mumblings about the 'roc's auk's egg' (*U* 658)?[4] We shall never know, and perhaps we do not need to know.

William Empson points out that Bloom clearly has a strategem for dealing with Boylan: he plans to use Stephen as a decoy to get Boylan out of the house.[5] Both the Blooms are well aware that the proposed exchange of singing lessons for Italian lessons would probably lead to sexual dalliance. In 'Eumaeus' Bloom shows Stephen Molly's photograph in evening dress with a 'liberal display of bosom' and 'more than vision of breasts, the full lips parted' (*U* 573). Later he gives 'Stephen Dedalus, professor and author' pride of place in his narration of the day's events (*U* 656). Molly falls for the bait and enjoys fantasizing about becoming the poet's lover and mistress. From Bloom's point of view this is an extremely roundabout way of slaughtering the suitors. In any case, there is no reason to expect Stephen to fall into the trap.

Bloom's only tangible triumphs – as we saw in Chapter 7 – consist in retaining Molly's fundamental affection and coming to terms with his feelings of jealousy. Marilyn French is one of those recent critics who discovers moral heroism in these actions: 'In accepting her affair with Boylan, Bloom does "slaughter the suitors". . . . Bloom's attitude permits him to remain the "unconquered hero", right to the end of the novel, and it is one of the few things in *Ulysses* that Joyce clearly labels "right" '.[6] These liberal sentiments belong in the same tradition as Richard Ellmann's championship of Bloom as a persistent opponent of 'chauvinism and force'.[7] Yet Joyce, who as ever refuses to be pinned down, is a little more ambivalent than this. Bloom's motives for renouncing traditional male domination are not entirely altruistic and rational. Molly – however much she respects him – is inclined to see him as a dirty-minded masochist who deliberately connived at her adultery. Neither she nor Bloom possesses the self-awareness, or lack of shame, of Richard and Bertha in *Exiles* where the husband's desire to be cuckolded is openly discussed. Nevertheless there are good grounds for thinking that *Ulysses* explores a similar emotional dilemma. At the level of the 'novel of manners' it is legitimate to say that Joyce endorses Bloom's non-violent and non-aggressive behaviour. But the inner meaning of the couple's emotions and of their continued commitment to one another is something the author can only tacitly (though compassionately) indicate. The central subject of *Ulysses*, French argues, is 'mysterious sexuality'.[8] The Blooms confront their deepest sexual problems less articulately and more instinctively than the characters of *Exiles* did. Bloom, unlike Richard Rowan, is not an advanced thinker in the Ibsen tradition. Hence the

mysteries of sex are explored through non-rational and poetic means
– through symbolic and sensual epiphanies – instead of stage-
dialogue. Any reading of the symbols (and they have given rise to
innumerable readings) is bound to be provisional and to some extent
subjective. Stuart Gilbert pointed out long ago that within the larger
odyssey of Bloom we could trace the mini-odyssey of his cake of soap,
a 'Saponiad'.[9] His own study, however, is a *Gilbertiad*, and a similar
rule is likely to apply to any deliberately symbolic account. In this
chapter we shall pursue some implications of a single symbol in *Ulysses*
– that of the kiss.

The notion of the kiss was foregrounded early in the *Portrait of the
Artist*, when Wells asked Stephen whether or not he kissed his mother
at night. Stephen was too young to understand that this was a trick
question, and afterwards he brooded over what it involved:

What did that mean, to kiss? You put your face up like that to say goodnight
and then his mother put her face down. That was to kiss. His mother put her
lips on his cheek; her lips were soft and they wetted his cheek; and they made
a tiny little noise: kiss. Why did people do that with their two faces? (*P* 15)

In *Ulysses* we can no longer view the kiss as innocently as this. For
Stephen, the idea of a mouth-to-mouth kiss with his mother now carries
the horrific implications seen in his vampire-poem. The Blooms' kiss
on Howth Head was mouth-to-mouth, and for Molly 'theres nothing
like a kiss long and hot down to your soul almost paralyses you' (*U*
661–2). Yet Leopold Bloom seems long ago to have lost interest in
kissing his wife's lips. He prefers to kiss other parts of her anatomy,
which excite him sexually without the need for the full reciprocal
emotion experienced on Howth Head ('Kissed, she kissed me'). The
'four cardinal points' of the female body around which, as Joyce wrote
to Budgen, 'Penelope' revolves do not include the lips, which are
common to both sexes. But adult kissing does not necessarily conjoin
two faces, as Stephen once thought. Like other forms of loveplay, it
involves the expressive conjunction of two bodies.

Joyce told Frank Budgen that *Ulysses* was 'among other things . . .
the epic of the human body'.[10] The body referred to, as we saw in
Chapter 1, is not the classical body portrayed in the statues outside the
National Library or in the '*Bath of the Nymph*', 'Given away with the
Easter number of *Photo Bits*: Splendid masterpiece in art colours' (*U*
67), hanging over the Blooms' bed. Joyce is not interested in physical
perfection but in a body which is the scene of constant activity, with
its orifices open and even its entrails on show. His is a tangible body,

felt, smelt and lived in rather than idealized; divisible like butcher's meat into its separate parts, but also merging with its surroundings and permeating the whole of art and life. The 'Linati schema' that Joyce drew up shows that each episode after the Telemachiad bore its appropriate bodily organ: kidneys for 'Calypso', the lungs for 'Aeolus', the brain for 'Scylla and Charybdis', the ear for 'Sirens', fat for 'Penelope' and so on. In these terms to read through *Ulysses* is to progress from one hypertrophied organ to another.

One of the first things Bloom encounters in Nighttown is his 'composite portrait' in a pair of distorting mirrors. In between the concave and convex mirrors is one which shows him 'level, Bloom for Bloom' (*U* 428). *Ulysses* as a whole combines the plain and the distorting mirrors. On one level is the realistic portrayal of trivial bodily acts such as defecation, micturition, and nose-picking. Realism also dictates the presence in *Ulysses* of a vigorous cast of the naturally disabled and deformed: the blind stripling, the one-legged sailor, the gnomes and pygmies of 'Circe', Gerty MacDowell. At another level the book is pervaded by metaphorical bodily distortions, arising out of the ribaldry of ordinary Dublin speech:

– By Jesus, she had the foot and mouth disease and no mistake!   (*U* 134)

– It's as uncertain as a child's bottom, he said.   (*U* 92)

Hoho begob, says I to myself, says I. That explains the milk in the cocoanut and absence of hair on the animal's chest.   (*U* 317)

Examples of actual bodily torture and deliberate mutilation are surprisingly rare in *Ulysses* (in this respect, the book belongs to the high noon of pre-First World War liberalism, whose passing was recorded by Yeats in 'Nineteen Hundred and Nineteen'). The one striking exception is the discussion of British imperial flogging and hanging in 'Cyclops', which gives rise to one of Joyce's most memorable mixtures of realism and grotesque comedy. At the opposite extreme from the priapic image of the 'Ruling passion strong in death' (*U* 303) is Bloom's vision of Palestine and the Dead Sea, 'the grey sunken cunt of the world' (*U* 63). Palestine was the home of the 'oldest, the first race', but it is now

A barren land, bare waste. Vulcanic lake, the dead sea: no fish, weedless, sunk deep in the earth. No wind would lift those waves, grey metal, poisonous foggy waters. Brimstone they called it raining down: the cities of the plain: Sodom, Gomorrah, Edom. All dead names. A dead sea in a dead land, grey and old.

(*U* 63)

Barrenness – not death or mutilation or the horrors of dying that
Stephen imagines – is the worst evil Joyce shows us in *Ulysses*. The fear
of barrenness and of racial and species death is the context of the book's
endorsement of 'Warm beds: warm fullblooded life' (*U* 116–17),
however promiscuous or anarchic.

The images of a 'dead sea in a dead land' and 'the grey sunken cunt
of the world' establish a connection, which is found time and again in
Joyce's book, between the body and water. We have seen *Ulysses*
described as the epic of the human body and the odyssey of a lump of
soap; but it might also have been described as a poem about water. One
of the finest things in 'Ithaca' is the great passage enumerating the
qualities of water (*U* 592–3). Water is to *Ulysses* what storms are to
Shakespeare and the heath is to Hardy. It takes us beyond the febrile
complexities of civilized life, 'setting behind the small action of [the]
protagonists', as D. H. Lawrence wrote of Hardy, 'the terrific action
of unfathomed nature'.[11] *Ulysses* very nearly begins with the sea
('*Thalatta! Thalatta!*', *U* 11) and ends, as Molly drifts towards her final
'yes', with 'the sea the sea' (*U* 704). The water of the sea is 'our great
sweet mother'; it is the element symbolically sailed upon by
Ulysses–Bloom and flown over by Stephen Dedalus. The sea itself is
admittedly only a marginal presence – viewed from the beach, or
rhapsodized over in faraway accents – at the literal level in *Ulysses*.
But Joyce misses no opportunity of reminding us how intimately the
natural element helps to shape our urban lives. Not only does it flow
through the city and via pipes and taps into our houses. We live
immersed in water because of its 'ubiquity as constituting 90% of the
human body' (*U* 592–3).

Bloom, Stephen and Molly are all judged by their attitudes to the sea
and to water. Bloom's actual experiences of the sea have not been very
happy ones. He remembers a trip to Holyhead (*U* 547) and a pleasure
cruise on the *Erin's King* which hit perilous seas around the Kish
lighthouse (*U* 551). Molly remembers – though Bloom has
conveniently repressed – his foolhardy attempts to handle a rowing-
boat at Bray (*U* 686). Bloom in 'Eumaeus' remarks on the 'eloquent
fact . . . that the sea was there in all its glory and in the natural course
of things somebody or other had to sail on it' (*U* 550). Nevertheless,
he would rather the 'somebody or other' were not himself.

It is on the 'stream of life' (*U* 88) that 'Seabloom' (*U* 289) displays
rather more proficiency as a sailor. 'Life, love, voyage round your own
little world', he jauntily reflects (*U* 374). Like all the Dubliners he has

an eye for the seaside girls of Blazes Boylan's song. From a safe distance he admires the sea's 'vastness', its 'unplumbed profundity', its 'restlessness' (*U* 592). But Bloom, 'waterlover', prefers water in its municipal and domestic manifestations, in the public baths, in the kettle, or on its remarkable route to the kitchen tap (*U* 591).

Stephen, of course, is 'hydrophobe'. His refusal to wash before drinking his cocoa forces Bloom to admit the 'incompatibility of aquacity with the erratic originality of genius' (*U* 593). Stephen claims he does not need to bathe because 'All Ireland is washed by the gulfstream' (*U* 22). This draws our attention to another of the prime functions of water and the sea in modern society – as a carrier-away and a receptacle for waste-products. Among these are the 'Elijah is coming' leaflet (thrown into the Liffey), Stephen's nosepickings left on the beach, and the body's extrusions left in dirty clothes. Stephen's noserags are no longer white but 'snotgreen' (*U* 11); Molly's bedroom is cluttered with 'soiled linen' (*U* 64); but Bloom, as we might expect, has a penchant for washing such items. He has 'washed his wife's undergarments when soiled', and sees it as a sign of love: 'Love me, love my dirty shirt' (*U* 557). It would only be Joycean to reflect on the consequences of dropping an 'r' from that quotation, since Bloom's coprophiliac tastes are something Molly has not failed to register. For him, love and excrement belong together almost as inevitably as water and dirt.

H. G. Wells, in an influential and favourable review of *A Portrait of the Artist*, accused Joyce of a 'cloacal obsession', *cloaca* being the Latin word for a drain, sewer, or excremental cavity.[12] The phrase stuck, and it is no accident that Joyce himself employed it in *Ulysses*. Here, using Professor MacHugh as his spokesman, he turns the allegation back on his accusers:

– What was their civilisation? Vast, I allow: but vile. Cloacae: sewers. The Jews in the wilderness and on the mountaintop said: *It is meet to be here. Let us build an altar to Jehovah*. The Roman, like the Englishman who follows in his footsteps, brought to every new shore on which he set his foot (on our shore he never set it) only his cloacal obsession. He gazed about him in his toga and he said: *It is meet to be here. Let us construct a water-closet*. (*U* 132)

The ancient Irish, Lenehan adds, were partial to the 'running stream' (*U* 133). Yet the Irish since Swift have the reputation of being Yahoos engaged in a perpetual 'dirty protest', while their English rulers are fixated on water-closets. No. 7 Eccles Street does not contain a water-closet – Bloom and Molly have to make do with a chamber-pot under the bed, and an earth-closet in the back garden – though Bloom's dream cottage, Flowerville, is equipped with them (*U* 634). Neither of Joyce's protagonists possesses what Freud described as the 'anal character' – one of 'orderliness, parsimony and obstinacy'[13] – and indeed these qualities strike us immediately as Anglo-Saxon rather than Celtic. The anal character derives from the sublimation of anal-eroticism, and is therefore not to be expected in someone like Bloom who has retained this zone's erotogenic properties in adult life.[14] Bloom conspicuously fails to regard the faeces as unclean and disturbing matter that should not be part of the body. On Ben Howth he is clearly stimulated by the nanny goat's currants. At the same time he is a 'waterlover' who pays general attention to cleanliness. Conceivably there is a source of his psychosexual conflicts in this, since Bloom's anal-eroticism affects the reader as masochistic and self-degrading.

Ulysses in this respect offers a prolonged meditation on the subject of Yeats's lines:

> But love has pitched his mansion in
> The place of excrement;
>   ('Crazy Jane talks with the Bishop')

For Bloom, the paradoxical affinity of love and excrement is redeemed by his love of water. Water, in the shape of bodily fluids, is the subject of a profound fascination which is both admissible and shameful. For example, he likes grilled kidneys because they 'gave to his palate a fine tang of faintly scented urine' (*U* 57). Among the affinities between the moon and woman of which he is aware is 'her potency over effluent and refluent waters' (*U* 623). The twin summits of sexual experience – kissing and copulation – involve not merely physical conjunction but the mingling of bodily fluids. Our attention is drawn to this by his memory of the exchange of the seedcake, 'sweet and sour with spittle'. Such mingling, however, has ceased to be part of his relationship with Molly. The exact nature of their sexual activities is unclear but it evidently stops short of full intercourse. Bloom's last physical act before going to sleep is to kiss the 'plump mellow yellow smellow melons of her rump' (*U* 656). The fact that they sleep head-to-toe seems a measure of their physical deviance and emotional estrangement.

Ulysses begins with images of the body in water: the drowned man, the shaving-bowl, Buck Mulligan swimming, the sybaritic pleasure with which Bloom in 'Lotos-Eaters' looks forward to soaking his body in the bath. There is also, in Stephen's memory of his mother retching up bile, a horrifying image of the 'bitter waters' in the body. Towards the end of the book Stephen's meeting with Bloom and the entry of Molly as a narrator produce a series of benign images of fluids in the body. Bloom and Stephen perform two tangible acts of fellowship, drinking cocoa together and then urinating together under the stars. Molly in 'Penelope' begins to menstruate − a manifestation of the most tabooed of the bodily fluids and a sign that she has not been impregnated by Boylan. Not only is her monologue written in liquid, unpunctuated prose but her thoughts return again and again to such fluids as blood, milk, urine, saliva, sweat, and semen. Her romantic reconstruction of her life, in the course of the monologue, consists of a series of kisses and approaches to sexual intercourse.

Ulysses is thus a hymn to human fertility and procreation − though far more compassionate and circumspect in its tone than the crude braggadocio of 'Oxen of the Sun'. The facts of life that the book as a whole recognizes are the fragility of human emotions and the necessary 'limitation of fertility' (*U* 657). We may draw inspiration from the animal elements in our natures but − despite the propagandism of the 'Oxen' chapter − we are not animals. Bloom and Molly's emotional estrangement has unleashed the more anarchic elements in their sexual make-up, driving Molly into the arms of Boylan and Bloom to masturbation, coprophilia and promiscuous fantasy. We cannot say what their future will be but we do know, by the end of the book, that they both retain undimmed memories of that from which they have become estranged.

In the 'Oxen of the Sun' fertility and procreation are viewed as public concerns, even if this leads to the crudity of anti-birth control propaganda and the vulgarity of Buck Mulligan's 'National Fertilising Farm'. Perhaps it is typically Joycean that the more sensitive and subtle handling of the theme of fertility in *Ulysses* is also a very private matter. Molly's final 'yes' to anarchic sexuality does not prevent her from handling her love life prudently and taking steps to avoid unwanted pregnancies. Bloom, sadly, seems to have had little wish to engender a son after Rudy's death. He and Molly must face their problems of sexual adjustment as solitary individuals cut off, to a great extent, from the social continuities around them. That is their fate, as bourgeois characters. Their consolation is that the mysteries of sexuality are − at least, within the perspectives of *Ulysses* − best examined within the home. Molly observes disapprovingly of her sleeping husband that 'he came somewhere Im sure . . . he must do it

somewhere and the last time he came on my bottom' (*U* 659–61). The
kiss on Howth Head led to the Blooms' decision to marry and set up
home together; and Molly, who was then in her teens, did not achieve
full sexual enjoyment until the age of 22 (*U* 688). That homecoming and
home coming are both desirable, and both difficult, is therefore one
of the messages of *Ulysses*. (Another is that Stephen, if he is to become
a genuine artist, cannot remain in the bourgeois home.) The truth of
the ultimate symbol in *Ulysses* is therefore a somewhat narrow one –
not so much a spiritual or a religious revelation as the 'Fundamentals
of Sexology or the Love Passion which Doctor L. B. says is the book
sensation of the year' (*U* 478). But the symbol leads not only to pungent
and perhaps sordid mysteries but to an expansive, richly imaginative
vision of life. Bloom's sensuality is intimately connected with his
sensitivity, his curiosity about people and things, his poignant
awareness of the loss of his son. Molly's sensuality is linked to her
capacity for poetic rhapsody. Her moments of transcendent sexual
experience are indissolubly connected with the landscapes of her life.
Having grown up on the Rock of Gibraltar and chosen her marriage-
partner on the Hill of Howth she is an earth-goddess permeated by the
meeting of the land and sea. 'I gave him all the pleasure I could leading
him on till he asked me to say yes and I wouldnt answer first only looked
out over the sea and the sky I was thinking of so many things he didnt
know' (*U* 703). Her memories are as irresistible as falling water and as
salty and uncontainable as the sea. Molly, however, is Joyce's creation
and her multitudinous internal life is something that only his book can
give access to. In *Ulysses* the 'bread of everyday life' is transformed,
not into a Communion wafer, but into the seedcake which is an emblem
of joy and fertility but also 'Mawkish pulp her mouth had mumbled
sweet and sour with spittle' (*U* 176). The young Stephen Dedalus had
argued that beauty could be found in a place as unlikely as the clock
on the Ballast Office. The author of *Ulysses* looked for beauty in
private rather than public places, and was concerned with bodily as well
as spiritual manifestations; but he too had the audacity to look for it
in the commonest objects at which no-one else had looked.

PART III

Finnegans Wake: List of chapters

(This outline gives no more than the barest indications of the scope of each chapter; when reading the *Wake* a fuller summary or textual guide should be consulted.)

10   The nightmare of history

Work in Progress

Joyce had spent most of the First World War in Zurich. After the war he returned to Trieste, but soon moved to Paris, where he was to stay until 1939. In Paris he was no longer a lone exile: the city was becoming a legendary home for expatriate American and English writers. It was here that *Ulysses* found a publisher, and on 2 February 1922, the morning of his fortieth birthday, he received the first two copies. His sense of fulfilment, however, was short-lived. The most arduous task of his life was about to begin.

In Paris Joyce's reputation as a banned writer made him an instant literary celebrity. He became an acknowledged leader of the avant-garde. At the same time, he was less far removed from Dublin, and began to meet a steady flow of visitors from Ireland. One of the first, Desmond Fitzgerald, was Minister of Information in the new Free State government. Fitzgerald asked him if he would return to Ireland now that the twenty-six counties had received their independence, but Joyce refused for the time being.[1] Soon afterwards Nora Barnacle and his children went home on a visit, in the course of which they were caught in crossfire between Free State troops and the rebel forces of De Valera. Echoes of the 'devil era' (*FW* 473:8) and the Irish Civil War are to be found throughout *Finnegans Wake*. For the rest of his life Joyce refused to visit his native country, his nearest approaches being to stay at London's Euston Hotel and at such English watering-places as Bognor Regis.

Though not as dramatic as the upheavals in Ireland, the changes in Joyce's life in the years 1918–22 were substantial enough. The banning of *Ulysses* greatly delayed the financial rewards he could expect from his work. On the other hand, he had had the extraordinary good fortune to attract a patron, Harriet Shaw Weaver, who most generously supported him from 1917 to his death. Miss Weaver's patronage, based only on a belief in his genius, has been justifiably

represented as a literary miracle of Dickensian proportions.[2] It made
his move to Paris possible, and greatly aided his transition from being
an obscure language teacher in a Mediterranean backwater to an
influential and established major writer. It secured his independence
both from the world of employment and from the literary market. Yet
inevitably, in view of the esoteric nature of his last book, the question
must be asked whether this anachronistic form of literary financing did
not in the long run incur its own penalties. Joyce, though scarcely an
example of prudence as far as money was concerned, was scrupulously
aware of his obligations towards his patron. These obligations were not
artistic – since he knew of Miss Weaver's reservations about the
direction his work was taking as early as the 'Sirens' episode of *Ulysses*
– but moral. He took immense pains to explain himself to Miss
Weaver, and showed patience and charm over her lack of
understanding. We shall never know how he would have responded had
he found a publisher as loyal and steadfast as Miss Weaver, for her
part, turned out to be. As a professional full-time writer blessed with
a patron, Joyce was almost uniquely secure from the need to find an
audience outside a small coterie of friends and admirers. This cannot
be discounted when we consider the extravagant demands *Finnegans
Wake* makes on the reader's attention. As he began his new task, Joyce
told one of his Paris friends that he 'might easily have written this story
in the traditional manner. Every novelist knows the recipe'. Instead,
he was 'trying to build many planes of narrative with a single esthetic
purpose'.[3] This is not to say that he had ever actually considered the
idea of writing a traditional novel. He pursued his own path with the
astonishing self-confidence expressed in a remark he reportedly made
to Samuel Beckett in the late 1930s: 'I have discovered I can do anything
with language I want'.[4] Unlike many less fortunate writers he had the
opportunity to exercise and vindicate this self-confidence.

Even so, Joyce in his later years endured a good deal of hardship. He
began writing *Finnegans Wake*, in one of his most remarkable bursts
of creative energy, in 1923–4. Had all gone to plan it should have been
finished well before the end of the decade; but a succession of personal
troubles overtook him. His eye complaint, which had begun during the
war years, led to long spells of enforced rest and a series of painful
operations to preserve his sight. His daughter Lucia slowly succumbed
to schizophrenia. No sooner had *Ulysses* begun to find acceptance in
the literary world than the early portions of *Finnegans Wake* were
greeted with dismay by some of his most faithful admirers, among them

his brother Stanislaus who stated his objections in typically cantankerous fashion.

His new book, Joyce told Miss Weaver at their first meeting (in London in 1922) was to be a 'history of the world'.[5] Though centred on an innkeeper and his family, it would abandon chronology and conventional characterization, even of the sort he had employed in *Ulysses*. 'Time and the river and the mountain' were to be its real heroes.[6] Nevertheless, the earliest drafts are sketches of Irish historical and mythological figures such as St Kevin, Tristan and Isolde, King Roderick O'Conor, St Patrick, and the 'archdruid' Berkeley. These were to represent aspects of the members of the 'Chapelizod family' – a family consisting of a father and mother, two quarrelling sons and a daughter, living over a pub by the banks of the Liffey in one of Dublin's western suburbs. Soon the father and mother took shape as HCE (the mountain) and ALP (the river); the actual names being variable but tending towards universality, as in 'Haveth Childers Everywhere' and 'Anna Livia Plurabelle' (the titles of two early published fragments) – and the initials always the same. What led Joyce to choose these sets of initials is unknown (why, for example, is ALP a river not a mountain?). But it is most likely that they are a deliberate anagram of the word CHAPEL,[7] presumably because Chapelizod is composed of 'Chapel' and 'Izod' (Isolde, the Irish bride of King Mark of Cornwall). If father and mother are mountain and river, the two brothers in *Finnegans Wake* are represented as a tree and a stone (tree + stone = treestone or Tristan). From this we may deduce that Isolde or Issy is the apex of two of the triangular relationships within the Chapelizod family. As daughter and sister she is an object of secret and repressed desire both to her father (for whom she may be supplanting her mother) and to her two brothers. Such triangular relationships within the family had already been found in *Ulysses*, where they were highlighted by Stephen's Shakespeare theory, and in the 'family romance' theme in the *Portrait*. In *Finnegans Wake* the family romance becomes a 'family umbroglia' (*FW* 284:4). And just as Stephen in *Ulysses* had assumed the roles of Hamlet, Icarus, Telemachus, and so on, the family structure in the *Wake* would be made to incorporate the widest possible range of history and legend. Once again a microcosm of human life was to be centred in the bourgeois home.

From 1924 fragments of the early drafts of the *Wake* began appearing in little magazines and in pamphlet form under the title

Work in Progress. 'Anna Livia Plurabelle', the most celebrated section of all, first appeared in the French magazine *Le Navire d'Argent* in October 1925. Here Joyce's technique of fusing character and landscape – the archetypal mother as the River Liffey – was made public for the first time. 'Anna Livia' was frequently revised and reprinted as part of Joyce's battle to gain acceptance for his new mode of writing. In England, for example, it should have appeared in the prestigious *Calendar of Modern Letters*, but publication was stopped when the printers refused to typeset certain passages, presumably on the grounds of suspected obscenity. Joyce allowed it to be printed in *Experiment*, a Cambridge undergraduate magazine edited by William Empson, and then – thanks to Eliot's good offices – it was brought out as a 'Criterion Miscellany' pamphlet produced by Faber and Faber. The Criterion pamphlet had a modest success, being reprinted twice in 1930 and again in 1932. Despite the disapproval of most of the English literary establishment a large number of people were curious as to what Joyce was up to.

These early readers cannot have seen *Work in Progress* as a 'history of the world'. It would have seemed barely conceivable that the slender episodes published in pamphlet form could join together in a book still more encyclopaedic than *Ulysses*. Inevitably it was not the 'family umbroglia' or Joyce's fusion of motifs and identities, but his fusion of words which attracted most comment. Not only historical and mythological characters but language itself is melted down, joined together and remoulded in the 'museyroom' (*FW* 8:9) of the *Wake* – an imaginary museum which is also a 'musicroom' (as in the brothel in 'Circe', *U* 469) and a waxworks (*FW* 113:22). Joyce's decision to experiment with words, as he had earlier done with character and narrative form, has its own justifications, as we shall see. Yet it is powerful evidence of the influence on his work of a particular time and place. If ever linguistic experiment was in vogue it was in the early 1920s, in the centres of the European avant-garde such as Paris.

Paris in 1920 was the home of a successful revolution in the visual arts. Not only the method of representation but the whole traditional conception of the meaning of the painted surface had been abandoned. Not surprisingly there were those who sought to unleash the energies of Cubism and abstraction in the literary arts. Foremost among them were writers associated with Picasso and his circle, such as Apollinaire and the expatriate American writer Gertrude Stein. Stein's *Tender Buttons* (1914) developed an experimental, patterned and hypnotic prose-style long before Joyce had begun the 'Sirens' episode of *Ulysses*. At the same time modern poets in many countries began to concentrate on rhythm, assonance, repetition and image-association at the expense of easy intelligibility. In England 1922, the year of *Ulysses*, was also the year of Eliot's *Waste Land* and of Edith Sitwell and William Walton's *Facade*. The reciprocal influence of Joyce on Eliot and of Eliot on Joyce is well-known.[8] Joyce wrote his first parody of *The Waste Land* (ending 'Shan't we? Shan't we? Shan't we?') in a letter to Miss Weaver in 1925 (*SL* 309). Subsequent parodies of Eliot's last line appear in several places in the *Wake*. They should remind us that the sheer daring of Eliot's collage of fragments —

> London Bridge is falling down falling down falling down
> *Poi s'ascose nel foco che gli affina*
> *Quando fiam uti chelidon* — O swallow swallow
> *Le prince d'Aquitaine à la tour abolie*
> These fragments I have shored against my ruins
> Why then Ile fit you. Hieronymo's mad againe.
> Datta. Dayadhvam. Damyata.
>   Shantih shantih shantih

— was a more economical and revolutionary method of epitomizing world culture than anything Joyce had aspired to in *Ulysses*.

Equally, though he chose not to acknowledge their work, it is hard to believe that the example of other 'experimental' writers such as Gertrude Stein and Edith Sitwell exerted no influence on Joyce. In *Facade*, for example, Sitwell abandons logic and sense for a garrulous, light-hearted verbal music incorporating familiar dance-rhythms. Is it merely Joyce's comparable interest in dance-music and popular song which accounts for the following Sitwellian cadences in *Finnegans Wake*?

dear Sir Armoury, queer Sir Rumoury   (*FW* 96:7)

Here she is, Amnisty Ann! Call her calamity electrifies man. (*FW* 207:27–8)

You should pree him prance the polcat   (*FW* 513:12–13)[9]

In *Work in Progress* Joyce was adding his authority to a movement of linguistic experiment which had begun without him. *Ulysses* experiments with narrative forms, with prose styles and the rhetoric of fiction; *Finnegans Wake* is much closer to the modernist ethos of 'free verse' and 'prose-poetry'. Much of that ethos was fairly frivolous, a modish response to the 'jazz age' and the age of the flapper. Even Eliot was soon in full retreat from his earlier extravagances. Joyce, however, went on. Such support as he could muster came largely from the

Parisian review *transition*, which opened its first number (in April 1927) by declaring 'The Revolution of the Word'. The manifesto, drafted by Eugene Jolas, declared war on 'the banal word, monotonous syntax, static psychology, descriptive naturalism'. Among its pronouncements were the following:

The literary creator has the right to disintegrate the primal matter of words imposed on him by textbooks and dictionaries.

He has the right to use words of his own fashioning and to disregard existing grammatical and syntactical laws.

The 'litany of words' is admitted as an independent unit.

We are not concerned with the propagation of sociological ideas, except to emancipate the creative elements from the present ideology.

The writer expresses. He does not communicate.

The plain reader be damned.[10]

Joyce, following his invariable practice, did not sign the 'Revolution of the Word'. But he was content, by and large, to have his work championed by *transition* along lines laid down in its manifesto. His friend Frank Budgen, for example, declared that the difficulties of *Work in Progress* arose not from any 'unessential obscurity' but from 'our own atrophied word-sense'.[11] A good deal of the acrimony aroused by *Work in Progress* may have been due to its association in the public mind with the outpourings of surrealists and 'verbal revolutionaries'. Joyce's pamphlets were seen not as fragments of a unique work, but as part of a vociferous – and, in the short run, not very successful – campaign to subvert the authority of 'textbooks and dictionaries' over what writers could write.

The hostility to his new work was something Joyce felt very intimately. Whatever his opinion of his brother's tact and literary judgment it cannot have been pleasant to receive a letter from Stanislaus describing the first published instalment as 'unspeakably wearisome'.[12] (Later, Stanislaus refused a presentation copy of the completed *Finnegans Wake*.) Other reactions were more delayed but, when they came, no less dismaying. Given that the *Wake*, with its three books and short *ricorso* chapter, was not completed until November 1938 it is startling to find that Joyce had almost finished Books I and III by the end of 1926. Unfortunately the speed and assurance of his first four years' work could never be regained. His eye trouble grew more serious in 1926 and, at the same time, he was shaken by the defection of Ezra Pound, who (he told Miss Weaver) 'has written turning it down altogether, can make nothing of it, wading through it for a possible joke, etc' (*SL* 317). Shortly afterwards came the critical broadsides of Wyndham Lewis in *Time and Western Man* and of

Rebecca West in *The Strange Necessity*.[13] Miss Weaver herself came as close as she ever would to deserting the standard. In September 1926, anxious to retain her allegiance, Joyce invited her to 'order' a piece to be incorporated in the book. Miss Weaver played the game and sent him a photograph of the Giant's Grave at Penrith in Cumberland. Joyce, who (after much else) was then drafting the opening chapters, responded by giving a prominent place to the burial of the giant Finn MacCool with his head at Howth and his toes in Phoenix Park.[14] Now and later his letters to Miss Weaver were stuffed with glosses and explanations of what he was doing. By the beginning of February 1927, however, she had written to him frankly expressing her misgivings:

I am made in such a way that I do not care much for the output from your Wholesale Safety Pun Factory nor for the darknesses and unintelligibilities of your deliberately-entangled language system. It seems to me you are wasting your genius. But I daresay I am wrong and in any case you will go on with what you are doing, so why thus stupidly say anything to discourage you? I hope I shall not do so again.[15]

Joyce was deeply shaken by all this, but its perhaps predictable effect in the long run was to make him retreat into a still more 'deliberately-entangled language'. Difficult enough before, the *Wake* now became cautious, self-doubting, and impenetrably obscure. Wyndham Lewis, Rebecca West and their attacks on him were incorporated into the book's rhetoric. Already Shem the Penman, Joyce's *alter ego* in the *Work in Progress*, had been told by his brother that 'You are mad!' (*FW* 193:28). Once his initial four-year burst of energy was over, Joyce's compositional technique seems to have become increasingly laborious. 'Such an amount of reading seems to be necessary before my old flying machine grumbles up into the air', he complained in 1931.[16] As his eyesight deteriorated the reading became more difficult and friends had to be drafted in to help him – but, being perhaps wary of the world's judgment, he was deaf to all hints that he should bring his work to a speedy conclusion.

These anguished middle years of the *Wake*'s composition have a profound irony for the modern student. The passages to which Joyce's earliest readers objected are those which – thanks to scholarly aids and to théir own inherent momentum, even where Joyce greatly added to them after 1927 – we can now fairly easily master. 'Anna Livia Plurabelle', for example, has been widely recognized as one of the most beautiful prose-poems in English. The worst and most disorienting quagmires in the *Wake* do not come in Books I and III, which he had already roughed out before the disastrous winter of 1926–7, but in

Book II which at his most optimistic he had hoped to complete in a further year or so (*SL* 315). The extreme difficulties of the book, that is to say – difficulties which several experienced commentators have hinted may be irresolvable – were a response to Joyce's disheartenment with his first readers' impatience with its easier passages. The pattern of exile and lonely withdrawal was reasserting itself and, for the first time, adversely affecting his life's work.

One immediate consequence of the crisis of the winter of 1926–7 was the publication of *Pomes Penyeach*. Both Joyce and Miss Weaver saw the value of a volume which, however slim (it contains only thirteen brief lyrics) would place his capacity for soulful emotional expression once again before the public. The book was rushed out in July 1927. Its most striking and distinguished poem, 'Tilly', dates from 1904 (see Chapter 2); the others are mainly from the war years, though their manner belongs to the 1890s. They are love-poems, including some memorable expressions of his love for his son and daughter, and their most consistent device is the emotional landscape; most of them are either 'night-pieces' or 'sea-pieces'. 'Simples', 'A Flower Given to My Daughter', 'On the Beach at Fontana' and others are polished if slightly pallid exercises which reveal the shape of some of Joyce's emotional obsessions. These poems had little effect on his reputation, though Rebecca West in *The Strange Necessity* belaboured them on the grounds of tastelessness and 'reactionary sentimentality'.[17] Joyce was wrong if he thought his avant-garde fiction would be accepted the more readily for being the work of a distinctly conventional poet.

At about the time *Pomes Penyeach* was published Joyce conceived the extraordinary idea that *Finnegans Wake* might be handed over to the Irish writer James Stephens, who had expressed his liking for its way with language. 'Of course he would never take a fraction of the time or pains I take but so much the better for him and me and possibly for the book itself. If he consented to maintain three or four points which I consider essential and I showed him the threads he could finish the design' (*SL* 323), Joyce wrote. 'Any duffer ought to be able to pick the threads for part 2 out of the immense sombre *melopées* of 1 and 3' (*SL* 327). A much happier result of his loss of self-confidence in 1927 was the time and trouble he began to devote to explaining what he was doing. The more complications he put into *Work in Progress*, the more anxious he became to give some help to its first readers. The 'help' that he offered over the years was both internal and external to the work. Internally, the *Wake* is full of statements which invite us to interpret them as self-commentary:

You is feeling like you was lost in the bush, boy? You says: It is a puling sample
jungle of woods. You most shouts out: Bethicket me for a stump of a beech
if I have the poultriest notions what the farest he all means. Gee up, girly! The
quad gospellers may own the targum but any of the Zingari shoolerim may pick
a peck of kindlings yet from the sack of auld hensyne. (*FW* 112:3–8)

'Gee up, girly!' was in effect what Joyce said, at very great length, in
his letters to Miss Weaver. He encouraged the editors of *transition* to
reply to his critics and, when a concerted volume of essays was planned,
he both invented the title – *Our Exagmination Round His
Factification for Incamination of Work in Progress* (1929) – and
directed the whole operation. In *Our Exagmination* and his letters to
Miss Weaver we see Joyce constructing, not only the *Wake* itself, but
the foundations for the extensive network of scholarly platforms and
scaffolding from which it has come to be viewed.

We shall go on to examine the grounds of a critical approach to the
Wake, but one of Joyce's justifications of his method deserves to be
mentioned in this review of the book's history. This is the idea – on
which he placed great stress when forced to defend himself after 1927
– that the *Wake* is a 'night-piece'. Night-language, he maintained, is
as different from day-language as dreaming is from waking life. This
claim, which is still heard from time to time,[18] is crucial to the extent
that it leads us to explore Joyce's notions of the nature of language and
to relate his work to the Freudian and Jungian analysis of dreams.
Freud himself had written of the 'amusing and curious neologisms'
thrown up by the process of word-formation in dreams.[19] Yet, since it
cannot be said that neologism is a major feature of the dreaming
process, such a justification for the language of *Finnegans Wake*
smacks dangerously of expediency. It reflects the same rather crude
notion of imitative form that Joyce invoked to defend some of the later
chapters of *Ulysses* (for example, the prose of 'Eumaeus' was flatulent
and cliché-ridden 'because Bloom was tired'). It is always hard to draw
the line between dogged conviction and outrageous practical joking in
his adherence to such ideas. Frank O'Connor tells of an evening when,
as a guest in the Joyce flat, he touched the frame of one of the pictures
on the wall. The following dialogue ensued:

What's this?
Cork.
Yes, I see it's Cork. I was born there. But what's the frame?
Cork.

When O'Connor reported this to Yeats (who had been defending

Joyce's 'necessary idiosyncrasy'), the poet's response was appalled:
'That is mania. That is insanity'.[20] Certainly it is a wonderful Irish
story. We may recognize the idea of Wakeian 'night-language' as an
example of Joyce's grotesque humour even if we can never be quite sure
who was kidding whom over the Cork picture.

The interpretation of fables and dreams

What sort of book is *Finnegans Wake*?

It is, to start with, a remarkable example of intertextuality. *Ulysses*
refers on the face of it to a single literary predecessor, yet the Homeric
parallel, though structurally important, is only one of many that the
reader comes to recognize. In *Finnegans Wake* the wealth of literary
reference is such that one of the best scholarly studies yet to appear is
devoted simply to *The Books at the Wake*.[21] There is no single and
inescapable literary model, though to search for one is undeniably
instructive. The title *Finnegans Wake* (which remained a close-kept
secret until publication day) suggests a combination of heroic
mourning for a dead Celtic chieftain, a call to insurrection addressed
to his followers, and an Irish night's entertainment commemorated in
a ballad. The idea of a collection of stories and entertainments written
in 'night-language' and bound together in a single volume reminds us
irresistibly of the *Arabian Nights*. Joyce had been familiar from
childhood with the Arabian stories, notably in the form of the
pantomime 'Turko the Terrible'. His own story 'Araby' hints at some
of the glamour they may have held for him. J. S. Atherton lists fifteen
references in the *Wake* to Sir Richard Burton's translation (*The
Thousand Nights and a Night*, 1885–8), and I believe this is a
conservative estimate.[22] Some of the allusions belong to the category
of Wakeian 'self-commentary', to which we have already referred.
Joyce's book is well described as a 'scherzarade of one's thousand one
nightinesses' (*FW* 51:4–5), and as 'one thousand and one stories, all
told, of the same' (*FW* 5:28–9). The 'ideal reader suffering from an
ideal insomnia' is sentenced to nuzzle over the text 'a full trillion times
for ever and a night' (*FW* 120:12–14). The ten thunderwords in the
Wake could be combined as a single word of a thousand and one
letters.[23] A body of stories jumbled together, story within story, with
some strange compulsion masked in the telling: that is a plausible
description of a modern *Arabian Nights*.

The *Arabian Nights* is a thoroughly secular work, full of lust and also of cruelty and greed. *Finnegans Wake*, though a bawdier production than *Ulysses* (for those who have learned to read it) is also a further attempt to realize the 'Sacred Book' of the Symbolists. It is what Synge called an 'elaborate book . . . far away from the profound and common interests of life'.[24] It contains manifold references to some of the world's scriptures, including the Bible, the Koran, and the Egyptian Book of the Dead. It also refers to such primary epics as the Celtic legends and Norse sagas, though not, except incidentally, to Greek mythology. There may be two reasons for this. One is that the Greeks had already provided so much material for the *Portrait* and *Ulysses*; the other is that the Greek myths had been comprehensively mined in the book which may be the most substantial precursor of *Finnegans Wake*: the *New Science* of Giambattista Vico (1744). Vico had sought, through etymological examination of the Homeric poems and Greek fables, to reconstruct the history of the gentile nations excluded from the Old Testament. Joyce, turning to other mythological sources – including a wide range of world literature, Dublin folklore, popular song, and modern stories of his own and his father's invention – seeks to reconstruct a 'history of the world' more fundamental and far-reaching even than that of Vico.

It was *Our Exagmination*, in 1929, which first drew attention to the Viconian elements in the *Wake*. Vico's thought is expounded in Samuel Beckett's essay 'Dante . . . Bruno. Vico . . . Joyce', and also in Stuart Gilbert's 'Prolegomena to *Work in Progress*'. These essays remain essential texts for any would-be or struggling readers of Joyce's book. Nevertheless, their account of the kind of debt Joyce owed to Vico is a little one-sided. According to Beckett and Gilbert, what was important to him in the work of the 'practical roundheaded Neapolitan'[25] was Vico's theory of the three ages of human society – Theocratic, Heroic, and Human or Democratic – and of the origins of civilization and language. Thus Vico, who may well be seen as the greatest pioneer in the history of sociological thought,[26] was viewed as the author of a fable rather than as the analyst of fables. Beckett and Gilbert give pride of place to his suggestion that early men, surprised by a thunderstorm in the midst of their enjoyment of an 'infamous promiscuity of things and women',[27] retreated into their caves where they constructed a society based on shelter and paternal authority. It was only after the primal thunderclap that they began to babble in language, as a way of expressing their fear of, and reverence for, the gods. Vico speculates that the first intelligible sounds produced by the human voice were 'pa! pape!'[28] The human *paterfamilias* then uses language to inspire respect in his dependants and hence to ape the divine authority (Jupiter = *jus* + *pater*, or, as Gilbert puts it, 'the sky is not merely the allfather but also the source of law and justice, of the family tie and social consciousness'[29]). Thus Vico's fable associates the origins of language with what, following Freud, we may see as the origins of psychic repression. Joyce certainly made use of it in this sense. Time and again in *Finnegans Wake* we come back to the hundred-lettered thunderword, to the repression of promiscuous sexuality and to the guilty attempts of the protagonists of the heroic and democratic ages (HCE, Shem and Shaun) to usurp 'majestate' (*FW* 478:12) or 'genuine authorship and holusbolus authoritativeness' (*FW* 118:3–4). But Joyce responded to other aspects of Vico as well.

The *New Science* hides its greatness amid an astonishing farrago of misplaced ingenuity. Vico's professed aim was to construct a historical anthropology which could be squared with a literal reading of the Old Testament. To do this he distinguishes between historical narratives – such as those of the Old Testament and of Homer – and the cryptographic history which he finds buried in the Greek fables. Both Homer and the fables are to be viewed, not as the work of individual authors, but as the literary expressions of whole peoples. In the fables, he says, 'the nations have in a rough way and in the language of the human senses described the beginnings of this world of sciences, which the specialized studies of scholars have since clarified for us by reasoning and generalization'.[30]

The 'esoteric wisdom' of the fables, then, consists of an understanding of history which is both alternative and complementary to the 'official' history embodied, for Christians, in the Old Testament. Similarly, when Joyce said he was writing a history of the world, he meant (needless to say) an alternative history to the modern rationalistic account exemplified by the synoptic historians such as Wells and Toynbee. The alternative history does not *refute* the 'official' account – it adds on to it. (And it may in the end undermine it; *The New Science*, rediscovered in Germany in the nineteenth century, added weight to the 'scientific' criticism which destroyed the literal reading of the Old Testament, which Vico himself had been at such pains to uphold.)

The New Science, however weird and barbarous to modern eyes, is a work of scholarship which deconstructs already existing fables. *Finnegans Wake* is a work of fiction which combines a body of fables (the 'thousand and one stories') with the work of analysis and deconstruction. This accounts for the centrality in the *Wake* of the 'Letter' — both an actual letter, which may be a joint plea by the Chapelizod family to exonerate HCE from his 'crime' or sense of guilt, and a microcosm of the *Wake* itself. Joyce's book frequently parodies a style of lecturing or scholarly inquisition, most notably in the chapter (I.v) devoted to the interpretation of the Letter. If the *Wake* is an *Arabian Nights* entertainment, its pervasive deconstruction of its own stories also reveals it to be a 'thousand and one stories, all told, of the same'. This fictional combination of fable and deconstruction implies, not only that Joyce's weird jumble of stories could be made to yield a new sort of historical consciousness, but that both the new historical consciousness and the 'scientific' history it offers to complement are nothing other than forms of mythology. To this extent Isaiah Berlin is correct to regard Joyce as a 'modern irrationalist' follower of Vico, whose work 'would destroy, at least in theory, all distinction between history as a rational discipline and mythical thinking'.[31] There is only one error (comparable to Stuart Gilbert's error over *Ulysses*) in such an assessment. Joyce expected to be understood as a maker of fictions, not as a thinker. The justification of his Viconian (or post-Viconian) irrationalism is the *Wake* itself, and not its application to the writing of history.

One of the mistakes which have arisen from a too narrow assimilation of Vico and Joyce is the belief, first found in Beckett's article, that the structure of the *Wake* corresponds to Vico's three ages. In this view Book I is the Theocratic Age, Book II the Heroic, Book III the Democratic, and Book IV the *ricorso* by which history recycles back to the beginning. Campbell and Robinson, the pioneering authors of the *Skeleton Key to 'Finnegans Wake'* (1944), adopted a very similar scheme. Recent scholars have shown this to be untenable, since, as Roland McHugh puts it, 'there is little internal differentiation in the Viconian segments of *Finnegans Wake*'.[32] Joyce's 'commodius vicus of recirculation' (*FW* 3:2) or 'wholemole millwheeling vicociclometer' (*FW* 614:27) explains why everything in the *Wake* comes round again and the last sentence turns into the first. But it stops far short of determining the complexity of the book's structure.

Another curious assertion of Beckett's was that Joyce had somehow gone back beyond 'writing' to a more primitive form of 'direct expression', a gestural language such as was found in the earliest times after the thunderclap. 'Here is direct expression — pages and pages of it', Beckett wrote. 'And if you don't understand it, Ladies and Gentlemen, it is because you are too decadent to receive it'.[33] Such a view of the origins of language belongs to the heyday of modernism and its successor, the New Criticism. Beckett's implication that hieroglyphics are preferable to the alphabet is strictly comparable to Ezra Pound's well-known interest in the Chinese ideogram as a poetic medium. Even if he had been right about 'direct expression', it would have followed that Joyce and his fellow 'revolutionaries of the word' had singlehandedly found a way of bypassing the whole Western tradition. In more recent times a central theme of poststructuralist thinkers such as Jacques Derrida and Jacques Lacan has been that the notion of an 'authentic' language prior to written expression is a myth. Several Joyce scholars have drawn heavily on the work of the French poststructuralists. It would, in fact, be rather misleading to suppose that citations from Derrida and Lacan could provide independent confirmation for Joyce's insights into language, since both thinkers have acknowledged their indebtedness to him.[34] What Derrida and Lacan do offer is an influential model of language which tells us a good deal more about the *Wake* than Beckett's model could.

Joyce's deconstruction of language, it is argued, is in the service not of 'direct expression' but of 'indeterminacy', 'freeplay' or 'unlimited semeiosis'. In the *Wake* the notion of the subject expressing himself in language is 'decentered'.[35] The existence of authority is undermined not merely at the social and familial level – the usurpations of Shaun, the guilty stutter of HCE – but also in the figure of the writer or 'author', Shem the Penman, who (like his *alter ego* Joyce) is unable to assert any commanding presence in language. Instead of controlling, he is himself seen to be controlled by the systems of writing. As Stephen Heath puts it, 'first and last, the *Wake* remains writing, goes on with the interminable play of language, comes back to no origin, knows no break between world and book'.[36] At the level of literary appreciation (rather than of models applicable to language as a whole) the virtues and pleasures of such a text became the subject of the later work of Roland Barthes – though Barthes, unlike Derrida and Lacan, showed no sign of having studied Joyce. The psychoanalytic meaning of the decentered text, which seeks to undermine official and authorized language-modes by 'childish' devices such as the pun, has been expounded by Jacques Lacan. Lacan equates the infant's access to its mother's body with 'direct expression' or 'presence'. The child's banishment from the mother's body entails its entry into the symbolic order of language, an 'endless process of difference and absence'.[37] The moment of conscious banishment from the mother is that of the 'mirror-phase', when the child learns to recognize its reflection in the mirror. Whatever the merits of this as a contribution to the clinical practice of psychoanalysis (the question is rarely discussed or even, apparently, deemed relevant by Lacan's English followers), it is eminently compatible with the *Wake*, and especially with the 'Nightlessons' chapter (II.ii), which shows how writing and learning stem from the recognition of the sexual difference between the father and the mother. With the aid of Derrida and Lacan the garrulousness of the *Wake* and the infinite regress of its Letter may be seen to result from the impossibility of 'direct expression'; what are to be expressed are tabooed matters associated with the physical secrets (phallus and vagina) of the father and mother. Other commentators, however, had reached this point without Derrida's and Lacan's aid. Indeed, it is something of a commonplace in *Wake* scholarship.

We may express Joyceian 'freeplay' or 'unlimited semeiosis' in terms of a rather different metaphor, by invoking Jorge Luis Borges's well-known short story 'The Library of Babel'. The Library of Babel consists of an enormous number of identical rooms housing identical shelves of identical-sized books containing every possible permutation of printed characters over 410 pages. This finite library − a metaphor for the universe itself − is so large that none of its inhabitants will ever determine its boundaries or even (unless intuitively) discover its structure. The Library is a nightmare vision of 'freeplay' (defined by Derrida as 'a field of infinite substitutions in the closure of a finite ensemble'[38]) taken to its logical conclusion. No sooner have we proposed such a model, however, than we notice its discrepancies with *Finnegans Wake*.

Margot Norris touches on a significant feature of Joyce's book − of its length and difficulty and the reader's possible boredom − when she speaks of its 'extraordinary redundancy'. She quotes Hugh Kenner's statement that 'Joyce worked seventeen years to push the work away from "meaning", adrift into language; nothing is to be gained by trying to push it back'. She justifies the redundancy, however, on the grounds that 'a work with an unprecedented amount of "interference" requires an unprecedented amount of seemingly gratuitous repetition in compensation'.[39] Perhaps these comments illustrate the difficulty of avoiding self-contradiction in writing on the *Wake*; what is clear, however, is that both Kenner and Norris (and, I think, all other exegetes) regard Joyce's work on the book as purposive, even where the apparent result is to produce Babel. However much 'noise' and 'interference' the book may contain, it is an infinitely smaller proportion of the whole than would be the case in Borges's Library. In that Library we should be extremely lucky to find sentences and pages, let alone books, written in a recognizable language. What is the language of the *Wake*? 'Are we speachin d'anglas landadge or are you sprakin sea Djoytsch?' (*FW* 485:12–13). If 'Djoytsch' is the answer – it is certainly a possible answer – then this should be identified with what is elsewhere called 'rutterdamrotter' ('I can beuraly forsstand a weird from sturk to finnic in such a patwhat as your rutterdamrotter', *FW* 17:13–15), in other words Double Dutch, which as every child knows is a form of English. We are in the realm of 'nonsense-language', such as that used by Lewis Carroll, in which manifest nonsense is the vehicle of a good deal of latent sense. Nonsense, joking and foolery have a more deliberate purpose in Joyce than in Carroll; the result is 'Ibscenest Nansence!' (*FW* 535:19), or the sort of obscene nonsense which Joyce conceives to be worthy of a great explorer and a great artist. Unlike the Library of Babel, the freeplay of *Finnegans Wake* is leading somewhere – though the goal tends to elude definition and the route is evidently a circuitous one.

In discussing *The New Science* it was suggested that Joyce's book is at once a body of fables, and the interpretation of those fables. Joyce, in addition, insisted that it was a 'nightpiece' – a dream or collection of dreams. There seems no reason to dissent from Frederick J. Hoffman's conclusion, in the appropriately-titled 'Infroyce' (in *Freudianism and the Literary Mind*, 1945) that Joyce 'employed all of the devices which Freud explained in chapter seven of *The Interpretation of Dreams*'.[40] Not only does *Finnegans Wake* use such dream devices as displacement, condensation, substitution, and overdetermination but it also alludes to particular dreams (such as the famous dream of Irma's injection) reported by Freud's patients. Joyce was surely affected by Freud's unravelling of the 'dream-work' in writing *Finnegans Wake*, and in III.iv he hints at a Freudian primal scene (the child watching the parents copulate), or at least the image of such a scene. Freud's professional concern with individual sickness and health leads inevitably to the vexed question which critics have usually posed as follows: if *Finnegans Wake* is the book of a dream, then who is the dreamer? Edmund Wilson – mistakenly, it now seems – entitled his influential 1939 essay on the *Wake* 'The Dream of H. C.

Earwicker'. The dream, however, cannot be definitely allocated to any individual member of the Chapelizod family; it seems to bear the multiple imprints of HCE, of Shem and Shaun and Issy, and even of ALP. Moreover, it incorporates matter which no Chapelizod innkeeping family dreaming according to Freud's rules could ever have succeeded in encompassing. If it is a dream (something which is far easier to assert than to prove) then it is an archetypal dream of Everyman, constructed out of the Jungian 'collective unconscious' rather than the personal symbolism analysed by Freud.

Freud does not pretend to be an infallible interpreter of his patients' dreams. He shows how it takes deep knowledge and trust to learn how to crack the dream-code in each individual case; and even then, he never claims to have brought *all* the patient's repressed material to light. *Finnegans Wake*, by contrast, is a 'transparent' dream in which the most shocking and tabooed material is scarcely repressed at all. It is, as it were, both the dream and the analysis.[41] The art critic and Freudian Adrian Stokes wrote of the distorting processes of mental life as exhibiting 'an intense subtlety at the service of an intense crudity'. The 'crudity' is not a simple or easily definable thing; it is the 'vast acrimonious territory' of the unconscious, which makes itself felt at every moment; 'our conscious minds are vessels on the seas of the unconscious'.[42] *Finnegans Wake*, like Stokes's view of the mind, displays the subtlety and the crudity side by side. The crudity is that of 'one's thousand one nightinesses'; that is, it is protean and never quite to be pinned down. It takes the various forms of sexual curiosity, sibling rivalry, parricide, incest, and all kinds of sexual deviance: voyeurism, undinism, coprophilia and so on. The Letter promises time and again to let us in on the 'secret workings of natures' (*FW* 615:14) and to give us the keys to nature's crudity. But the Letter, like the *Wake* itself, is an almost illegible palimpsest. It contains everything from Alpha to Omega, but by the same token it is 'A..........! ?.........O!' (*FW* 94:21–2), that is to say a possible zero. The version given in the final chapter is full of irrelevancies and digressions; the 'message' has somehow got mixed up in 'messes of mottage' (*FW* 183:22–3), including gossip, catch-phrases, snatches of song and bits of the morning paper. If the 'keys to dreamland' (*FW* 615:28) have been 'Given!', as the last complete statement in the book assures us (*FW* 628:15), they have also got irretrievably lost.

Freud's *Interpretation of Dreams* shows how the endless processes of distortion and evasion govern mental activity. Yet in the very act of distortion and evasion the mind is apt to confess its fraudulence and to give itself away. Joyce makes a similar point in his reiterated use of the word 'hesitancy' — the misspelling of which, as 'hesitency', was what identified Pigott as the forger of some notorious letters attributed to Charles Stewart Parnell. 'Hesitancy' is suggestively close to the acronym HCE, and HCE, taking up another of Freud's theories, is a chronic stutterer. He and the other members of his loquacious family give themselves away because, thanks to Joyceian punning, to bear false witness is to 'bare whiteness' (*FW* 364:1–2) and to 'bare full sweetness' (*FW* 615:33). The injunction 'to shall not bare full sweetness' is 'stringstly . . . forbidden by the honorary tenth commendmant' (*FW* 615:32–3). The implication that self-exposure is the ultimate shame is another highly Freudian theme, since Freud gives particular prominence to the class of 'Embarrassing Dreams of Being Naked'.[43]

Towards the end of *The Interpretation of Dreams* Freud invokes the fundamental principle of evolutionary biology that ontogeny recapitulates phylogeny, or the development of the individual recapitulates the development of the species. Ultimately, the analysis of dreams disinters not only the childhood of the individual but of the human race. Buried and distorted within the protean shapes of the night-time imagination there is concealed 'a knowledge of man's archaic heritage, of what is psychically innate in him'. Thus the psychoanalyst, like the archaeologist, can help to piece together the story of human development.[44] Freud with characteristic humility professes himself scarcely equipped for such a task. The determination to uncover a buried history in fables and dreams had earlier inspired Vico and, in turn, it was to be both copied and parodied by Joyce. (Archaeological concepts, like psychoanalytic ones, are among the multifarious sources of the *Wake*'s vocabulary.) *Finnegans Wake* is concerned throughout with the idea of a buried universal history which in Freud's book, with its clinical origins, emerges as little more than an afterthought. The 'messes of mottage' are imaged as a midden-heap, such as hens and archaeologists peck over. The secret shame is also a public crime (though of indeterminate nature) committed in Dublin's Phoenix Park. The 'crudity' of the Freudian unconscious becomes, in Joyce, a shady historical obsession, an 'utterly unexpected sinistrogyric return to one peculiar sore point in the past' (*FW* 120:27–8). The child's banishment from the mother is also the Fall of Man and the collapse of a dynasty. The dream-analysis becomes a Wake.

A wake is a fuddled affair, an opportunity for merriment, music-making and forgetfulness. Yet however lavish the entertainment the mind will keep coming back to the crudity of its prompting: a *funferal* (*FW* 120:10) is occasioned by a corpse. The biological inevitability of death and succession is an ineradicable part of our consciousness:

Life, he himself said once, . . . is a wake, livit or krikit, and on the bunk of our breadwinning lies the cropse of our seedfather, a phrase which the establisher of the world by law might pretinately write across the chestfront of all manorwombanborn. (*FW* 55:5–10)

But if death is ordained by universal law it does not inspire the morbidity and despair sometimes associated with biological themes in *Ulysses*. Joyce's resolute banishment of gloom from the narrative of the *Wake* (at least, until ALP's final monologue) is a measure of the extent of his desertion of realism for comic satire and farce. Human failings are the subject of innumerable invectives, vituperations and tirades exchanged by the quarrelling twins; the broader sense of life's futility, however, is faced with noisy equanimity. Instead of the gross scientific 'facts' of our bodily state – as recalled in the 'Hades' chapter of *Ulysses* and in Stephen's memories of his mother – *Finnegans Wake* exhibits the grotesque body through mythology, totemism and pornographic fantasy. Yet the primitive habit of thought which portrays the man as a mountain and the woman as a river must be set against the rhetoric of history which is espoused from time to time by every member of the Chapelizod family. ALP, for example, is author of the 'untitled mamafesta memorialising the Mosthighest' – in other words, the Letter (*FW* 104:4); what Shem wrote all over his own body 'slowly unfolded all marryvoising moodmoulded cyclewheeling history' (*FW* 186:1–2); mistress Kathe the charwoman seems to be the guide who shows us round the 'Willingdone Museyroom' (the museum commemorating the Battle of Waterloo, *FW* 8:10); and the four old men, Matthew Gregory, Mark Lyons, Luke Tarpey and Johnny MacDougall (with his donkey) are the Four Masters who were the ancient historians of Ireland. The view of history offered in the *Wake* varies from minutiae of interest only to antiquarians – and Irish antiquarians at that – to the broad perspectives of Vico and Herder, whose philosophy of history inspired the quotation from Edgar Quinet reproduced (uniquely for the *Wake*) in its entirety on page 281.[45] The basic literary mode of the *Wake*, indeed, is historical – the sifting of evidence, the unfolding of memory, the recall of the past (including the very distant past), the telling of tales and retailing of gossip. Where

the action is set in the present it often takes the form of quizzes,
riddles, lessons, dramas, séances, courtroom scenes and acts of
literary and musical composition which invariably take us back into
the past. Such an unfolding of the 'history of the world' was not
a wholly unprecedented exercise for Joyce. It was already implicit
in 'The Dead' with its use of a plot-structure from Ibsen, and in
the portrayal of Bloom, Stephen, and Molly in *Ulysses*. With
hindsight Joyce's earlier protagonist might have said that 'History
is a nightmare from which I am entwining a *Wake*'.

11   Reading the *Wake*

The first-time reader of *Finnegans Wake* needs to acquire some feeling both for Joyce's methods of word- and sentence-formation and for the book's larger structures. At all levels repetition is the key. It is the repeated elements, such as sound-patterns, images, catch-phrases, book- and song-titles and agent- or character-relationships which sustain the spiralling flights of Joyce's narrative. In any analysis of the *Wake* we are liable to find ourselves extracting words and phrases from their immediate contexts and juxtaposing them with widely separate textual items. The reason for this almost cavalier disregard for context is Joyce's systematic disruption of the integrity of paragraph, sentence, word, and phrase. Formal English syntax is maintained but the result, as often as not, disturbs our conventional and logical expectations as to meaning. Sentences may expand into enormous lists or wilt under a load of repeated parentheses. Sometimes the very statements which seem to be telling us things we need to know are those most tampered with, most subject to interference:

(Stoop) if you are abcedminded, to this claybook, what curios of signs (please stoop) in this allaphbed! Can you rede (since We and Thou had it out already) its world? It is the same told of all. Many. Miscegenations on miscegenations. Tieckle. They lived und laughed ant loved end left. Forsin. (*FW* 18:17–21)

This is the first of several occasions on which the *Wake*'s expository style pauses (stoops?) for what seems a direct address to the reader. It is the 'same told of all' and also the Writing on the Wall ('Mene. Mene. Tekel. Upharsin'). As we continue with the book we become aware of a second fourfold pattern of interjections ('stop, please stop, do please stop, and O do please stop respectively', *FW* 124:4–5), of which the first two are present in the above quotation – which means that we may confidently expect to encounter the other two later in the same paragraph. These four interjections are one of several types of allusion to *The Book of Kells*, the early Irish manuscript of the Gospels, which is one of the principal sacred books subsumed in the *Wake*. Sir Edward Sullivan in his edition of *The Book of Kells* distinguished between four types of full stop that he claimed to find in the manuscript.[1] Such information, which is the staple of all Wakeian exegesis including that

219

offered by Joyce himself, must usually be retrieved by collating widely separate instances and relating them to a common source. Yet if we are ignorant of it we are far from finding the sentence unreadable. We are merely reading it in a simpler (and quite possibly an earlier) version.

The *Wake* begins with a decapitated but still legible sentence, which is not completed until 625 pages later:

riverrun, past Eve and Adam's, from swerve of shore to bend of bay, brings us by a commodius vicus of recirculation back to Howth Castle and Environs.

A way a lone a last a loved a long the

There are a number of things to be said about this. It goes from 'A way' to 'recirculation', in other words from A to O or Alpha to Omega. It divides before 'riverrun', but when reunited we perceive another division:

A way a lone a last a loved a long the riverrun, past Eve and Adam's, from swerve of shore to bend of bay, // brings us by a commodius vicus of recirculation back to Howth Castle and Environs.

Here the side-to-side wave-rhythm of ALP, the serpentining river, disappears without warning into the pompous abstractions of the 'historian'. It is one of many broken-backed sentences in the *Wake*, though the verbal drift in this case helps to evoke the discharge and dissipation of the waters into the bay. The Environs of Howth Castle consist of a hilly promontory, so that we have gone from the river (ALP) and its banks to the sea and the mountain (HCE).

The historian continues:

Sir Tristram, violer d'amores, fr'over the short sea, had passencore rearrived from North Armorica on this side the scraggy isthmus of Europe Minor to wielderfight his penisolate war: nor had topsawyer's rocks by the stream Oconee exaggerated themselse to Laurens County's gorgios while they went doublin their mumper all the time: nor avoice from afire bellowsed mishe mishe to tauftauf thuartpeatrick: not yet, though venissoon after, had a kidscad buttended a bland old isaac: not yet, though all's fair in vanessy, were sosie sesthers wroth with twone nathandjoe. Rot a pack of pa's malt had Jhem or Shen brewed by arclight and rory end to the regginbrow was to be seen ringsome on the aquaface.

When Joyce wrote this paragraph in November 1926 he provided a very full commentary (*SL* 315–17), which need not be repeated here. Following his directions one can painstakingly unravel the multiple meanings. Freud said of dreams that 'It is not . . . easy to form any conception of the abundance of the unconscious trains of thought, all striving to find expression, which are active in our minds'.[2] Joyce was not alone in applying this principle to literary language, for it was the basis of the mode of poetic analysis pioneered by William Empson in *Seven Types of Ambiguity* (1930). The problem is, how many of the semantic levels that we can theoretically admit, or laboriously unravel, can be held in the mind in anything resembling a conventional reading process? The image of the *Wake* as a kaleidoscope is sanctioned in the text ('collideorscape', *FW* 143:28) and has been repeated by several of its critics. It is possible to spend many hours over each paragraph of the book, though a much faster reading is also needed to give the sense of overall shape and structure. A kaleidoscope, after all, offers moving images.

The keyword of the paragraph is 'passencore' or 'not yet'. We are, in other words, at the beginning. Among the things which have not yet happened are Tristan's arrival, the Peninsular War, the settlement of America, the rise of Parnell, the baptism of St Patrick, the establishment of Jameson's distillery and the amorous friendships of Jonathan Swift. Such a random jumble of disparate events is typical of the *Wake*'s encyclopaedism. Each of those listed will be a recurrent motif, but the list barely scratches the surface of Wakeian history. It does, however, indicate the mixture of genres in that history – romance, sacred history, historical geography (the River Oconee flows through Dublin, Laurens County, Georgia, founded by an Irish settler), war, politics, literature and so on – as well as its predominantly Irish complexion. This riddling paragraph is a hasty, almost breathless, preliminary statement of the book's themes.

Implicit in the historical events, just as Stephen found Shakespeare's emotional dilemmas implicit in his plays, are the recurrent psychological conflicts of the Chapelizod family. The passage offers glimpses of the war of the sexes and of father and son, not to mention the 'penisolate' struggles of a lonely penman. These family discords are the results of the 'fall' into history heralded by the hundred-lettered Viconian thunderword at the beginning of the next paragraph. The fall is any number of things: the death of a giant, a social disaster such as the 1929 Wall Street crash, a personal calamity such as befell Old Parr (said to have died in 1635 at the age of 150) and the still more legendary Humpty Dumpty, and the collapse of a building and its builder. One such builder was the bricklayer Tim Finnegan, who fell off a ladder while carrying his hod and whose Wake was the subject of an Irish–American ballad.

'Phall if you but will, rise you must' (*FW* 4:15–16). The giant's toes stick up in the appropriately-named Phoenix Park, where the gratitude of a subservient nation has found expression in the great obelisk of the Wellington Monument. But 'Bygmester Finnegan, of the Stuttering Hand' (*FW* 4:18) is HCE, and he is also Ibsen's Master Builder. The alternation of rising and falling (or of construction and deconstruction) helps to determine the pattern of the *Wake* as a whole. No simple model of its structure is quite adequate, but Clive Hart and Roland McHugh have usefully described the lateral inversion of Books I and III, the parts of the *Wake* that Joyce wrote first. In McHugh's words there is a 'simple equilibrium of two symmetrical half-arches supporting a keystone of greater complexity'.[3] The keystone is Book II. The fall of HCE early in Book I is paralleled by his resurrection towards the end of III.iii, in the section originally called 'Haveth Childers Everywhere', when his ghost speaks forth in the middle of a séance. Like all *Wake* personages, his ghost is familiar and compound; we know from Joyce's own testimony, for example, that this section draws on a book entitled *Psychic Messages from Oscar Wilde*.[4] Yet the abiding impression from both sections is of Finn or HCE as Master Builder, and hence as the founding father of civilization.

Starting out as an inspired and reverent builder of churches, Ibsen's Bygmester Solness paid a terrible price for his creative achievements. The play begins with him in late middle age, prosperous and respected but occasionally troubled by his conscience. A young woman comes knocking at his door and luring him, once again, to pit his strength against the unknown. Something similar has happened to HCE. Like Solness, he is conscience-ridden and threatened by the young ('When the youngdammers will be soon heartpocking on their betters' doornoggers', *FW* 572:2–3). His buildings were the expressions of his love and reverence for his wife, the River Liffey. HCE's version of the 'castles in the air' that Solness dreamed of building is an idealized vision of Dublin – a utopian city of 'twinminsters' and 'stavekirks' (*FW* 552:3–4), 'carpet gardens' and 'lecheworked lawn' (a reference to the English Garden City movement, *FW* 553:9), which incorporates the seven wonders of the world and the works of fourteen named Dublin architects. HCE's Dublin, '*Urbs in rure*' (*FW* 551:24), is a bourgeois paradise, like Bloom's Flowerville and Solness's house with its tower. But from the tower or 'upservatory' he has a clear view of what is either an earth-closet or flush-toilet, 'wherewithin to be squatsquit in most covenience', and built 'for minne elskede [my beloved]' (*FW*

551:24–7). Hence the landscape of the city is also a landscape of tabooed desire, of an infantile 'cloacal obsession'. *Urbs in rure* is a much grander design than Flowerville, but the design has led to squalor and decay worse and more far-reaching than any encountered in 7 Eccles Street. Ibsen's Master Builder gave up building churches – he was scared of heights – and decided to concentrate on homes for human beings; yet even these he found disillusioning: 'Human beings haven't any use for these homes of theirs. Not for being happy in'.[5] HCE has built the city of Dublin for the sake of its people – in Joyce's version they are the characters of Ibsen's plays: 'For peers and gints, quaysirs and galleyliers, fresk letties from the say and stale headygabblers, gaingangers and dudder wagoners, pullars off societies and pushers on rothmere's homes' (*FW* 540:22–5). He has given the city a motto, 'Obeyance from the townsmen spills felixity by the toun' (*FW* 540:25–6); this is of course Dublin's motto *Obedientia civium urbis felicitas*. He has secured a royal charter (*FW* 545:14–23); this is the charter of Henry II granting Dublin to the citizens of Bristol. Yet the citizens are oppressed rather than happy. Their social conditions are detailed in some extraordinary pages quoting and parodying B. Seebohm Rowntree's *Poverty* (1902), a social survey of York. HCE's people, like Rowntree's, are judged by the bourgeois standard of respectability; indeed, Joyce's use of the word 'respectable' as a constant, sardonic refrain almost certainly explains what caught his eye in Rowntree's work.[6] Yet their life is sordid and miserable and their city has become a wilderness of tenements and hovels. (Since Book III inverts Book I, however, the collapse of HCE's efforts as builder of cities is narrated backwards.) When a city finally collapses it becomes a pile of rubble, or the *Wake*'s archetypal midden-heap. Dublin is also 'Dirtdump' (*FW* 615:12).

Ibsen's *Master Builder* ends not with the collapse of buildings but with the fall of their architect. Solness, egged on by the young temptress, Hilde Wangel, climbs the tower of his new house to hang the customary wreath on the weathervane. At the top he is assailed by devils – at least, that is how Miss Wangel sees it – and falls to his death. Solness's fall is reflected in the opening pages of the *Wake*, which describe HCE's greatest achievement,

a waalworth of a skyerscape of most eyeful hoyth entowerly, erigenating from next to nothing and celescalating the himals and all, . . . with a burning bush abob off its baubletop and with larrons o'toolers clittering up and tombles a'buckets clottering down.   (*FW* 4:35–5:4)

The *Wake* here is a *Mirror for Magistrates*, reminding us that *hubris* with its associated fall is the potential fate of Everyman. Thomas à Becket is one of those who fell, so is Tim Finnegan, and so, we shall find out a page or two later, was Napoleon. The principle of substitutability allows that the Wellington Monument in Phoenix Park is also the museum on the battlefield of Waterloo, and that the terrain of the battle, shown to us as a scale model, is also a much more intimate landscape. A second principle, that of the identity of opposites ('Extremes meet', a doctrine which Joyce derived from Giordano Bruno) entails that, if HCE by rights ought to be the fallen Napoleon, he may also be the victorious Wellington. In the 'museyroom' sequence he appears as 'Sraughter Willingdone' (*FW* 8:16), while his opponents (thanks to Napoleon's famous hat) are the 'three lipoleum boyne', two of whom are deadly rivals, 'the bog lipoleum mordering the lipoleum beg', while the third is 'nayther bag nor bug' (*FW* 8:24–6). Also present is (are?) the seductive 'jinnies':

This is the jinnies with their legahorns feinting to read in their handmade's book of stralegy while making their war undisides the Willingdone. The jinnies is a cooin her hand and the jinnies is a ravin her hair and the Willingdone git the band up. (*FW* 8:31–4)

We have here references to the crime in Phoenix Park, and also to the three children of the Earwicker family. The crime (HCE's voyeurism or indecent exposure) was witnessed either by two girls or three fusiliers. The three fusiliers are the children (Issy being 'nayther bag nor bug', or the odd one out – though the phrase also means 'neither mother nor father'). The two girls are Issy and her mirror-image.

Since we are visiting a museum, this passage is one of a series of episodes in the opening chapter which offer a symbolic entry both into the 'family umbroglia' and the *Wake*'s historical narrative. Yet it can only be understood retrospectively, and even then our understanding will remain incomplete. The 'jinnies', for example, might be jinnees (from the *Arabian Nights*), Germans, Guinness, or genitals. Their main significance, however, is that they encode the two-in-one mirror-image of HCE's daughter. So why are they the 'jinnies'? We shall find the right clue if we look far enough, though even so dedicated an exegete as Roland McHugh, in his *Annotations to 'Finnegans Wake'*, does not explicate the word. The answer can be made out on page 359 when we hear a radio broadcast of a nightingale's song (a well-known item in the BBC's early repertoire). The nightingale's song suggests Issy divided into two 'naughtingels' (*FW* 359:32) – Florence Nightingale of Crimean War fame, and Jenny Lind ('Jinnyland', *FW* 359:35) the 'Swedish Nightingale'.[7] The two 'jinnies' are also 'jinnyjos' (*FW* 526:17) and the 'jenny's' upon which Glugg or Jerry (Shem) has his 'eyetrompit trained' (*FW* 247:32–3). 'Making their war undisides' signifies female micturition − something which is invariably associated in the *Wake* with male voyeurism and sexual arousal (French *bander*). Thus by playing the game of textual hide-and-seek we can tentatively reconstruct the logic of a meaning which many, no doubt, will have grasped intuitively. As so often, prying beneath the surface of the *Wake* yields a thinly disguised infantile sexual content. What is the whole thing − like *Tristram Shandy* − but a 'cock and a biddy story' (*FW* 519:8)? And what else is 'Waterloo' but a place for urinating?[8]

After we leave the museyroom the scene dissolves into a deserted battlefield (a midden-heap) on which the hen is scavenging; then to an excerpt from the annals of Dublin and a meeting between Mutt and Jute, the primordial Celt and Dane; and then to an interpolated folktale, the story of Jarl van Hoother and the Prankquean. Like two of the other interpolated tales in *Finnegans Wake* − the Mookse and the Gripes (I.vi) and the Ondt and the Gracehoper (III.i) − this tale has a bearing on the two sons of HCE, the 'jiminies' Tristopher and Hilary (*FW* 21:11–12). (Is it a coincidence that 'jinnies' are to 'jiminies' as Shaun to Shem or John to James?) The tale concerns the prankquean's riddle ('Why do I am alook alike a poss of porterpease?', *FW* 21:18–19), and once again − as Bernard Benstock's analysis makes clear[9] − the riddle is covertly concerned with urination.

'Like pah, I peh' (*FW* 296:28). Book II chapter ii, by common consent the central chapter of the *Wake*, shows one of the twins (Shem) instructing the other (Shaun) in the nature of the sexual difference between men and women. This is the basis of 'gramma's grammar' (*FW* 268:17) and of the 'nightlessons' which, nevertheless, take us through every branch of the intellectual curriculum. Margot Norris sums up the view of life that Joyce thus conceals in *Finnegans Wake*: 'Joyce, like Freud, seems . . . to have believed that we would be as polymorphously perverse as babies if only we didn't feel so guilty about it and try so hard to repress it'.[10] A 'cloacal obsession', then, is at the kernel of the *Wake* since both polymorphous perversity and the recognition of sexual difference centre on the physiological association of pleasure with urine and faeces. The repression to which this is subjected generates the whole verbose structure of metaphor and euphemism, of evasion and rationalization, which is language or, at least, *Wake* language. This language, like Freud's dream narratives, is at once the medium of alibi and the medium of confession. Alibi and confession come together, for example, in the story of the Phoenix Park crime which, in either of its two versions, involves micturition.

G. V. L. Slingsby – the contributor of a 'Letter of Protest' to *Our Exagmination*, and possibly a Joyceian alias – asked the pertinent question 'Is Mr Joyce's hog latin making obscenity safe for literature?'[11] To some extent *Finnegans Wake* is a Great Debate (profusely illustrated by the offending material) over pornography and obscenity. For Joyce, pornography and obscenity are the distorted and displaced adult forms taken by the all-consuming and perfectly healthy interests of the infant. Joyce's attitude to this is different from the scientific impartiality of Freud, and different again from the hectoring solemnity of the inverted puritan D. H. Lawrence. Unlike them, he finds it grotesque, and unlike them, he admits that it is both irresistibly curious and intensely comic. Just as the adult is made out of the child, so is civilization made out of barbarism by repressing the curiosity and pleasure of the infant. Civilization is thus reared out of the contradiction between the acknowledgement of anarchic sexuality, and its necessary repression. In *Finnegans Wake*, the warring contraries are represented by the two brothers (whose explicit polarity is implicit in the father). The father stands for achieved (and precarious) civilization; but without the dynamic of brotherly rivalry civilization would never have come to exist.

One of the principal contrasts between the two brothers is, as we should expect, in their respective attitudes to sin and dirt. Shaun (Stanislaus Joyce) appears as the hermit 'Saint Kevin, Hydrophilos' (*FW* 606:4–5) taking his bath. He is connected with the rite of baptism and also, no doubt, with more modern sanitary rites. He is popular with Issy and her twenty-eight fellow-virgins, who call him 'dear sweet Stainusless' (*FW* 237:11). He is a politician aspiring to be the new broom to sweep up now that HCE is gone. Shem (James Joyce) is a portrait of the artist as polluter and pornographer. His 'lowness' is described in revolting detail in I.vii, the most scatological chapter of *Finnegans Wake*. Like Mr Bloom's, his lowness 'creeped out first via foodstuffs' (*FW* 170:25–6). Later we hear of his method of making ink – a method which the prurient narrator attempts to conceal in the time-honoured manner of learned treatises by putting it in Latin (*FW* 185:14–26). Having mixed his urine and faeces together he fulfils his literary vocation by writing 'over every square inch of the only foolscap

available, his own body' (*FW* 185:35–6). His writing is not only a Dirty
Protest but a filthy form of self-concealment, like the squid lurking
behind its cloud of ink.[12] Yet it does not deceive the narrator of the
passage, who is Shaun in his favourite role of prosecuting counsel.

The 'Shem the Penman' chapter presents a hypertrophied and
Rabelaisian version of Stanislaus Joyce's condemnation of *Work in
Progress*. We may even judge that his brother, as he wrote *Finnegans
Wake*, was too much oppressed by his experience of fraternal quarrels.
The *Wake* contains some explicitly autobiographical fragments and a
great deal more that seems to originate in Joyce's personal obsessions.
'Sudds for me and supper for you and the doctor's bill for Joe John'
(*FW* 215:17–18) – the scolding voice of Nora Barnacle? – is an
example of the former kind. The endless brotherly quarrels, while not
nakedly autobiographical, are the transmutation of a personal
obsession. Among the *Wake*'s bickering pairs are Caddy and Primas,
Mutt and Jute, Tristopher and Hilary, Kevin and Jerry, Treacle Tom
and Frisky Shorty, Shaum the Posed and Shun the Punman, Mick and
Nick, the Mookse and the Gripes, Burrus and Caseous, Justius and
Mercius, Glugg and Chuff, Dolph and Kev, Butt and Taff, and the
Ondt and the Gracehoper. The tone of invective and disguised polemic
emanating from these Tweedledum-and-Tweedledee pairs is extremely
widespread in the *Wake*. It is true that denunciation and vituperation
as rhetorical exercises – 'flyting', satire, the arts of political
lampooning and judicial impeachment – are deeply ingrained in the
literary tradition, though less at home under liberal democracy where
they tend to be replaced by more subtle and insidious propaganda
techniques. Joyce, to a modern taste, overworks these traditional
literary resources. It is amid the *Wake*'s endless binary divisions and
brotherly tirades that the reader's attention is most likely to wander.

The *Wake* offers little genuinely impartial narration. McHugh
suggests that Book I may be seen as Shaun's presentation of Shem and
his works whilst Book III is Shem's presentation of Shaun and his. The
actual narrators are the 'Four Masters', biassed towards Shaun or
Shem as the case may be.[13] Book II is also largely concerned with the
brothers, who (following Bruno's principle) change places halfway
through II.ii. In II.iii, disguised as Butt and Taff, the television comics
who tell the story of Buckley and the Russian general, they can
eventually be found merged into one.

Buckley, an Irish soldier in the Crimea, happened on a Russian
general who had taken his pants down to defecate. The Irishman had

him in his sights but 'adn't the arts' (*FW* 345:2–3) to pull the trigger. Only when the general tore up a clod of peat to wipe himself did Buckley, like a patriotic Irishman, let him have it. The story was one of Joyce's father's anecdotes. It has its place in *Finnegans Wake* both on account of its scatology and because it is a parable of father-killing. Both Shem and Shaun could approve of shooting the Russian general, who is at once an embodiment of self-indulgent dirtiness and a man anxious to clean himself up. The shooting is a cataclysmic act (rather like the throwing of the biscuit-tin in *Ulysses*). It is the end of the world and the 'abnihilisation of the etym' (*FW* 353:22) or splitting of the atom by Lord Rutherford; another version, in fact, of the fall.

The fall, in Vico, was a fall into language. The thunderword is 'The hundredlettered name again, last word of perfect language' (*FW* 424:23–4). This means both that it is the model of language, and that all that follows it must be imperfect language. The difference, perhaps, is that perfect language is a spell or incantation, imperious and magical in its effects; imperfect language is mere miscellaneous patter or hocus-pocus. J. S. Atherton has traced Joyce's interest in the theories of the primitive mind put forward by the anthropologist Lévy-Bruhl. Naming, for Lévy-Bruhl's primitives, is a mode of appropriation or possession. To name a thing is to have power over it. The *Wake* suggests that Shem and Shaun, at least, no longer have this power. Shem is not a shaman but a simple 'Sham' (*FW* 170:25). Shaun's language, as his inquisitors point out in III.iii, has no authority since it possesses no term 'to signify majestate' (*FW* 478:12). The language of both brothers is degraded, for if one glibly speaks 'slanguage' the other is a hesitant writer of 'sinscript' (*FW* 421:17–18). Does the 'miscegenated' style of the *Wake* itself show the taint of the brothers' language?

Where Joyce comes closest, it would seem, to the magical use of language is in his systematic employment of lists and names. All the books of the Bible are named in the *Wake* – as if to name them were, somehow, to claim them.[14] In quantitative terms the *Wake*'s intertextuality is very much less a matter of quotation or pastiche than of simple allusions to authors and titles, including hundreds of once-popular titles now known only to the specialist and bibliophile. Another form of quasi-magical appropriation comes in the 'Anna Livia Plurabelle' chapter, which is filled with hundreds of river-names (some of them very obscure) from all over the world. Yet it is as impossible to name all the world's rivers as it is to name all the world's books or even its works of scripture — however much Joyce might have liked to do so. The result is not genuine magic or 'perfect language' but an entertainer's patter; fallen language, that is, aspiring only to imitate a source of original power and to produce the momentary illusion that that power is not lost.

This point is illustrated further by the crucial issue of polyglottism in the *Wake*. A world of perfect language would be monolingual. *Finnegans Wake* has been viewed by semioticians as a model of language, comparable with those offered by modern linguistic theorists. But the grand theories of Chomsky and Saussure are monolingual theories, based on an ideal homogeneous speech-community in which there is a constant relationship between the language and the individual speaker. In this perspective conditions such as bilingualism are regarded as exceptional.[15] It is Joyce's great merit — as well as his great difficulty — that in *Finnegans Wake* he does more than any previous writer had dared to do to reflect the actual linguistic confusion of modern cultures. Roland McHugh in his *Annotations* has discovered elements drawn from 65 different languages and sub-languages in the vocabulary of the *Wake*. Some of these Joyce simply mugged up for a particular passage; others, notably French, German, Italian, the Scandinavian languages and Gaelic, are so pervasive that, if one happens to know them, the experience of reading the *Wake* is immensely enriched. Now the *Wake*'s 65 languages, like its book-titles and river-names, may be a doomed attempt to encompass, by naming, all the world's languages — how else, for example, can we explain the passage on pages 470–1 in which 'Peace' is written in 29 of them? But the attempt is hopeless given the fallen condition of man 'after Babel'. It is profoundly appropriate that one of the symbolic entries into history provided in I.i is a meeting between a primordial Celt and Dane who have great difficulty in understanding one another:

Scuse us, chorley guy! You tollerday donsk? N. You tolkatiff scowegian? Nn. You spigotty anglease? Nnn. You phonio saxo? Nnnn. Clear all so! Tis a Jute. Let us swop hats and excheck a few strong verbs weak oach eather yapyazzard abast the blooty creeks. *(FW* 16:5–9)

Mutt's 'linguistic competence', here, is not that of any given culture or nation but rather that of the chaotic marketplace in which every *lingua* is *franca* enough for its denizens to exchange repartee and swop hats. So it is throughout the *Wake*. Communication is highly imperfect and is constantly interrupted, but — even when we can 'beurally forsstand a weird' *(FW* 17:13–14) — it does take place.

Language-levels in the *Wake* vary enormously. Sometimes, as in the 'river' chapters, Joyce allows an intense lyricism, a 'natural magic' which he associates with female voices. Then the beautifully modulated style has the phrasing and the cadences of the professional tenor that Joyce might have become. But far more often we are aware of a deliberate debasement, of a style with has abandoned all claims to lyricism and authority in favour of a polyglot jumble of mixed registers, mixed metaphors, ephemera and noise. It would be wrong, however, to see Joyce as perversely straining after such effects. Frequently he is merely recording, and giving artistic shape to, kinds of discourse he could hear all around him — but which conventional literary people had trained themselves not to notice. Newspaper headlines, advertising and media-language, not to mention the conversation of polyglot cities such as Trieste, Paris and Zurich, all display the sort of verbal promiscuity that is rife in the *Wake*; only Joyce pushes it to its logical conclusion, in the heterogeneity not only of the sentence but within the individual word.

When *Work in Progress* began appearing Joyce, as he must have expected, was accused in some quarters of wanting to destroy the English language. The same accusation is levelled against Shem who, if he lived long enough, would 'wipe alley english spooker, multaphoniaksically spuking, off the face of the erse' (*FW* 178:6–7). But Shem, and Joyce, were starting not from language as it is defined in dictionaries and academies but from language as it actually is and was. Compare, for example, a famous passage of 'literary' English —

A good book is the precious life-blood of a master spirit . . .

— with modern media-prose. Milton's sentence can be parodied and travestied, it can become dulled by commercial repetition, for the very reason that it has a drive and eloquence which make it worth parodying and worth stealing. But say we were to take the following 'sentence' (from a recent BBC television announcement):

The museum that's a Mecca for the bike brigade.

With its jumbled concepts, dead metaphors and tired alliteration, such a sentence cannot be travestied or debased. It is already a grotesque specimen except that, far from being suggestive and intriguing as *Wake* language invariably is, it is merely pointless and flat.

Joyce's principal method of reclaiming dead and debased language is by means of puns and portmanteau-words. These are used much too systematically to be considered, save in exceptional cases, as 'jokes' even though the deformation of language they embody is inherently derisive and comic. They direct attention to the physical reality of words and their relationships with other words. Such relationships have a sort of illusory magic, and indeed to a fanatical etymologist like Vico they appear as genuine magic, or at least as containing the vital clues to human history. But in fact etymologies based solely on verbal resemblance are notoriously unreliable, a form of fools' gold. Many if not most such resemblances are simply coincidental and fortuitous. Yet to pursue them is to rediscover the physicality of words and the reservoir of unrealized and unexploited meaning which is needed to sustain any language or sign-system. For example, the flatness of the above specimen of BBC English arises from its search for epigrammatic concision and deliberate exclusion of redundancy. To reactivate its language we should want to find some way of drawing together the concepts of *museum* and *Mecca*, perhaps by building a portmanteau-word including the two-way associations of *muezzin*. 'Bike brigade' is another arbitrary coinage, which must be first disassembled and then reassembled to make anything of it. (Presumably it is the militarism of motorcycling gangs which is implied, though why should militarists be in search of a 'Mecca'?) By pursuing some implications of 'bike' and 'brigade' we can arrive at a transformation such as the following:

Museomuezzin, the bikers' Micah, helmetsangels' headquarters . . .

We have arrived at something like *Wake*-language by a grotesque verbal doodling process, subjecting an already debased language to still further – but far more deliberate – deformations.

Two conclusions may be drawn from the foregoing discussion. The first is that the basic language of *Finnegans Wake* is not only English but, specifically, modern English – a language (like the sample given above) which is full of dead significations and of miscellaneous cultural debris. Famous snatches of literary English, such as the Miltonic sentence quoted above, have become part of the debris, together with a vast quantity of more recent and much more ephemeral accretions. The *Wake* bristles not only with literary reference but with popular songs, catch-phrases, the names of men and women who enjoyed a brief notoriety, and references to sport and games.[16] (At this level the book belongs so much to the 1920s and 30s that already the reader who can take a 'hillman minx' (*FW* 376:3) or a 'Belisha beacon' (*FW* 267:12) in his stride has an advantage over younger contemporaries.) In addition, just as newspaper culture was endemic in *Ulysses*, the *Wake* is full of the newer culture of the airwaves. Its linguistic anarchy is more than a journalistic clash of styles; discourses are scrambled, and signals oscillate in strength, much as they do when we run through the wavelengths on a radio. The format of television programmes, too, appears in Joyce's book long before it became a familiar part of cultural experience; though the word *television*, which Joyce uses, dates from 1909, the first demonstration of a television image did not take place until 1926. Shortwave wireless communication ('Calling all downs', *FW* 593:2) is heard at the beginning of IV.i, while the 'pub' chapter, II.iii, is interrupted by a BBC broadcast with weather forecast, news, and a police message complete with the telephone number to contact ('Clontarf, one love, one fear', *FW* 324:20–1, which is an echo of Whitehall 1212). If broadcasting offers a pervasive metaphor for the disembodied voices of the *Wake*, so does another characteristic tool of modern communications, the telephone. Much of the séance in II.iii is conducted over the telephone, and the whole of *Finnegans Wake* may be imaged as a 'tellafun book' (*FW* 86:14). The 'dreariodreama' (*FW* 79:28) is, in fact, a remarkable prophecy of electronic culture.

The second conclusion to be drawn from Joyce's deformation of an already deformed language is that he had found an effective way (and conceivably the only way) of injecting it with new life. That it is a morbid, decadent, even parasitic mode of life may not greatly matter. The pun is a universally despised linguistic device, and yet the process of punning and portmanteau word-creation is astonishingly fecund in his hands. The midden-heap (the debris of everyday English or 'alley english spooker') becomes a compost-heap, the scene of an endless fermentation process in which are concentrated all hopes of renewal. Among the many symbols affirming renewal in the *Wake* is the Letter, which corresponds in turn to Joyce's own book.

In its simplest version, the Letter (written down by Shem the Penman and delivered by Shaun the Post) is ALP's plea in defence of her husband, HCE, who is accused of public indecency. As a restorative or instrument for the rehabilitation of a fallen hero it is not unlike the legendary drop of whiskey, spilt over the corpse at Tim Finnegan's wake, which caused the dead man to revive. The kind of life which it promotes, in other words, is a reprieve or after-life, a late second flowering or even (bearing in mind the quantity of infantile material in the *Wake*) a second childhood. HCE may be revived towards the end of Book III, but he will never regain the vigour of his younger self. He achieves sexual intercourse with ALP (III.iv), but in a laboured and safely contraceptive fashion. In her last monologue ALP views him in a disillusioned way, as a 'bumpkin' and a 'puny' (*FW* 627:23–4). The old man is not what he was. The same feeling is present in other strands of the revival- or resurrection-theme in the *Wake*. An Easter Rising, Joyce reminds us from time to time, has led to the creation of an Irish Free State, but there is little indication that post-treaty Eire with its 'devil era' (*FW* 473:8) should be regarded as a nation equal in stature with the Ireland of old. The limits of the succession or resurrection are evident also in one of the *Wake*'s more curious symbols – that of eggs.

Eggs are associated with Humpty Dumpty (HCE) as well as with Easter and the hen which scratches in the midden-heap. The younger generation has pushed Humpty off his wall ('Move up. Mumpty! Mike room for Rumpty!' *FW* 99:19–20), and he will never be the same even if he can be reassembled. Broken eggs, however, have their uses. You cannot make an omelette without breaking eggs (a political proverb which is found in the *Wake*, and whose significance was not lost on Joyce). A pun is a sort of scrambled egg or word-omelette, which is one reason why the Letter is written on eggshells ('scribings scrawled on eggs', *FW* 615:10). Eggs signify dawn and breakfast, and therefore a release from the nightmare of dream-history: 'iggs for the brekkers come to mournhim, sunny side up with care' (*FW* 12:14–15). Sunrise and the promise of eggs, in Book IV, mark the end of the night – which has descended, not at the beginning of the *Wake*, but at the close of 'Anna Livia Plurabelle' and the succeeding chapter, 'The Mime of Mick, Nick and the Maggies', in which the children are called indoors for bed. But the broken eggs are also the mark of a continued recycling, in which there is no escape from the dream-world. For it is by means of the egg that HCE's genotype is handed down to his successors.[17] Resurrection implies succession.

The opening chapter of the *Wake* ends with the mourners reassuring Finnegan, whose wake it is, that an orderly succession is taking place – he must lie easy since there is no need for his resurrection. His wife is sitting in her chair reading the *Evening World*. (The headline, 'Angry scenes at Stormount' (*FW* 28:22) implies that the date is shortly after Partition.) As for his son, there is a 'big rody ram lad' (*FW* 28:36) ready to take over. This is HCE, the historical version of the legendary Finn. We hear of his crime, his public trial, his burial and then of the brothers squabbling over the succession. As we have seen, late in Book III HCE is given a second lease of life. Sexually he is revitalized by the growth to puberty of ALP's successor, Issy. Issy is short for Isolde and is also an oral palindrome. In the Tristan legend there were two Isoldes;

Issy's name suggests Narcissus, and also urination. She is a 'kissmiss' (*FW* 624:6), which in the Scandinavian languages yields a pun on urination, a 'youngdammer' like Ibsen's Hilde Wangel, and a cloud or tiny rivulet beside her mother, the great river. As the 'peepette', 'meeting waters most improper' (*FW* 96:14) she shares HCE's voyeurism, and as a 'nippy in a noveletta' (*FW* 87:23) her dialogues with her mirror-image are conducted in a style strongly reminiscent of Gerty MacDowell. Indeed the triangle Bloom–Molly–Gerty (given that Gerty is much the same age as Milly, Bloom's daughter) is a close analogue to the father–mother–daughter relationship in the *Wake*.

Both in *Ulysses* and *Finnegans Wake* Joyce registers a deep generic difference between male soliloquy and female soliloquy. Margot Norris suggests that in the *Wake* the distinction is between male competitiveness and female narcissism.[18] In the case of Issy versus her brothers this is plain enough. ALP, however, has no need of self-admiration since the whole book resounds with praise of 'Annah the Allmaziful' (*FW* 104:1). To the washerwomen of I.viii she is a legendary figure, the universal mother, about whom they could never hear too much. To Shem and Shaun she is the 'eternal geomater' (*FW* 296:36–297:1), the fount of all secret knowledge. 'Anna Livia Plurabelle' and the final monologue, the two most lyrical and poetic sections of the *Wake* (and hence the most accessible to new readers), are both devoted to her.

Of all Joyce's chapters it is 'Anna Livia Plurabelle' which, in the opinion of most readers, comes closest to the genuinely magical use of language. The vivid brogue of the gossiping washerwomen and the majestic, everlasting flow of the river are one of Joyce's most triumphant conceptions. What he offers here is (as always) human and literary, not 'natural' enchantment. The chapter begins:

O

tell me all about

Anna Livia! I want to hear all

about Anna Livia. Well, you know Anna Livia? Yes, of course, we all know Anna Livia. Tell me all. Tell me now. You'll die when you hear. (*FW* 196:1–5)

Padraic Colum wrote that this passage 'gives us the river as it is seen and heard and felt', and A. Walton Litz, seconding Colum, describes it as an 'onomatopoeic *rendering* of the river'.[19] But the magic is that of the 'Tell me' theme – of storytelling, that is, not of the rendering of nature. The side-to-side rhythm of the river serpentining down to the sea is subdued here, although it is a characteristic effect later in the chapter. No simple evocation of a river would find room for the grotesque humour of the 'Anna Livia Plurabelle' chapter – the slogan 'Ireland sober is Ireland stiff' (*FW* 214:18), for example, and the 'manzinahurries' (*FW* 214:3) which combines a public convenience with a river in Spain. Joyce celebrates the bounteousness and fecundity of Anna Livia with such feats of invention as the list of 111 presents she hands out to her children, and the splendid series of variations on the theme of generation and succession. Renewal is implicit in the actions of the washerwomen – 'Wring out the clothes! Wring in the dew!' (*FW* 213:19–20) – and the process is truly 'allalluvial' (*FW* 213:32) in that it embraces us all: 'Gammer and gaffer we're all their gangsters' (*FW* 215:14–15). The washerwomen's curiosity about the old folk and their stained sheets, not to mention their less shop-soiled successors ('my tennis champion son, the laundryman with the lavandier flannels', *FW* 214:27–8), is as natural and inevitable as it is inexhaustible. Our interest in the act of conception, prurient though it may sometimes seem, is an interest in origins and thus an example of the fundamental historical impulse; and it is the root of all literature, being the basis of our quickened attention when we hear the promise of a tale. 'Anna Livia Plurabelle' is (unlike a good deal of *Finnegans Wake*) a highly suitable text for oral performance, as Joyce's own recording shows; and it is an example of the Joyceian grotesque celebration of life at its most magisterial.

Very different in tone is ALP's final monologue, which ends not with a lifegiving 'yes' but with the resignation, the self-yielding, of the river flowing out to sea. Here ALP is 'passing out' (*FW* 627:34), in a celebration not of fertility but of succession. It is an epilogue to history, in which the whole tale of human life that has been told is surveyed and found wanting: 'How small it's all!' (*FW* 627:20). Anna Livia knows that her time is up, and like a dying person she is already estranged from the life she has led and ready to embrace an essential loneliness. Her second childhood, as she rushes into the arms of her father, the sea-god ('Far calls. Coming, far!' (*FW* 628:13)) is quite inescapably an intimation of death. Death, which has been faced with curiosity, anguish, mockery and farce in Joyce's earlier work, is here the subject of a painful excitement, a terrible rapture. It is a new awakening, like that of Gabriel at the end of 'The Dead', in which human identity – though conscious and garrulous to the last – is received back into the symbolic landscape from which throughout civilization and throughout the *Wake* it has struggled to distinguish itself:

I am passing out. O bitter ending! I'll slip away before they're up. They'll never see. Nor know. Nor miss me. And it's old and old it's sad and old it's sad and weary I go back to you, my cold father, my cold mad father, my cold mad feary father, till the near sight of the mere size of him, the moyles and moyles of it, moananoaning, makes me seasilt saltsick and I rush, my only, into your arms. I see them rising! Save me from those therrble prongs! Two more. Onetwo moremens more. So. Avelaval. My leaves have drifted from me. All. But one clings still. I'll bear it on me. To remind me of. Lff! So soft this morning, ours. Yes. Carry me along, taddy, like you done through the toyfair! If I seen him bearing down on me now under whitespread wings like he'd come from Arkangels, I sink I'd die down over his feet, humbly dumbly, only to washup. Yes, tid. There's where. First. We pass through grass behush the bush to. Whish! A gull. Gulls. Far calls. Coming, far! End here. Us then. Finn, again! Take. Bussoftlhee, mememormee! Till thousendsthee. Lps. the keys to. Given! A way a lone a last a loved a long the   (*FW* 627:34–628:16)

Joyce finished this passage in November 1938, so that it is the last piece of fiction he ever wrote. He died, worn out before his time, on 13 January 1941, a few weeks short of his sixtieth birthday and the twentieth anniversary of *Ulysses*.

In the introduction to his *Annotations* Roland McHugh declares – perhaps with undue severity – that 'In *Finnegans Wake* the novice always misses the point'.[20] Our judgement of the book must take account of the extent to which it is capable of being understood, and at what cost. It may or may not comfort the novice reader that – for all the gains of *Wake* scholarship over the years – nobody now claims that every word of the book can be understood and assimilated. Some commentators, as we have seen, suggest that the persistence of a residue of pure untamed verbal wilderness – noise, or interference, or unlimited semeiosis – is actually a virtue. Certainly it is inescapable, though it should be added that this foreground feature of the *Wake* may be a background element of our response to all great literary works. As Joyce's lifetime recedes from us, and with it the likelihood of recovering those of his more fugitive and ephemeral allusions which have yet to be detected, the *Wake* is in some ways getting more difficult, even as scholarship renders it easier to master.

One of the most pessimistic accounts of *Wake* exegesis was that given by Bernard Benstock at the beginning of *Joyce-Again's Wake* (1965): 'Time, which was expected to bring all evidence eventually to the surface in an ordered pattern, so far has had the opposite effect'.[21] That is still true, though clearly it does not diminish the fascination of the book, nor the possibilities of writing about it. What is very clear, however, is that a certain amount of our present-day knowledge has emerged from the comparison of Joyce's manuscripts and early drafts with the final version, and could not have been arrived at otherwise. This is true of the interpretation of so central and important a passage as the Balkelly–Patrick dialogue in IV.i, which Joyce himself said contained the 'defence and indictment of the book itself'.[22] It would doubtless be entertaining to compare various scholarly summaries of this dialogue, which I myself would read as a defence of the esoteric artist (Berkeley or the druid) against the robustly practical imperatives of St Patrick. Admittedly, the dispute over the interpretation of the passage is not more extreme than some other disagreements in the notoriously contentious field of literary criticism. In order to interpret it at all, however, it is more or less necessary to refer to the earlier and simpler drafts which Joyce later overlaid with pidgin English. A. Walton Litz called this a 'damning commentary' on Joyce's method.[23] It certainly suggests an experiment which may, at some points, have gone astray.

Nevertheless, the rewards of reading the *Wake* are immense. A good deal of initial commitment is needed; Joyce, after all, taught himself Dano-Norwegian in order to read Ibsen in the original. It is unwise not to possess a chapter-by-chapter commentary or working outline when one attempts the book for the first time. (Later, one can construct one's own commentary.) Once launched into the text, the greatest challenge is the astonishingly miscellaneous and diverse range of knowledge, allusion, and reference that Joyce worked into it. The encyclopaedic nature of this knowledge is what makes *Finnegans Wake* a 'history of the world', yet Joyce had utterly abandoned any preconceived ideas of a canon or hierarchy of knowledge. He omitted nothing, that is, on the grounds that by some external standard it was too trivial or ephemeral for inclusion. His alternative history displays, instead, a voracious appetite for what orthodox historians would see as trivial and ephemeral. The *Wake*, like a vast crossword puzzle, sets up a hierarchy of knowledge which is all its own. The choice is dictated by its intricate poetic logic and also, it must be admitted, by Joyce's own private tastes. (For example, *Finnegans Wake* may possibly have extra appeal for those to whom Dublin and Ireland are the centre of the universe – and at least one scholar has written that 'to appreciate the book fully one needs to live in Dublin'[24] – yet this has, of course, left the great majority of Dublin's population unmoved.)

Until very recently, the problem that any individual reader's stock of general knowledge was unlikely to coincide very closely with Joyce's was usually overcome by communal reading — in reading circles, study sessions, and in seminars and classes. Reading the *Wake* was an eccentric but highly enjoyable form of group activity. Various people recognized the need for a comprehensive set of interlinear glosses to the book, and now, since the publication of McHugh's *Annotations* in 1980, such a volume is conveniently available. Thanks to the *Annotations* silent, not communal, reading can now become the norm for most purposes. McHugh brings together a far greater range of knowledge than any single group of people is likely to have readily on call; it would be a rare seminar group, for example, which could detect allusions in 65 languages. McHugh's own commitment to a silent reading-process is exemplified by his preference for identifying the main characters by their 'sigla' — the symbols Joyce used to distinguish them in his manuscripts and letters — rather than by name. There are good reasons for using the sigla but they would be useless for group reading, being purely visual symbols with no sounds attached.

McHugh's compilation is by no means complete. Any persistent reader will find himself in a position to add to it.[25] Nevertheless, it marks the most substantial attempt yet made to bridge the gap between the exegetical labours of *Wake* specialists, and the needs of the ordinary reader. The very necessity for volumes of line-by-line annotations to the later Joyce is, of course, a palpable sign of his difference from virtually every other twentieth-century writer. *Ulysses* and *Finnegans Wake* have remained unique performances, partly because the laws of supply and demand in the literary market-place would be unlikely to permit more than two or three such books in any century. Joyce's genius was that he felt called upon to write, and found appropriate forms and answerable styles for, such works. With the reading aids now available, anyone with sufficient determination can read *Finnegans Wake* with a very substantial degree of understanding. The poetic richness of the most easily accessible passages should be enough to suggest the rewards of such a full reading, and the enrichment of life and literary experience that it can offer; though such rewards, admittedly, are not for the impatient.

PART IV

12   Recourse

'There can be no reconciliation . . . if there has not been a sundering', says Stephen in *Ulysses* (*U* 195). Joyce (as Vivian Mercier has shown) may be plausibly viewed as a quintessentially Irish writer, drawing both on the Celtic reverence for poetry and scholarship, and on Celtic traditions of grotesque obscenity.[1] *Finnegans Wake* marks his reconciliation with Irish culture; the very title makes this evident. An Irish wake was an occasion for dancing, singing, revels and horse-play, including elaborate burlesques on the theme of fertility.[2] It was a pagan ritual, owing nothing either to the Sassenach or the Roman. Joyce was a product of the British and Roman Catholic hegemony in Ireland and, like most if not all modern Irishmen, was profoundly and indelibly affected by them. But he sought to invert the English language and literature and the categories of the Christian religion in such a way that they could be used to express a pagan and comic vision – one which, by the standards of its time, was at once impious and shockingly 'nonliterary'. His refusal to compromise with the moral, literary, and political orthodoxies of his age makes him an avant-garde writer still today, and perhaps for a long time to come. His work attracts fanatical devotees, many of them drawn from outside the ranks of formal students of literature. He is revered by linguists and practising writers, as well as by literary critics.

Where Joyce arouses resentment today it is not, on the whole, because of his irreverence or 'obscenity' but because of his extreme difficulty. There are precedents for such difficulty. Derrida, for example, has described him as 'the most Hegelian of modern novelists', while Bakhtin said of Rabelais that, of all classical authors of world literature, he is 'the least popular, the least understood and appreciated'.[3] The author of *Finnegans Wake*, at least, seems determined to dispute this place with the author of *Gargantua and Pantagruel*.

Joyce's attitude to writing was not that of a journalist but of a scholar. Mercier represents him as fighting 'the old battle of the wandering scholar against the clergy, who must inevitably tend to dominate intellectual life in a Catholic country'.[4] He has the pride and

241

self-absorption of the scholar, feeling, for example, that the astonishing labour he put into his books was in itself sufficient to justify the reader's labour in comprehending them. He had taught himself Dano-Norwegian in order to read Ibsen, so why should not others have to learn 'Djoytsch' in order to read *Finnegans Wake*? He showed no false modesty in foreseeing the generations of lesser scholars who would devote themselves to Joyceian exegesis.

Joyce in his later books writes *of* and *about* – though not *for* – the common man and woman. The broad theme of creation and fertility is pursued in its linguistic, dynastic, and sexual – not merely its artistic – aspects. The building of houses and cities and the triumphs and tribulations of family life take their place beside more literary and intellectual labours. Perhaps because his own life was so single-mindedly devoted to his art, he was able to incorporate in it life's broader concerns seen with an unfailing gusto, and a pervading innocence. The gusto is Dickensian; the innocence is not. For the contrast of Joyce and Dickens as comic and visionary writers[5] would be incomplete if we failed to observe that Joyce lacks the luridly and violently Gothic strain of Dickens's imagination. For Dickens, and many of his successors, the grotesque implies terror and murderous hatred and mental and physical torture. The sufferings of Bloom and the 'crimes' of HCE are wholly lacking in the more brutal forms of sadism and masochism. Like much of the best comedy, there is something deliberately childlike about Joyce's banishment of horror and fear.

It is curious that *Ulysses* ends with Bloom and Molly eating the seedcake, since the seedcake, in one of its implications, may represent the Fall of Man. *Finnegans Wake* takes place after the Fall but presents history as an unending sequence of degradation and regeneration, which avoids the finality of the Christian revelation. The sermon in the *Portrait* shows that Joyce associates torture and suffering with a Christian view of the world. His own art uses some of the Christian imagery and terminology in the service of a vision which is not merely secular and post-Christian but rampantly pagan. HCE, ALP, Bloom and Molly are grotesque, morally suspect, and yet irrepressible figures, who are certainly not orthodox saints or heroes and yet are untouched by the violence and villainy of which actual history (both sacred and secular) is full. They are bourgeois characters who transcend bourgeois society to become, not Christian icons, not classical statues like those Bloom ogles in the National Museum, but symbols of human fertility and succession − modern equivalents, perhaps, of the phallic and steatopygous stone images found in the world's great prehistoric temples. Like the stone figures, they are found in elaborate edifices constructed with enormous labour, and like them, their appeal is one of sheer carnality, permanence, and mystery.

Notes

1. Introduction

1. John Forster, *The Life of Charles Dickens*, Charles Dickens edn., London (Chapman & Hall) n.d., I, p. 290.
2. Frank Budgen, *James Joyce and the Making of 'Ulysses' and Other Writings*, London (Oxford University Press) 1972, p. 69.
3. Forster, *Life*, II, p. 195.
4. G. H. Lewes, 'Dickens in Relation to Criticism', reprinted in *The Dickens Critics*, ed. George H. Ford and Lauriat Lane, Jr., Ithaca (Cornell University Press) 1961, p. 66.
5. Richard Ellmann, *James Joyce*, new edn., New York (Oxford University Press) 1982, p. 554.
6. See Gissing's diary, published as *London and the Life of Literature in Late Victorian England*, ed. Pierre Coustillas, Brighton, Sussex (Harvester Press) 1978, p. 23.
7. Charles Dickens, *Little Dorrit*, London (Oxford University Press) 1953, p. 143.
8. T. S. Eliot, *Selected Essays*, London (Faber & Faber) 1951, p. 289.
9. Ellmann, *Joyce*, p. 61.
10. Arthur Power, *Conversations with James Joyce*, ed. Clive Hart, London (Millington) 1964, p. 69.
11. Ibid, p. 89.
12. Quoted in *The Joyce We Knew*, ed. Ulick O'Connor, Cork (Mercier Press) 1967, p. 107.
13. W. B. Stanford, *The Ulysses Theme*, Oxford (Basil Blackwell) 1954, p. 223.
14. Vitruvius, *On Architecture*, trans. Frank Granger, London (Heinemann) 1934, II, p. 105.
15. Wolfgang Kayser, *The Grotesque in Art and Literature*, trans. Ulrich Weisstein, Bloomington (Indiana University Press) 1963, p. 102.
16. Vivian Mercier, *The Irish Comic Tradition*, Oxford (Clarendon Press) 1962, p. 48.
17. Mikhail Bakhtin, *Rabelais and His World*, trans. Helene Iswolsky, Cambridge, Mass. (MIT Press) 1968, pp. 320, 318.
18. Friedrich Nietzsche, *The Birth of Tragedy and The Genealogy of Morals*, trans. Francis Golffing, Garden City, NY (Doubleday Anchor) 1956, pp. 238–9.
19. Kayser, *The Grotesque*, p. 157.
20. Ibid.
21. Eliot, *Selected Essays*, p. 303.
22. George Orwell, *Collected Essays, Journalism and Letters*, ed. Sonia Orwell & Ian Angus, London (Secker & Warburg) 1968, II, p. 163.

23. Cf. Bernard O'Donoghue, 'Irish Humour and Verbal Logic', in *Critical Quarterly*, xxiv no. 1 (Spring 1982), p. 35.
24. Bakhtin, *Rabelais*, p. 58.
25. Cf. J. S. Atherton, *The Books at the Wake*, London (Faber & Faber) 1959, pp. 162–5, 278–9.
26. Mercier, *Irish Comic Tradition*, p. 48.
27. W. B. Yeats, *Autobiographies*, London (Macmillan) 1955, p. 315.

2. The Student

1. See Ellmann, *Joyce*, pp. 101–4.
2. Stanislaus Joyce, *The Complete Dublin Diary*, ed. George H. Healey, Ithaca & London (Cornell University Press) 1971, p. 3.
3. A. Dwight Culler, *The Imperial Intellect: A Study of Newman's Educational Ideal*, New Haven (Yale University Press) and London (Oxford University Press) 1955, pp. 168–9.
4. Fergal McGrath, SJ, *Newman's University: Ideal and Reality*, London (Longmans, Green & Co) 1951, p. 118.
5. Kevin Sullivan, *Joyce Among the Jesuits*, New York (Columbia University Press) 1958, pp. 149, 162.
6. C. P. Curran, *James Joyce Remembered*, Oxford (Oxford University Press) 1968, p. 37.
7. Sullivan, *Joyce Among the Jesuits*, pp. 167–8.
8. Stanislaus Joyce, *My Brother's Keeper*, ed. Richard Ellmann, London (Faber & Faber) 1958, p. 126.
9. Ellmann, *Joyce*, p. 104.
10. Ibid, pp. 266–7.
11. Yeats, *Autobiographies*, p. 316.
12. Ellmann, *Joyce*, p. 240.
13. Ibid, p. 149.
14. Ibid, p. 136.
15. Oliver St John Gogarty, *As I Was Going Down Sackville Street*, Harmondsworth (Penguin) 1954, pp. 298–9.
16. Curran, *Joyce Remembered*, p. 49.
17. S. Joyce, *Dublin Diary*, p. 51.
18. Ellmann, *Joyce*, p. 266.
19. Ibid, p. 163.
20. Ibid, p. 150.

3. *Dubliners*

1. Curran, *Joyce Remembered*, p. 49.
2. H. G. Wells, Introduction to *The Country of the Blind and Other Stories*, London (Nelson) n.d., p.v.
3. Edmund Wilson, *Axel's Castle*, New York (Scribner's) 1948. p. 155.
4. George Moore, *The Untilled Field*, London (Fisher Unwin) 1903, p. 416.

5. Wells, *The Country of the Blind*, p. vii.
6. Marvin Magalaner and Richard M. Kain, *Joyce: The Man, the Work, the Reputation*, New York (Collier Books) 1962, p. 92.
7. *Letters*, II, pp. 305–6.
8. Arthur Symons, *The Symbolist Movement in Literature*, New York (E. P. Dutton & Co.) 1958, p. 1.
9. Richard Levin and Charles Shattuck, 'First Flight to Ithaca', in *James Joyce*, ed. Givens, 2nd edn., pp. 47–94.
10. Seamus Deane, 'Joyce and Nationalism', in Colin MacCabe, ed., *James Joyce: New Perspectives*, Brighton (Harvester Press) and Bloomington (Indiana University Press) 1982, pp. 181–2.
11. Quoted in Magalaner and Kain, *Joyce*, p. 100.
12. Magalaner and Kain, *Joyce*, pp. 100–1.
13. Ibid, pp. 101–2.
14. See François Laroque, 'Hallowe'en Customs in 'Clay': A Study of James Joyce's Use of Folklore in *Dubliners*', in *Cahiers Victoriens et Edouardiens* no. 14 (October 1981), pp.47–56.
15. Florence L. Walzl, '*Dubliners*: Women in Irish Society', in Suzette Henke and Elaine Unkeless, eds., *Women in Joyce*, Brighton (Harvester Press) 1982, p. 33.
16. See Burton A. Waishen and Florence L. Walzl, 'Paresis and the Priest: Joyce's Symbolic Use of Syphilis in 'The Sisters', in *Annals of Internal Medicine* lxxx (June 1974), pp. 758–62.
17. Hugh Kenner, *The Pound Era*, London (Faber & Faber) 1975, pp. 34–9.
18. O'Connor, ed., *The Joyce We Knew*, p. 97.
19. Henrik Ibsen, *Ghosts*, in *Four Great Plays*, trans. R. Farquharson Sharp, New York (Bantam Books) 1959, p. 99.

4. *A Portrait of the Artist* and *Exiles*

1. For Pound's role in establishing Joyce's literary reputation, see *Pound / Joyce*, ed. Forrest Read, London (Faber & Faber) 1968.
2. The Italian texts have been published as *Scritti Italiani*, ed. Gianfranco Corsini and Giorgio Melchiori, Milan (Mondadori) 1979.
3. Gustave Flaubert, *Letters*, ed. Richard Rumbold, London (Weidenfeld & Nicolson) 1950, p. 98.
4. Oscar Wilde, *The Picture of Dorian Gray*, World's Classics edn., Oxford (Oxford University Press) 1981, p. 5.
5. Joyce, 'A Portrait of the Artist', in *A Portrait of the Artist as a Young Man: Text, Criticism, and Notes*, ed. Chester G. Anderson, New York (Viking Press) 1968, pp. 257–8.
6. Ibid, p. 260.
7. Ibid, p. 265.
8. Ibid, pp. 257–8.
9. In 1907 Joyce, presumably finding the name 'Dedalus' too artificial, had thought of changing it to Daly (see Ellmann, *Joyce*, p. 264).
10. Symons, *The Symbolist Movement*, p. 5.

11. Hugh Kenner, 'The Portrait in Perspective' in *James Joyce: Two Decades of Criticism*, ed. Seon Givens, 2nd edn., New York (Vanguard Press) 1963, p. 137.

12. Ibid, p. 169.

13. Ellmann, *Joyce*, p. 264.

14. Mark Schorer, 'Technique as Discovery', in *Forms of Modern Fiction*, ed. W. Van O'Connor, Minneapolis and London (University of Minnesota Press) 1948, pp. 9 ff.

15. Sigmund Freud, 'Family Romances', in *On Sexuality*, Harmondsworth (Penguin Books) 1977, pp. 222–3.

16. Maud Ellmann, 'Polytropic Man', in *James Joyce: New Perspectives*, ed. MacCabe, p. 94.

17. See Richard Brown, 'James Joyce: The Sexual Pretext', unpublished PhD thesis, University of London, 1981, Ch. 4.

18. Quoted in Samuel Levenson, *Maud Gonne*, London (Cassell) 1977, p. 308.

19. H. G. Wells, 'James Joyce', in *H. G. Wells's Literary Criticism*, ed. Patrick Parrinder and Robert M. Philmus, Brighton (Harvester Press) and New York (Barnes & Noble) 1980, p. 174.

20. For a full discussion of the villanelle, see e.g. Robert Scholes, 'Stephen Dedalus, Poet or Esthete?', in *A Portrait: Text, Criticism, and Notes*, ed. Anderson, pp. 468–80.

21. See Ruth Bauerle, 'Bertha's Role in *Exiles*', in *Women in Joyce*, ed. Henke and Unkeless, pp. 108–31.

22. Ellmann, *Joyce*, p. 704.

5. A Dublin *Peer Gynt*

1. Ellmann, *Joyce*, pp. 229–30.

2. Ibid, p. 230.

3. Ibid, p. 265.

4. A. Walton Litz, 'The Genre of *Ulysses*', in *The Theory of the Novel: New Essays*, ed. John Halperin, New York (Oxford University Press) 1974, p. 110.

5. J. M. Synge, *Plays, Poems and Prose*, Everyman edn., London (Dent) 1941, pp. 107–8.

6. Georg Lukács, *The Historical Novel*, trans. Hannah and Stanley Mitchell, Harmondsworth (Penguin Books) 1969, p. 36.

7. Budgen, *Joyce and the Making of 'Ulysses'*, p. 15.

8. E. A. Bennett, 'Mr George Gissing', in *Fame and Fiction*, London (Grant Richards) 1901, pp. 201–2.

9. George Gissing, *New Grub Street*, World's Classics edn., London (Oxford University Press) 1958, p. 149.

10. George Eliot, *Middlemarch*, World's Classics edn., London (Oxford University Press) 1947, p. 207.

11. Ellmann, *Joyce*, p. 266.

12. H. G. Wells, *Tono-Bungay*, London (Macmillan) 1909, pp. 6, 7.

13. Erich Auerbach, *Mimesis*, trans. Willard Trask, Garden City, NY (Doubleday) n.d., p. 481.
14. T. S. Eliot, '*Ulysses*, Order and Myth', in *Joyce: Two Decades*, ed. Givens, pp. 201–2.
15. Ellmann, *Joyce*, p. 618.
16. Stuart Gilbert, *James Joyce's 'Ulysses'*, Harmondsworth (Penguin Books) 1963, p. 49.
17. Ibid, pp. 48, 55.
18. Ellmann, *Joyce*, p. 528n.
19. See Patrick Parrinder, 'The Strange Necessity', in *James Joyce: New Perspectives*, ed. MacCabe, pp. 151–67.
20. Georg Lukács, *The Meaning of Contemporary Realism*, trans. John and Necke Mander, London (Merlin Press) 1963, p. 18. Cf. Alick West, *Crisis and Criticism*, London (Lawrence & Wishart) 1937, p. 179. West's whole discussion of *Ulysses* is of great interest and has yet to be improved upon from a Communist standpoint.
21. Brown, *Joyce: The Sexual Pretext*, p. 282.
22. A. Zhdanov, Maxim Gorky, N. Bukharin, K. Radek, and A. Stetsky, *Problems of Soviet Literature: Reports and Speeches at the First Soviet Writers' Congress*, London (Martin Lawrence) n.d., p. 154.

6. Stephen in *Ulysses*

1. For the Linati schema see Richard Ellmann, *Ulysses on the Liffey*, London (Faber & Faber) 1972.
2. Budgen, *Joyce and the Making of 'Ulysses'*, p. 107.
3. Weldon Thornton, *Allusions in 'Ulysses'*, New York (Simon & Schuster) 1973, pp. 22–3.
4. Cf. Thornton, *Allusions*, pp. 30–1. Thornton points out that Stephen's riddle is not a Joyceian invention.
5. Robert Humphrey, *Stream of Consciousness in the Modern Novel*, Berkeley and Los Angeles (University of California Press) 1954, p. 4.
6. Robert Scholes and Robert Kellogg, *The Nature of Narrative*, New York (Oxford University Press) 1966, pp. 183–4.
7. Ibid, p. 189.
8. Gilbert, *Joyce's 'Ulysses'*, pp. 24–5.
9. Thornton, *Allusions*, pp. 41–2.
10. Ibid, p. 62.

7. Bloom and Molly

1. See John Henry Raleigh, *The Chronicle of Leopold and Molly Bloom*, Berkeley, Los Angeles and London (University of California Press) 1977. The paragraph which follows draws on Raleigh at several points.
2. Virginia Woolf, 'Modern Fiction', in *The Common Reader: First Series*, London (Hogarth Press) 1925, p. 191.

3. Robert Martin Adams, *Surface and Symbol: The Consistency of James Joyce's 'Ulysses'*, New York (Oxford University Press) 1962, p. 106.

4. For a discussion of Bloom's 'evasions' in rather different terms see Shari Benstock, 'The Evasion Principle: A Search for Survivors in *Ulysses*', in *Modern Fiction Studies* xxiv no. 2 (Summer 1978), pp. 159–79.

5. Marilyn French, *The Book as World: James Joyce's 'Ulysses'*, Cambridge, Mass., and London (Harvard University Press) 1976, p. 106. See also Hugh Kenner, *Ulysses*, London (Allen & Unwin) 1980, pp. 73–5.

6. Cf. Benstock, 'The Evasion Principle', p. 173.

7. Roderick Gradidge, *Dream Houses: The Edwardian Ideal*, London (Constable) 1980, p. 224.

8. Quoted in Ellmann, *Joyce*, p. 629.

9. Ibid.

10. French, *The Book as World*, p. 255.

8. The Styles of *Ulysses*

1. Arnold Goldman, *The Joyce Paradox*, London (Routledge & Kegan Paul) 1966, p. 96.

2. The phrase is Ezra Pound's. See *Pound/Joyce*, ed. Forrest Read, p. 157.

3. An Irish bull is defined by Bernard O'Donoghue as 'something which is logically sound according to the detailed sequence of its verbal argument but not true of the real world of observed common sense'. O'Donoghue, 'Irish Humour and Verbal Logic', p. 37.

4. Joyce used the phrase in a 1919 letter to Harriet Shaw Weaver (*SL* 242).

5. Litz, 'The Genre of *Ulysses*', in *The Theory of the Novel: New Essays*, ed. John Halperin, p. 116. Two very stimulating readings of *Ulysses* along these lines are Colin MacCabe, 'A Radical Separation of the Elements' in *James Joyce and the Revolution of the Word,* London (Macmillan) 1979, pp. 69–103, and Karen Lawrence, *The Odyssey of Style in 'Ulysses'*, Princeton, NJ (Princeton University Press) 1981.

6. A. Walton Litz, *The Art of James Joyce*, London (Oxford University Press) 1961, p. 49; Michael Groden, *'Ulysses' in Progress*, Princeton, NJ (Princeton University Press) 1977, p. 32.

7. Budgen, *Joyce and the Making of 'Ulysses'*, p. 20.

8. Kenner, *Ulysses,* p. 4.

9. Subliterary in the sense that they were once literary. They are 'dead' allusions to famous book-titles, Dryden's *All for Love* and Adam Smith's *Wealth of Nations*.

10. Ellmann, *Joyce*, p. 521.

11. Cf. (e.g.) Wolfgang Iser, *The Implied Reader*, Baltimore and London (Johns Hopkins University Press) 1974, p. 192.

12. Groden, *'Ulysses' in Progress*, p. 165.

13. David Hayman, 'Cyclops', in *James Joyce's 'Ulysses': Critical Essays*, ed. Clive Hart and David Hayman, Berkeley, Los Angeles and London (University of California Press) 1974, p. 264.

14. Stanley Sultan, *The Argument of Ulysses*, Athens, Ohio (Ohio State

University Press) 1964, pp. 272–4.

15. Peter Trudgill, *Sociolinguistics*, Harmondsworth (Penguin Books) 1983, p. 24.

16. See J. S. Atherton, 'Oxen of the Sun', in *James Joyce's 'Ulysses': Critical Essays,* ed. Hart and Hayman, pp. 313–39.

17. Cf. Iser, *The Implied Reader*, p. 189.

18. Cf. Sandra Gilbert, 'Costumes of the Mind', in *Critical Inquiry* vii, no. 2 (Winter 1980), p. 399.

19. See Goldman, *The Joyce Paradox*, p. 96; French, *The Book as World*, p. 186; Hugh Kenner, *Joyce's Voices*, London (Faber & Faber) 1978, pp. 91–2.

20. Thornton, *Allusions*, pp. 393–4.

21. Kenner, *Ulysses*, p. 130.

22. French, *The Book as World*, pp. 208–10.

23. Henry James, preface to *Roderick Hudson*, Chiltern Library edn., London (John Lehmann) 1947, p. viii.

24. Ellmann, *Joyce*, p. 501.

25. Ibid.

26. Woolf, 'Modern Fiction', in *The Common Reader: First Series*, p. 189.

27. Kenner, *Joyce's Voices*, p. 88.

9. The Ultimate Symbol

1. Brown, *Joyce: The Sexual Pretext*, p. 300.

2. Ellmann, *Joyce*, p. 163.

3. Budgen, *Joyce and the Making of 'Ulysses'*, p. 287.

4. Kenner, *Joyce's Voices*, p. 87.

5. William Empson, 'The Ultimate Novel', Pt 2, in *London Review of Books* iv no. 16 (2–15 September 1982), pp. 6–10.

6. French, *The Book as World*, p. 47.

7. Ellmann, *Joyce*, p. 379.

8. French, *The Book as World*, p. 53.

9. Gilbert, *Joyce's 'Ulysses'*, p. 360.

10. Budgen, *Joyce and the Making of 'Ulysses'*, p. 21.

11. D. H. Lawrence, 'Study of Thomas Hardy', in *Lawrence on Hardy and Painting*, ed. J. V. Davies, London (Heinemann Educational) 1973, p. 31.

12. Wells, 'James Joyce', in *H. G. Wells's Literary Criticism*, ed. Parrinder and Philmus, p. 172.

13. Freud, *On Sexuality*, pp. 212–13.

14. Ibid, p. 215.

10. The Nightmare of History

1. Ellmann, *Joyce*, pp. 533–4.
2. Christopher Ricks, '*Great Expectations*', in *Dickens and the Twentieth Century*, ed. John Gross and Gabriel Pearson, London (Routledge & Kegan Paul) 1962, p. 211.
3. Ellmann, *Joyce*, p. 554.
4. Ibid, p. 702.
5. Ibid, p. 537.
6. Ibid, p. 554.
7. See Bernard Benstock, *Joyce-Again's Wake*, Seattle and London (University of Washington Press) 1965, p. 85.
8. On Joyce and Eliot, see Timothy Materer, *Vortex: Pound, Eliot, and Lewis*, Ithaca and London (Cornell University Press) 1979, pp. 163–97.
9. Joyce attended a public reading by Edith Sitwell in January 1931 (*Letters*, III, p. 210n).
10. Ellmann, *Joyce*, p. 588n.
11. Samuel Beckett and others, *Our Exagmination Round His Factification for Incamination of Work in Progress*, London (Faber & Faber) 1972, p. 41.
12. Ellmann, *Joyce*, p. 577.
13. Lewis and West were principally concerned with attacking the Joyce of *Ulysses* (and, in West's case, of *Pomes Penyeach*), though they disapproved of *Work in Progress* as well. See Parrinder, 'The Strange Necessity', in *James Joyce: New Perspectives*, ed. MacCabe, pp. 151–67.
14. Ellmann, *Joyce*, p. 582.
15. Ibid, p. 590.
16. *Letters*, I, p. 300.
17. Rebecca West, *The Strange Necessity*, London (Cape) 1928, pp. 15, 20.
18. E.g. Anthony Burgess, *Here Comes Everybody*, London (Faber & Faber) 1965, p. 264.
19. Sigmund Freud, *The Interpretation of Dreams*, in *Standard Edition of the Complete Psychological Works of Sigmund Freud*, ed. James Strachey, London (Hogarth Press) 1953, IV, p. 296.
20. Quoted in L. A. G. Strong, *The Sacred River: An Approach to James Joyce*, London (Methuen) 1949, pp. 144–5.
21. Atherton, *Books*.
22. Ibid, p. 238.
23. William York Tindall, *A Reader's Guide to 'Finnegans Wake'*, London (Thames & Hudson) 1969, p. 225.
24. See Chapter 5, note 5.
25. *Our Exagmination*, p. 4.
26. See Isaiah Berlin, *Vico and Herder*, London (Hogarth Press) 1976, pp. 56, 68–9.
27. Giambattista Vico, *The New Science*, trans. Goddard Bergin and Max Harold Fisch, revised edn., Ithaca (Cornell University Press) 1968, p. 420.
28. Ibid, p. 150.
29. *Our Exagmination*, p. 53.

30. Vico, *The New Science*, p. 297.
31. Berlin, *Vico and Herder*, p. 112.
32. Roland McHugh, *The Sigla of 'Finnegans Wake'*, London (Edward Arnold) 1976, p. 119. See also Margot Norris, *The Decentered Universe of 'Finnegans Wake'*, Baltimore and London (Johns Hopkins University Press) 1976, p. 24.
33. *Our Exagmination*, pp. 11–13.
34. See, for example, Jacques Derrida, *Writing and Difference*, Chicago (University of Chicago Press) 1978, p. 153, and *La Dissémination*, Paris (Seuil) 1972, p. 99n.
35. Norris, *Decentered Universe*, p. 123.
36. Stephen Heath, 'Joyce in Language', in *James Joyce: New Perspectives*, ed. MacCabe, p. 131.
37. Terry Eagleton, *Literary Theory: An Introduction*, Oxford (Basil Blackwell) 1983, p. 167.
38. Norris, *Decentered Universe*, p. 123.
39. Ibid, pp. 125–6.
40. Frederick J. Hoffman, 'Infroyce', in *Joyce: Two Decades*, ed. Givens, p. 422. Cf. Norris, *Decentered Universe*, passim.
41. Cf. Norris, *Decentered Universe*, p. 103.
42. Adrian Stokes, *Inside Out*, London (Faber & Faber) 1947, p. 41.
43. Norris, *Decentered Universe*, p. 6.
44. Freud, *Interpretation*, pp. 548–9.
45. See Atherton, *Books*, pp. 34–5.

11. Reading the *Wake*

1. Atherton, *Books*, p. 66.
2. Freud, *Interpretation*, p. 523.
3. McHugh, *Sigla*, p. 6.
4. Atherton, *Books*, p. 48.
5. Henrik Ibsen, *The Master Builder and Other Plays*, trans. Una Ellis-Fermor, Harmondsworth (Penguin Books) 1958, p. 205.
6. Atherton, *Books*, p. 76.
7. See Benstock, *Joyce-Again's Wake*, pp. 171–2.
8. Cf. Norris, *Decentered Universe*, p. 7.
9. Benstock, *Joyce-Again's Wake*, pp. 267ff.
10. Norris, *Decentered Universe*, p. 104.
11. *Our Exagmination*, p. 191.
12. Norris, *Decentered Universe*, p. 80.
13. McHugh, *Sigla*, p. 31.
14. Atherton, *Books*, p. 179.
15. Roy Harris, 'Theoretical Ideas', in 'On Translation – A Symposium', *Times Literary Supplement* no. 4202 (14 October 1983), p. 1119.
16. For the latter see J. S. Atherton, 'Sport and Games in *Finnegans Wake*', in *Twelve and a Tilly*, ed. Jack P. Dalton and Clive Hart,

London (Faber & Faber) 1966, pp. 52–64.

17. McHugh, *Sigla*, p. 113.
18. Norris, *Decentered Universe*, p. 53.
19. Litz, *The Art of James Joyce*, pp. 112–13.
20. Roland McHugh, *Annotations to 'Finnegans Wake'*, Baltimore and London (Johns Hopkins University Press) 1980, p.v.
21. Benstock, *Joyce-Again's Wake*, p. 40.
22. *Letters*, I, p. 406.
23. Litz, *The Art of James Joyce*, p. 113. For a less pejorative view see McHugh, *Sigla*, p. 134.
24. McHugh, *Sigla*, p. 137.
25. Like the current text of the *Wake* itself, McHugh's *Annotations* contains printers' errors (for example, two items on page 480 have been transposed from the following page).

12. Recourse

1. Mercier, *The Irish Comic Tradition*, passim.
2. Ibid, pp. 49–52.
3. Derrida, *Writing and Difference*, p. 153; Bakhtin, *Rabelais*, p. 1.
4. Mercier, *The Irish Comic Tradition*, p. 221.
5. See above, Ch. 1.

Guide to Further Reading

(i) *Chronology of Joyce's published works*

1907   *Chamber Music*, London (Elkin Mathews)
1914   *Dubliners*, London (Grant Richards)
1916   *A Portrait of the Artist as a Young Man*, London (Egoist Press) and New York (B. W. Huebsch)
1918   *Exiles*, London (Grant Richards) and New York (B. W. Huebsch)
1922   *Ulysses*, Paris (Shakespeare & Co)
1927   *Pomes Penyeach*, Paris (Shakespeare & Co)
1939   *Finnegans Wake*, London (Faber & Faber) and New York (B. W. Huebsch) (N.B. A number of sections of *Finnegans Wake* had earlier appeared in serial and pamphlet form, under the generic title *Work in Progress*.)

Posthumous works

1944   *Stephen Hero*, ed. Theodore Spencer
1956   *Epiphanies*, ed. O. A. Silverman
1957   *Letters* [Vol. I], ed. Stuart Gilbert
1959   *Critical Writings*, ed. Ellsworth Mason and Richard Ellmann
1965   *The Workshop of Daedalus*, ed. Robert Scholes and Richard M. Kain. (Includes the *Epiphanies*, 'A Portrait of the Artist', and the Paris, Pola and Trieste notebooks.)
1966   *Letters*, Vols. II and III, ed. Richard Ellmann
1968   *Giacomo Joyce*, ed. Richard Ellmann
1975   *Selected Letters*, ed. Richard Ellmann
1979   *Scritti Italiani*, ed. Gianfranco Corsini and Giorgio Melchiori

(N.B. This list does not include the publication of manuscript materials relating to *Ulysses* and *Finnegans Wake*.)

(ii) Secondary works

In all the vast secondary literature on Joyce, one work (and one only) stands out as essential and indispensable reading. This is Richard Ellmann's biography, *James Joyce*, first published in 1959 and now available in a new edition (New York: Oxford University Press, 1982).

Further information about Joyce's biography is to be found in the memoirs of Stanislaus Joyce, Frank Budgen, Mary and Padraic Colum, C. P. Curran, Arther Power, and others.

Listed below are some of the most useful and accessible studies of Joyce's works. A number of books and articles of more specialist interest which have been drawn upon in the present study are cited in the Notes.

General

Burgess, Anthony. *Joysprick*, London (André Deutsch) 1973. (On Joyce's language.)

Costello, Peter. *James Joyce*, Dublin (Gill & Macmillan) 1980 ('Gill's Irish Lives').

Deming, Robert H., ed. *James Joyce: The Critical Heritage*, 2 vols., London and Boston (Routledge & Kegan Paul) 1970. (Contemporary reviews of Joyce's books.)

Givens, Seon, ed. *James Joyce: Two Decades of Criticism*, 2nd edn., New York (Vanguard Press) 1963. (Collection of essays first published in 1948; includes T. S. Eliot's '*Ulysses*, Order and Myth'.)

Henke, Suzette, and Unkeless, Elaine, eds. *Women in Joyce*, Brighton (Harvester Press) 1982.

Kenner, Hugh. *Joyce's Voices*, London (Faber & Faber) 1978.

Litz, A. Walton. *The Art of James Joyce: Method and Design in 'Ulysses' and 'Finnegans Wake'*, London (Oxford University Press) 1961.

MacCabe, Colin, ed. *James Joyce: New Perspectives*, Brighton (Harvester Press) and Bloomington (Indiana University Press) 1982.

Peake, C. H. *James Joyce: The Citizen and the Artist*, London (Edward Arnold) 1977.

The early Joyce

Joyce, Stanislaus. *My Brother's Keeper*, ed. Richard Ellmann, London (Faber & Faber) 1958.

Magalaner, Marvin. *Time of Apprenticeship: The Fiction of the Young James Joyce*, London and New York (Abelard-Schuman) 1959.

Sullivan, Kevin. *Joyce among the Jesuits*, New York (Columbia University Press) 1958.

Ulysses

Adams, Robert Martin. *Surface and Symbol: The Consistency of James Joyce's 'Ulysses'*, New York (Oxford University Press) 1962.

Budgen, Frank. *'James Joyce and the Making of "Ulysses" ' and Other Writings*, London (Oxford University Press) 1972. (Based on Budgen's close friendship with Joyce during the writing of *Ulysses*; first published 1934.)

Ellmann, Richard. *Ulysses on the Liffey*, London (Faber & Faber) 1972. (Includes the 'Linati schema'.)

French, Marilyn. *The Book as World: James Joyce's 'Ulysses'*, Cambridge, Mass. and London (Harvard University Press) 1976.

Gilbert, Stuart. *James Joyce's 'Ulysses'*, new edn., London (Faber & Faber) 1952. ('Authorized' critical study, first published 1930.)

Kenner, Hugh. *Ulysses*, London (Allen & Unwin) 1980.

Lawrence, Karen. *The Odyssey of Style in 'Ulysses'*, Princeton, NJ (Princeton University Press) 1981.

Thornton, Weldon. *Allusions in 'Ulysses'*, Chapel Hill, N.C. (University of North Carolina Press) 1968.

Finnegans Wake

Introductory guides to *Finnegans Wake* include Anthony Burgess, *Here Comes Everybody* (London: Faber & Faber, 1965) and William York Tindall, *A Reader's Guide to 'Finnegans Wake'*, London (Thames & Hudson) 1969. Burgess has also edited *A Shorter 'Finnegans Wake'*, London (Faber & Faber) 1962.

Atherton, James S. *The Books at the Wake*, London (Faber & Faber) 1959. (The intertextuality of *Finnegans Wake*.)

Beckett, Samuel, and others. *Our Exagmination Round His Factification For Incamination of Work in Progress*, London (Faber & Faber) 1972. (Guidebook orchestrated by Joyce himself, and first published − long before the *Wake* was completed − in 1929.)

Benstock, Bernard. *Joyce-Again's Wake*, Seattle and London (University of Washington Press) 1965.

Glasheen, Adaline. *Third Census of 'Finnegans Wake': An Index of Characters and their Roles*, Berkeley, Los Angeles and London (University of California Press) 1977.

Hart, Clive. *Structure and Motif in 'Finnegans Wake'*, London (Faber & Faber) 1962.

McHugh, Roland. *The Sigla of 'Finnegans Wake'*, London (Edward Arnold) 1976.

McHugh, Roland. *Annotations to 'Finnegans Wake'*, Baltimore and London (Johns Hopkins University Press) 1980.

Norris, Margot. *The Decentered Universe of 'Finnegans Wake': A Structuralist Analysis*, Baltimore and London (Johns Hopkins University Press) 1976.

Joyce in Context(s)

Auerbach, Erich. *Mimesis*, trans. Willard Trask, Garden City, NY (Doubleday) n.d. (Realistic narrative from Homer to Joyce.)

Humphrey, Robert. *Stream of Consciousness in the Modern Novel*, Berkeley and Los Angeles (University of California Press) 1954.

Kenner, Hugh. *The Stoic Comedians: Flaubert, Joyce and Beckett*, London (W. H. Allen) 1964.

Korg, Jacob. *Language in Modern Literature*, Brighton (Harvester Press) and New York (Barnes & Noble) 1979.

MacCabe, Colin. *James Joyce and the Revolution of the Word*, London (Macmillan) 1979. (Joyce via Derrida and Lacan.)

Manganiello, Dominic. *Joyce's Politics*, London and Boston (Routledge & Kegan Paul) 1980.

Mercier, Vivian. *The Irish Comic Tradition*, Oxford (Clarendon Press) 1962.

O'Brien, Conor Cruise, ed. *The Shaping of Modern Ireland*, London (Routledge & Kegan Paul) 1970. (Essays on Joyce's Irish contemporaries 1891–1916.)

Read, Forrest, ed. *Pound/Joyce*, London (Faber & Faber) 1968.

Scholes, Robert, and Kellogg, Robert. *The Nature of Narrative*, New York (Oxford University Press) 1966. (On the interior monologue.)

Watson, G. J. *Irish Identity and the Literary Revival*, London (Croom Helm) and New York (Barnes & Noble) 1979. (On Synge, Yeats, Joyce, and O'Casey.)

Wilson, Edmund. *Axel's Castle*, New York and London (Scribner's) 1948. (Classic study of modern writers as the heirs of naturalism and symbolism, first published in 1931.)

Index